REFORM AND
RETRENCHMENT

A Rand Educational Policy Study

REFORM AND RETRENCHMENT
The Politics of California School Finance Reform

RICHARD F. ELMORE
MILBREY WALLIN McLAUGHLIN

BALLINGER PUBLISHING COMPANY
Cambridge, Massachusetts
A Subsidiary of Harper & Row, Publishers, Inc.

This project has been funded by the Ford Foundation and the National Institute of Education, U.S. Department of Education, under Grant No. NIE-G-79-0152.

International Standard Book Number: 0-88410-196-7

Library of Congress Catalog Card Number: 81-12738

Printed in the United States of America

Library of Congress Cataloging in Publication Data

Elmore, Richard F.
  Reform and retrenchment.

  Includes index.
  1. Education—California—Finance. 2. Educational law
and legislation—California. I. McLaughlin, Milbrey Wallin.
II. Title.
KFC651.E44   344.794'076   81-12738
ISBN 0-88410-196-7   347.940476   AACR2

CONTENTS

                                                                   v

LIST OF TABLES

PREFACE

Equity, in its multitude of forms, has been the central concern of educational policy for nearly thirty years. Now, with shrinking resources and the practical difficulties of translating abstract principles into concrete decisions, the future of equity seems less certain. The two themes of this book—reform and retrenchment—reflect the commitment and optimism of the past as well as the doubt and uncertainty of the future. On one level, this is a book about the politics of school finance reform in California—a case study of limited pretensions. On another level, it can be read as one episode in the complex history of equity as an objective of educational policy. The questions raised here about the relationship between principles and political outcomes and about the fate of equity in the face of declining resources reflect both the special circumstances of California and the dilemmas confronting educational policymakers everywhere.

When we began this study in the spring of 1978, we had in mind a political analysis of how California Assembly Bill (AB) 65 came about. Neither of us is an expert in the technical side of school finance; our comparative advantage, if any, lies in the description and analysis of complex political decisions. We were interested in understanding how a major shift in policy occurs, and we wanted to describe it in such a way that scholars, policymakers, and influential people in other settings would find it useful.

No sooner had we begun than the study we originally envisioned began to transmute into a host of unexpected and fascinating problems. In June 1978 California voters passed Proposition 13, a tax limitation measure that invalidated most of AB 65's school finance reform measures. Suddenly, we were no longer simply reconstructing the history of a major reform; we were studying its undoing. Proposition 13 gave us an opportunity to observe whether the politics of retrenchment were different from the politics of reform.

Upon closer examination we discovered that AB 65 was not quite the monumental reform some had made it out to be. There was serious disagreement about the extent to which it actually remedied the defects in the school-financing system that the California Supreme Court had found constitutionally offensive and whether it was really a major departure from past policy. We were rediscovering that reform is incremental. Important and often unobtrusive changes precede major reforms and make them politically feasible. We became both more skeptical about the magnitude of the AB 65 reform and also more inquisitive about its roots in previous legislative actions.

Our initial research also revealed that there was little or no agreement on the objectives of reform among the lawyers who initiated the *Serrano* suit and the people in the legislative and executive branches of state government who formulated the legislative response to it. The two sets of actors hardly spoke the same language; we were often pressed to remember that they were talking about the same problem. Running through our interviews is a barely concealed mutual distrust, with the lawyers accusing the political actors of not being sufficiently responsive to the court's mandate and the political actors accusing the lawyers of not being sufficiently sensitive to the complexities of legislative reform. We soon realized that this lack of a common framework for reform was one of the most important features of the case, and we set about documenting it with increasing detail.

This book is considerably different—more complex, less decisive—from the one we had initially planned. It reflects our tentative and incomplete understanding of how school finance reforms are initiated and pared back to meet the demands of fiscal austerity and of how differences between the judicial and legislative areas affect the way policy is made.

We were determined, when we started, to write a book that would speak to both academics and practitioners—to people who study policymaking and people who do it. We have tried to tell a good story as well as to squeeze meaning out of that story for people who confront educational policy in their daily work. We have also tried to cast a critical eye on the beliefs and principles that guide reformers and to expose the problems that attend judicially induced reform. To legislators, legislative staff members, educational administrators, policy analysts, citizen activists, lawyers, and researchers we have tried to speak with a single voice calculated to expose the conceptual and practical difficulties of reform.

Our interviews with the key participants were organized around questions designed to reveal both the chronology and the content of each major episode in California's school finance history. After the initial round of interviews we searched newspapers, political periodicals, the files of our respondents, and published government documents to corroborate the evidence from interviews. Where gaps or inconsistencies appeared, we reinterviewed some respondents. Drafts of each chapter were circulated to a selected group of respondents; in many cases their comments, written and oral, were incorporated into the final text. Extensive references to contemporary journalistic accounts of events are included to give a sense of how the events were perceived and publicly communicated.

The substance of the narrative was gleaned from interviews with people directly involved, not from secondary sources. One of our most disappointing discoveries was that the California legislature, for all its real and apparent sophistication relative to other state legislatures, does not keep a systematic record of committee hearings and reports. Legislative staff members were enormously generous with their time and their files and were unfailingly patient with our questions about the sequence and meaning of events. The same is true of staff members in the Department of Finance, the Department of Education, the Legislative Analyst's Office, and the numerous interest groups involved with educational policy in Sacramento. This research should be of interest to policymakers involved with school finance, legislators who wish to understand the multiple forces that shape coalitions, and students of the policymaking process.

Studies of this kind draw heavily on the time and expertise of busy people. We are deeply indebted to the lawyers, legislative staff, state level administrators, state board of education members, interest group representatives, and school district personnel who played a role in this research. Their generosity and patience were extraordinary.

Lawyers John Coons, David Kirp, Harold Horowitz, John McDermott, Stephen Sugarman, Sidney Wolinsky, and Mark Yodof reviewed Chapter 2, the intellectual and legal history of *Serrano*. Paul McGuckin of the Assembly Office of Research provided comment on the legislative history. David Cohen of the Harvard Graduate School of Education, James Kelly of the Ford Foundation, and Michael Kirst of Stanford University School of Education and former president of the California State Board of Education, reviewed the entire manuscript. All of these people gave us many useful comments, which substantially improved the text. Lucy Wilson of the Rand Corporation was primarily responsible for preparation of the manuscript, a task she handled with remarkable care and skill. The editorial expertise and persistent good sense of Helen Turin of Rand's publication department are evident throughout the manuscript. Thanks also go to our anonymous reviewer, James Catterall of the University of California, Los Angeles whose insights prompted a new Chapter 6 and caused us an extra month of work.

The idea for this study originated with James Kelly of the Ford Foundation. Although the result may not be exactly what he expected, without his concern that the *Serrano* story be told and Ford's support, we could not have begun. The National Institute of Education's (NIE's) School Finance Project provided the support that allowed us to finish. We are grateful to our NIE project monitor, Lauren Weisberg and Suzanne's for their collective support. We also thank the Rand Corporation for supporting our preparation of the book. Although this study could not have been done without all of these helpful people, they are, of course, in no way responsible for any shortcomings.

Richard F. Elmore
Milbrey Wallin McLaughlin

1 THE POLITICS OF REFORM
AND RETRENCHMENT

In 1971 the California Supreme Court handed down a nationally noted decision, *Serrano* v. *Priest*, invalidating the state's school-financing system. Six years later, the California legislature passed Assembly Bill (AB) 65, which many observers regarded as one of the country's most far-reaching and comprehensive educational reform measures. How that bill came to be is a classic case of coalition politics in the context of a major reform. How it subsequently unraveled is a benchmark case of the politics of retrenchment in the aftermath of Proposition 13, California's tax-limitation measure. In between is a view of how the issue of school finance equity polarized along political and technical lines its advocates, who were unable to agree on the objectives of reform.

Three themes run throughout this analysis. The first theme is *technical problems, political solutions*. The *Serrano* lawyers seized on an obvious defect of the California school-financing system: It produced extraordinarily large differences in educational expenditures among school districts, and those differences could be traced to the arbitrary basis of local property wealth. The school-financing system, like any revenue-raising system, is a complex collection of technical components, each of which has its origin in political compromise. School finance experts specialize in constructing technical solutions to problems like the one posed by the *Serrano* lawyers, and, indeed, there were any number of technically adequate ways of meeting the court's mandate. But each technical change in the system undoes a political compromise and undermines the political feasibility of reform. The construction of solutions to the inequities of the school-financing system is only incidentally a technical problem; it is much more a problem of political calculation. Each change has to be measured in terms of its effect on the complex system of political compromises that supports the status quo.

The second theme is called *judicial remedy, legislative response.* The courts are limited agents of reform. They can provide a forum for people who are adversely affected by past legislative action, and they can even provide a judicial remedy for the damage in the form of an order requiring the legislature to change the law. Except in rare cases, they do not specify the exact form of the new law because to do so would usurp the legislature's constitutional role. Typically, as in the *Serrano* case, the court states a legal principle and charges the legislature to rewrite existing law consistent with that principle.

Legislators do not take kindly to having the courts tell them what to do. The legislature regards itself as an equal branch of government and bridles at judicial intervention in sensitive policy areas. Also, legislators often regard the courts' legal principles as abstract and politically impracticable and, thus, largely useless in the framing of new legislation or generating support for change. Consequently, judicial intervention sets up a natural tension between the courts and the legislature that may not always operate in the best interests of public policy.

The third theme in our analysis is called *political capacity and coalition building.* Any legislative reform, whether judicially mandated or not, requires the construction of a reform coalition, which consists of both legislators who want the reform and constituent groups and members of the executive branch of government whose influence and expertise are needed to make reform possible. Reform coalitions depend in part on the participants' political skill and in part on their ability to calculate the consequences of political choices. Coalition politics does not necessarily require an abundance of either, but it does require some of each. The greater the political skill and calculating ability of coalition members, the more successful one would expect the reform coalition to be, where success is defined in terms of both the coalition's maintenance and the accomplishment of its members' objectives.

THE SYSTEM AND THE SETTING

When the *Serrano* suit was filed in 1968, California's school-financing system was not very different from that of most other states. Of total expenditures on education in California, about 55 percent were financed with revenues raised by local school districts through the property tax, about 35 percent came from state revenues, and the remainder came from federal sources.[1]

The amount of money spent on individual students within school districts was, to a substantial degree, a function of local property wealth and the willingness of localities to tax themselves—in technical terms, assessed valuations and tax rate. Assessed valuation per pupil, the amount of property wealth available to finance school expenditures, varied by a ratio of 1 to 10,000 from the poorest to the wealthiest districts. The state legislature set a maximum tax rate on property, but a majority of district voters could override this maximum; in all but a handful of California districts, the property tax rate was higher than the statutory maximum, which meant that school districts depended on annual voter approval for a major portion of their budgets.

The state's share of school revenues was distributed through a foundation system designed to assure a minimum level of expenditure in each district and involving basic aid and equalization aid. Basic aid was a flat $125 per pupil grant to all districts, regardless of local property wealth. Equalization aid was computed by multiplying a computational tax rate ($1 per $100 of assessed valuation, for example) times the local assessed valuation per pupil, adding the $125 basic aid grant, and subtracting the result from the state-guaranteed foundation ($355 per elementary and $488 per high school student in 1969). If the result was positive, the state paid that amount to the district in equalization aid. If the result was zero or negative, the district received only the $125 basic aid grant. The state also paid a special bonus, called supplemental aid, to very poor school systems that were willing to tax themselves at a high rate.

1. The following description of California's school-financing system before *Serrano* is drawn from Serrano v. Priest, 487 P.2d 1241 (1971), and from the legislative analyst's report, *Public School Finance* (1971), which the California Supreme Court used in constructing its description.

The results of this equalized system were not equal by any standard of reckoning. Per pupil expenditures in 1969 to 1970 in unified school districts varied from a low of $612 to a high of $2,414, with a median of $766. Tax rates tended to be inversely related to local property wealth; low-wealth districts had to tax themselves at a higher rate to raise less money than high-wealth districts. The favorite contrast used by school finance reform lawyers was between Beverly Hills and Baldwin Park. Beverly Hills had a per pupil expenditure of $1,232 in 1968 to 1969, while Baldwin Park, a few miles away, spent $577 per pupil. Beverly Hills had assessed valuation per pupil of $51,000, Baldwin Park $3,700. Baldwin Park received about $300 per pupil in basic aid and equalization aid from the state; Beverly Hills received the minimum $125.

Not only did the state aid system fail to compensate for differences in local property wealth; the basic aid feature actually aggravated inequalities. About one-half of the state's foundation support was distributed as basic aid on a flat per capita basis, leaving the remaining one-half for reductions of inequalities.

This school-financing system contained inequalities in both taxation and expenditures. Differences in property wealth, coupled with the inequality-producing aspects of the state aid system, resulted in different per pupil expenditures. Some undetermined fraction of differences in expenditures could be explained by legitimate differences in local costs (teachers' salaries, maintenance, transportation, etc.). Some additional amount could be explained by disproportionate concentrations of students with exceptional needs. Absolute expenditure differences were not necessarily a sign of real inequalities— that is, inequalities in the actual resources brought to bear on an individual student's education.

In the debates over school finance reform, tax inequalities and expenditure inequalities were frequently confused. One of the major sources of confusion running though the whole history of the California case is whether taxpayers or school children were the intended beneficiaries of school finance reform. Should one be primarily concerned about equalizing school district tax effort? Or should one concentrate on remedying substantial expenditure differences? How much inequality should the state tolerate on either group?

An additional complexity appears when one looks at other types of state educational expenditures beyond the foundation program. As Table 1-1 shows, the period during which California was grap-

Table 1-1. K-12 Total Revenue[a] (in Millions).

Year	Local Property Tax Levies	State[b] Aid	Federal Aid	Miscel-[c] laneous	Total Funding	Percentage of Change	Average Daily Attendance (ADA)	Total Funding per ADA	Percentage of Change
1971–72	$2,898.7 (54.0%)	$1,662.8 (31.0%)	$435.0 (8.1%)	$371.6 (6.9%)	$5,368.1	—	4,686,340	$1,145	—
1972–73	2,190.1 (36.4%)	2,945.1 (48.9%)	399.5 (6.6%)	485.1 (8.1%)	6,019.8	12.1	4,655,974	1,293	12.9
1973–74	3,051.9 (45.5%)	2,683.0 (40.0%)	467.5 (7.0%)	509.1 (7.6%)	6,711.5	11.5	4,647,128	1,444	11.7
1974–75	3,348.2 (45.3%)	2,952.5 (40.0%)	570.3 (7.7%)	524.4 (7.1%)	7,395.4	10.2	4,714,154	1,569	8.7
1975–76	3,795.2 (47.2%)	3,247.5 (40.4%)	613.4 (7.6%)	391.1 (4.9%)	8,047.2	8.8	4,760,966	1,690	7.7
1976–77	4,256.1 (48.1%)	3,422.3 (38.7%)	669.0 (7.6%)	495.6 (5.6%)	8,843.0	9.9	4,718,800	1,874	10.9
1977–78	4,617.0d (48.7%)	3,620.5 (38.2%)	747.9 (7.6%)	500.0 (5.3%)	9,485.4	7.3	4,652,486	2,039	8.8
1978–79 (Budget)	2,434.0e (25.4%)	5,796.5 (60.6%)	845.7 (8.8%)	490.0 (5.1%)	9,566.2	.9	4,329,300	2,210	8.4
1979–80 (Budget)	2,600.0d (26.0%)	5,945.4 (59.4%)	966.8 (9.7%)	490.0 (4.9%)	10,002.2	4.6	4,261,700	2,347	6.2

a. Includes county superintendents of schools, state operations, State Teachers' Retirement System direct support, and debt service on public school building bonds.

b. Includes property tax subventions.

c. Includes food sales, sale of property, sale of bonds, interest, fees, and rentals.

d. Includes $25 million for prior year taxes and timber yield receipts.

e. Includes district reserves of $33 million and $25 million for prior year taxes and timber yield receipts.

Source: Office of the Legislative Analyst.

pling with school finance reform was one of enormous growth in educational expenditures. Part of the growth is explained by increases in the foundation program, but a large part is explained by the addition of special categorical programs, which are designed either to provide support for identifiable populations of students with special needs (compensatory education, special education, bilingual education, etc.) or to change the structure or enhance the capacity of schools (early childhood education, staff development, competency testing, etc.). The exact distribution of categorical funds depends on complex formulas built into their authorizing legislation.

In its narrowest terms, the California Supreme Court's decision in *Serrano* dealt only with the foundation system, which depends on property taxes, not with categorical programs. In fact, the court explicitly exempted categorical expenditures from its ruling. In political terms, however, categorical programs were an essential ingredient in the construction of a reform coalition.

From these fairly simple elements—extremes in property wealth, extremes in per pupil expenditure, and an increasing statewide educational budget—grew a large number of reform options. One group of options would alter the tax base from which expenditure inequalities originate. School district consolidation, countywide property taxes, and statewide property taxes were designed to average out the property wealth of rich and poor districts and equalize tax rates.

Another group of options would change the tax rate structure and revenue disbursement system. One such proposal was district power equalization in which the state collects local property taxes and distributes them to districts in proportion to their tax rates. Districts taxing themselves at the same rate receive the same amount of money, regardless of their tax base and their contribution to the general fund. Another proposal was a recapture mechanism in which the state takes a certain share of the property tax proceeds from wealthy districts and uses it to raise the expenditures of poor districts.

A third series of options would eliminate reliance on the property tax altogether. One proposal was to move the foundation program to another tax base—the state income tax, for example. Another was to eliminate the foundation program and channel all state funds through categorical programs. These broad options permit an infinite number of permutations and combinations, some that are modest increments on the existing system and some radical departures.

Forging a politically feasible reform proposal from this range of technical options requires a distribution of benefits broad enough to hold together a winning coalition. When revenue is plentiful, reform coalitions can be built by a process called leveling up—raising the foundation without lowering the expenditures in property-rich districts. Leveling up is very expensive, and in systems with large property wealth differentials it can only be expected to reduce extremes, rather than to equalize them. At some point, decisionmakers must acknowledge that equalization of expenditures with limited revenues requires some amount of leveling down or using the property wealth of rich districts to increase expenditures in poor districts. The balance of leveling up and down is one of the most sensitive problems of coalition building.

Focusing purely on property wealth in the construction of reform proposals overlooks the fact that many districts with above-average property wealth also have large revenue needs—greater numbers of students requiring special attention, competing demands from other municipal services for property tax revenues, and so forth. The process of leveling up and down on the basis of property wealth may leave these districts no better off, or even worse off, than they were under the old system. A chief function of categorical programs in the construction of reform coalitions is to offer inducements to these districts. Categorical funds, in other words, act as a reservoir of resources for binding marginal districts into the reform coalition and for compensating districts with high needs and high property wealth. California is atypical of most states in the proportion of state funding that flows through categorical programs. Bargaining over categorical funds played a prominent role in both reform and retrenchment.

Because of the financial inducements required to bind coalitions together, reform is really a luxury public good. As long as revenues are increasing, the state may purchase reform with surplus revenues for which it must find a use. When the threat of declining revenues enters the picture, as it did with the passage of Proposition 13 in California, the complexion of reform politics changes. This is a new phenomenon, so it is difficult to predict what will happen to carefully constructed reform coalitions in times of fiscal retrenchment. Clearly, downside politics will be different from upside politics. School system administrators, educational interest groups, and politicians may be willing to divide growing revenues in a generous and equitable way, but generosity and equity may not follow reduced expenditures and eliminated programs. Protecting one's turf against the encroachment of fiscal decline requires different political behavior than does sharing in the benefits of increasing revenues. The California case provides a glimpse of both sides.

ANALYZING REFORM POLITICS

Policymaking in the courts and policymaking in the legislature are two completely different activities. The lawyers' and the politicians' views of reform, conditioned by the settings in which they work, diverge on several points. *Serrano* lawyers were impressed with the absolute disparities in revenue-raising capabilities and expenditures among school districts and attracted by the opportunity to make a major advance in legal doctrine. They were preoccupied with the essential elements of the process of constitutional litigation: documenting the system's inequities, developing a legal theory that could be used to invalidate that system, and convincing the courts that the inequities were serious enough to merit judicial intervention. The legal strategy of the *Serrano* lawyers was expressly designed to avoid specifying a solution; that responsibility was left to the legislature. The litigation in *Serrano* was surprisingly lacking in concrete discussions of how the system's deficiencies should be remedied.

The legislative response to *Serrano* was the construction of a coalition of politicians and constituency groups with divergent interests, which is much different from the construction of legal theory and argument. The key elements of coalition building—political influence, money, and information about the consequences of political choices—are as concrete as the elements of constitutional litigation are abstract. Legislative politics is pragmatic and atheoretical. It focuses on the politically feasible, often to the exclusion of the technically, theoretically, or ideologically desirable.

Out of this tension between judicial and legislative policymaking grows one set of analytic issues for this study: How well does the litigation process work as a device for initiating reform? How much do lawyers and judges know about the system for which they are making policy and the consequences of their decisions for the way that system works? How well does the process of litigation work to expose the weaknesses of competing arguments? How do participants in the legislative process perceive the role of the courts in policy-making? How effective are judicial decisions as guides to legislative policymaking? How effective are the courts in monitoring legislative compliance with judicial decisions?

States grapple with the issue of school finance reform in different ways in different circumstances. Reform in New Jersey, North Dakota, or New Mexico is not the same as reform in California. Political conditions, history, financial resources, and constitutional language differ substantially from one setting to another. Within these broad constraints are other factors—information, analytic resources, organization, and political skill—that are subject to the control of people who work on policy. These controllable factors are called political capacity. Interest in the relationship between political capacity and reform is quite practical. The question is what can be learned from the California case about how political capacity develops and how it is used to affect policy.

By capacity, three simple things are meant: (1) staffing, (2) organization, and (3) information retrieval and analysis. Staffing is not only the number of people who specialize in school finance policy but also their experience, expertise, and political sophistication. Formal decisionmaking of school finance reform in the courts and in the legislature is the smallest part of the process. Behind it lies the work of people who assemble information, devise options, and negotiate the details.

California is exceptionally well endowed with political capacity. In this sense, it is an atypical state in which to study the politics of reform and retrenchment. Its unrepresentativeness is a virtue insofar as it gives one a picture of what a fairly advanced stage of development looks like and how it is achieved. One would not presume to offer California as a model for other states to emulate, but it is not improbable that the California case could offer useful hints to people in other states about how to nurture and use political capacity.

Behind this practical interest in political capacity lies a more academic interest in the analysis of coalition politics. In formal terms, the study of coalitions involves analyzing how individuals, groups, or blocs with differing interests coordinate their behavior to make authoritative decisions. The important parts of this definition are the terms *different interests, coordination*, and *authoritative decisions*. If all interests are identical, politics would be a trivial matter, and coalitions would be unnecessary. The more elaborate and specialized the political systems, the more difficult is coalition building. Coordination requires developing means of communication, norms of consultation and decision, and means of enforcing consensus.

Willingness to engage in coalition politics requires a fairly sophisticated form of political rationality. One has to be able to calculate that the benefits of cooperation are greater than the benefits of individual action. Benefits can be measured in terms of both political influence and monetary reward. Coalitions form to make or to influence authoritative decisions—ones that distribute money or grant authority. It is the payoff in money and increased authority of these decisions that gives members an incentive to coordinate their behavior. Bargaining among coalition members takes the form of dividing the expected benefits of authoritative decisions. The internal exchanges of these benefits among coalition members are called side payments. The more public resources to be divided, the greater the incentive to participate.

In the language of school finance politics, coalitions form around the expectation that cooperation increases the total return to education and that individual members stand to benefit from an increase in the total pot. Cooperation requires at least a temporary suspension of internal conflicts and some level of internal organization. Side payments take the form of altering the distribution of funds through both foundation and categorical programs. This exchange of benefits is the critical element holding the coalition together. Special interest participation in coalitions, therefore, should be greater when resources for education are increasing than when they are constant or declining. When school finance reform carries the promise of additional resources for schools, it can be expected to stimulate the formation of coalitions with an active education interest component. Fiscal retrenchment, which carries the necessity of dividing a constant or declining pool of resources among education concerns and among general government activities, can be expected to undermine the role of special interest participation and create general coalitions.

The academic literature on coalitions examines such questions as the optimum size of winning coalitions, the effects of differentials in power, and the calculation of benefits accruing to participants (Riker 1962; Gamson 1961: 373–382). Political scientists who study coalition formation have been interested mainly in how multi-party parliamentary systems form governing coalitions and how these coalitions behave once they assume power (Groennings, Kelley, and

Leiserson 1970). This book is concerned with the relationship between coalition formation and political capacity.

The amount and distribution of technical expertise and political sophistication among the various elements of the coalition greatly affect the outcome of policy decisions. Continuity of staffing allows individuals to specialize, develop a detailed understanding of the field, and cultivate strong working relationships with their counterparts. The command of detail and the ability to understand the consequences of technical changes in existing law are the most important kinds of expertise a staff person can possess. Beyond technical expertise, however, lies the capacity for political judgment. Political sophistication is not nearly as elusive and intangible as its possessors make it out to be. It consists mainly of a detailed knowledge of the personal and organizational contacts through which important decisions are made, the ability to predict how individuals and organizations will respond, and the ability to mobilize individuals and groups around a common proposal (Bardach 1972). Each element of staffing capacity depends on the next: There must be a certain basic level of staffing before continuity and expertise are possible; some level of continuity and expertise must be reached before the staff can establish the working relationships that make political sophistication possible.

Sustained bargaining and concerted influence in coalitions require what Graham Allison has called "action channels," established methods of contact among coalition members (1971). In the educational arena, these take the form of systems for mobilizing interest group constituencies in support of legislative proposals, methods of conveying information to legislators and citizens about the consequences of policy decisions, informal working groups in which consensus proposals are worked out, and agreements that certain actions will not be taken until certain consultations have been made.

These devices fall under the heading of "organization." They are not simply coincidental or haphazard arrangements but deliberate attempts to establish a structure within which coalition politics will occur. Without some level of deliberate organization, coalitions cannot sustain themselves, but the level of organization required to sustain a coalition is a good deal less than that required to sustain a bureaucracy. Members of a coalition retain a high degree of autonomy and resist organizational devices that compromise that autonomy. Keep it informal is the most commonly heard piece of political advice one hears about the organization of political coalitions. The maintenance of coalitions is a constant battle between the necessity to maintain some level of organization and the necessity for individual members to preserve their autonomy.

Finally, one's ability to participate intelligently in a coalition depends in some measure on one's ability to calculate the payoff for doing so. A basic economy that accrues to the organization of coalitions is the capacity for information retrieval and processing. In school finance, this usually means the ability to estimate the revenue gain or loss to school systems or interest groups resulting from specific legislative proposals. Because school financing systems are extraordinarily complex, the costs of retrieval and processing are high, and the possibilities for error and disagreement are great. Reliable estimates of the effects of alternative proposals become a valuable commodity and one of the strongest inducements for participating in a coalition.

Coalition politics can occur at any capacity level. In most states, one would predict, coalitions form and dissolve with great regularity around school finance issues and never reach a very high level of capacity on any of the characteristics which have been described. One thing that stood out about the California case, however, was the apparent robustness and political clout of the coalition that formed around school finance issues. It was a broad-based coalition that included the governor, key legislators and their staffs, a large number of educational interest groups, and the state education administration. This, by itself, was important. It did not seem to be decisive. Upon closer examination, however, it became clearer that the strength of the coalition had a great deal to do with the expertise and sophistication of its members, its organizational form, and its information retrieval and processing capability. Although a high level of capacity, as defined, may not be a necessary condition for the formation of reform coalitions, it explains their ability to maintain themselves and to exert influence. A more problematical issue is whether reform coalitions of the type observed in California can sustain themselves in the face of retrenchment.

This analysis traces the course of school finance reform from the state's first response to *Serrano*, Senate Bill 90, to the aftermath of Proposition 13 and legislative development of Assembly Bill 8 as a way to manage retrenchment. The intellectual and legal history of the *Serrano* decision provides the backdrop for our analysis of the legislative politics of reform and retrenchment.

2 JUDICIAL INTERVENTION IN POLICYMAKING
Serrano v. Priest

Law, says the judge as he looks down his nose,
Speaking clearly and most severely,
Law is as I've told you before,
Law is as you know I suppose,
Law is but let me explain it once more,
Law is The Law.

                    W.H. Auden, "Law Like Love"

THE DILEMMAS OF JUDICIAL INTERVENTION[1]

The story of school finance reform in California, and in most other states, begins with the deliberate, strategic use of the courts by reformers to initiate a change in policy. From roughly the mid–1950s through the late 1960s, the courts acted as the primary agents of reform on a broad range of issues dealing with equality of educational opportunity (Yudof 1973; Kirp 1977). The reason for this reliance on courts as agents of reform was simple enough. "Recourse

---

1. This section was written with the benefit of the draft of a book by Michael Rebell and Arthur Block, "Education Policy and the Courts: An Empirical Study of the Effectiveness and Legitimacy of Judicial Activism," which contains a much more thorough and exhaustive treatment of the arguments surrounding judicial intervention than can be presented here.

to the courts marked an end run around institutions"—notably state legislatures and local school boards—"which were politically unresponsive to the equity-based grievances of traditionally unrepresented interests" (Kirp 1977:119). *Serrano* v. *Priest*,[2] the case that initiated school finance reform in California, came quite late in this period of judicial activism. It represents a fairly advanced stage of development in both doctrine and strategy. The *Serrano* case is important for the purposes of this book because it set the agenda for the extended legislative debate, which will be discussed in following chapters. It is also important for what it tells about the conflicts between courts and legislatures over school finance reform.

Two basic attributes made school-financing systems an attractive target for judicial intervention. First, virtually all state systems, including California's, produced substantial variations in expenditure among local school districts. At the extremes, these variations seemed almost surely to be tied to local property wealth. Second, state legislatures had created and maintained these systems and in the eyes of reformers appeared unwilling to change them substantially. Together, these facts piqued the interest of a number of legal scholars and reform-minded lawyers all over the United States. Thus began the somewhat disorderly process of using the courts to change school-financing policy, of which *Serrano* is one important stage.

Arguments over the proper role of courts and legislatures are endemic to the American constitutional system, which deliberately creates overlapping functions among the legislative, executive, and judicial branches. From the beginning, American constitutional law has acknowledged implicitly that lawmaking is shared by both the courts and legislatures. Although courts and legislatures share the lawmaking function, they exercise it in completely different ways— the courts by deciding individual cases on the basis of legal principle, the legislatures by balancing competing political interests. How these competing methods of lawmaking do or do not mesh is a central subject of this book. How legal professionals use the judicial system to initiate broad changes in policy is the subject of this chapter.

Abram Chayes (1976) uses the term "public law litigation" to characterize the courts' increasing involvement in issues broader than the resolution of private disputes between clearly defined parties. Public law litigation centers on "the vindication of constitutional or

2. 487 P.2d 1241 (1971), and 557 P.2d 929 (1976).

statutory policies" (Chayes 1976:1284), which means that it puts judges and lawyers in the position of policymakers, whether they choose to acknowledge that role or not. Public law litigation is characterized by "a sprawling and amorphous party structure" (Chayes 1976:1284), in which the formal parties to the suit do not always represent all those affected by the outcome. It thrusts the judge into the role of "the dominant figure in organizing and guiding the case" (Chayes 1976:1284). Instead of passively umpiring private disputes, the judge in public law litigation is called upon to mobilize, evaluate, and utilize complex technical information in reaching decisions, to manage "complex forms of ongoing relief which have widespread effects on persons not before the court," and to exercise "continuing involvement in the administration and implementation" of complex remedies (Chayes 1976:1284). The debate over the legitimacy of public law litigation has been strident (see, for example, Glazer 1975; Nagel 1978; Horowitz 1977). Whatever its legal merits, however, it is guaranteed to inspire conflict between legislatures and courts when, as in the case of school finance litigation, its purpose is deliberately to force legislatures to act.

The political stakes that attend public law litigation or judicial intervention in policymaking are best stated as a series of dilemmas. The case for or against judicial intervention is not clear-cut, but the complexities, risks, and difficulties of using the courts to initiate policy can be clearly stated. The major dilemmas of judicial intervention have to do with the definition of parties to a suit, the power exercised by lawyers and judges in determining the outcome of litigation, the nature of the remedies that courts can offer, and the relative strengths and weaknesses of courts and legislatures as lawmakers.

Choosing Plaintiffs

To make a case in court, one must have a plaintiff, a real person who has suffered some real harm for which there is a legal remedy. When the courts intervene in public policy, the plaintiffs are chosen by lawyers to represent not only themselves but a whole class of people who are alleged to be harmed by existing policy. "The emergence of the group as the real . . . object of litigation" grows out of an "awareness that a host of important public and private interactions . . . are conducted on a routine and bureaucratized basis" and is reinforced by a general political "tendency to perceive interests as group interests" (Chayes 1976:1291). The main problem with using groups as litigants lies in defining who is harmed and, hence, to whom the legal remedy should apply. On the one hand, legal advocacy thrives on extreme cases, so lawyers might choose plaintiffs who represent the most aggravated instances of the alleged harm. Having done this, they put themselves in the way of criticisms that "there is no assurance that litigants constitute a random sample of the class of cases that might be affected by a decree" (Horowitz 1977:44). The resulting remedy "may be law for the worst case or for the best, but not necessarily for the modal case" (Kurland 1968:597). On the other hand, the class of plaintiffs may be broadened to include a wider range of interests, but this raises further troubling questions: "How far can the group be extended and homogenized?" And "to what extent and by what methods will we permit the presentation of views diverging from that of the group represented?" (Chayes 1976: 1291).

The dilemma takes the following form: If the object of litigation is sharply defined and clearly represented in a well-defined class of plaintiffs, the plaintiffs probably do not represent the broader population of those affected by the court's decision. If plaintiffs have a wider range of interests in the outcome, thus broadening the object of litigation, the harm resulting from existing policy is more difficult to define and the legal remedy more difficult to devise. Lawyers can sidestep this dilemma by avoiding a clear specification of the common interest that binds plaintiffs together. Public law litigation also spawns a large number of amici curiae—friends of the court—who are allowed to present briefs without actually joining one side or the other in the case. In the end, however, the remedy the court grants and, hence, the effect of public law litigation on public policy depends on how the plaintiffs are chosen.

The Power of Lawyers and Judges

Public law litigation puts substantial power in the hands of lawyers and judges. Lawyers choose the target of litigation, select the plaintiffs, and devise the legal theory from which the court, if it rules in their favor, will construct a remedy. Judges are called upon to guide litigation that is "extraordinarily complex and extended in time with a continuous and intricate interplay between factual and legal elements" (Chayes 1976:1298) and to devise complex remedies and supervise their implementation over long periods. The more technically difficult the issue, and school finance is among the most, the greater the responsibility that devolves to lawyers and judges. Safeguards against the abuse of this power inhere in the procedures of courtroom argument and the conventions of legal decision. The process of litigation is hedged by adversarial rules intended to assure that questionable information and faulty legal theory will be exposed to criticism. Judges' decisions are based on legal principle rather than on calculations of political expediency or individual preferences, and they are presented as extensions of existing legal authority.[3]

In reality, public law litigation never quite approximates this ideal. Imbalances occur in resources and skill between legal adversaries. Legal principle, because it is retrospective, is often not a very good guide for decisions, making it difficult to avoid applying individual preferences or making judgments of political expediency. Often the sheer magnitude of technical evidence makes the judge's job impossible, and the task of framing a decision is, in effect, delegated to one or both of the adversaries (Chayes 1976:1298). As a complex issue moves through the courts, the language of argument and decision becomes progressively more specialized, more obscure to the layperson, and more detached from the problem that created the occasion for litigation in the first place.

The dilemma is this: The more important the issue of public law litigation (the more visible, the broader its consequences, the more urgent the remedy), the more technically complex it is likely to be, and the greater is the likelihood that it will push against the limits of the courts' competence to solve it within the established norms of argument and decision. Yet the more important the issue, the more attractive it will be as a target of litigation for enterprising and entrepreneurial lawyers.

The Nature of Judicial Remedies

Except in rare instances, courts do not implement their own decisions.[4] They rely instead on legislators and administrators to carry

---

3. The clearest statement of this norm is Wechsler (1959:19). The debate over the neutral principles doctrine is carefully summarized in Rebell and Block.

4. For an important exception, see Lehne (1978) and footnote 7 in this chapter.

out the remedies they prescribe. In most cases this means that judicially initiated reform, in effect, is delegated to the very agencies of government that created the necessity for intervention in the first place (Yudof 1980). The courts continue to supervise the implementation of decisions long after they are handed down, but they do not have, in either practical or constitutional terms, the capacity to implement their own decisions. The courts are not unique in this regard. Legislatures frequently find themselves in much the same position when they turn the implementation of legislatively initiated reforms over to hostile and resistant administrative agencies (Bardach 1977).

The courts, however, do have one disability that is not shared by legislatures in the area of implementation. "If as is often true the [court's] decree calls for a substantial commitment of new resources, the court has little basis for evaluating competing claims on the public purse" (Chayes 1976:1309). Reforms cost money. The more ambitious the reform, the more costly. The costs of school finance reform are determined by the political tradeoff between leveling up and leveling down: Should expenditure increases in poor districts be financed out of general increases or out of the existing expenditures of rich districts? This is precisely the sort of tradeoff that lawyers and judges freely admit the courts are poorly equipped to make. Lawyers urge judicial intervention knowing that it will require substantial commitments of new resources—they may even list that as a beneficial outcome of litigation—but they displace the responsibility for making those commitments to the very legislators and administrators who created the occasion for intervention in the first place. Public law litigation puts the courts in the role of shadow players in the game of coalition politics. The court decides. Legislators or administrators respond by making political tradeoffs that approximate the court's intent.

The tradeoffs are designed also to galvanize political support. Lawyers find the resulting legislative or administrative action an inferior approximation of the court's intent, so they return to court to ask the judge for another decision to force further action. The process can occur several times. In each instance, lawyers and judges disown responsibility for political tradeoffs made by legislators and administrators, but they reserve the power to evaluate the outcome of each coalition-building episode. Legislators and administrators, who are charged with making the decisions necessary to carry out the court's decisions, seldom share either the sense of urgency or the implicit funding priorities of lawyers and judges. The more effective the courts become as agents of reform, the less competent they are in forcing the necessary political tradeoffs for those reforms, and the greater their tendency to intervene where they are least competent.

Strengths and Weaknesses of Courts and Legislatures

The arguments for and against judicial intervention in policymaking ultimately come down to a question of the relative competence and authority of courts and legislatures. One school of thought argues that judges are ill-equipped to make decisions with far-reaching public policy implications. "That judges are generalists," the argument says, "means, above all, that they lack the experience and skill to interpret such information as they may receive" (Horowitz 1977:31).

Another school of thought argues that the professional background and socialization of judges leaves them well-equipped to make important, policy-relevant decisions. Judges are "likely to have some experience of the political process and acquaintance with a fairly broad range of public policy problems" as well as training and practice that equip them with "a professional ideal of reflective and dispassionate analysis" (Chayes 1976:1308). The argument for the superiority of legislatures as policymakers stems mainly from their adherence to the norm of specialization. The institutional structure of legislatures focuses legislators' attention on narrow subject-matter areas, allowing them to develop, if they choose, a command of the technical and political complexities of public policy issues. Specialization, the argument continues, is closely connected with the political incentives of electoral politics. As Mayhew put it, "The quest for specialization is the quest for credit," and credit translates directly into votes (1974:95).

Against these legislative advantages are arrayed judicial assets. Courts, in the best of circumstances, can provide "solutions that can be tailored to the needs of the particular situation and flexibly administered or modified as experience develops" (Chayes 1976: 1308). At least in the Anglo-American tradition, courts have come to be identified as guardians of individual and minority interests against the excesses of majoritarian democracy. Further, in some circumstances courts can function effectively as fact-finding bodies because the adversarial process "furnishes strong incentives for the parties to produce information" on the competing claims of litigants (Chayes 1976:1308). "Unlike an administrative bureaucracy or legislature," which can delay action indefinitely, "the judiciary *must* respond to the complaints of the aggrieved" (Chayes 1976:1308, emphasis in the original).[5]

Reduced to its simplest form, the argument for separate judicial and legislative branches is that the two sets of institutions, based on different constitutional authority and characterized by different norms of discourse and decision, compensate for each other's weaknesses. The courts, with their heavy reliance on individual cases, adversarial argument, and principled decisions check the tendency of legislatures to slide toward political expediency and inattention to the claims of unrepresented minorities. Legislatures, with their reliance on political pressure by organized interests, trading of benefits (side payments), and bargained decisions check the courts' tendency to make decisions that lack sufficiently broad-based political support to be carried out.[6] Often, differences between the legislative and judicial view of important issues, as will be seen in the case of school finance policy, are irreconcilable—at least in the short run. In such cases the only strategy open to reformers bent upon using the judicial system to change policy is to maintain relentless pressure on the legislature. This pressure creates a curious double bind. Lawyers appear in court to criticize the legislature for elevating political considerations and mere feasibility above legal principle, which, of course, is exactly what legislatures are designed to do. Participants in the legislative process criticize reform lawyers and judges for focusing on legal principle to the exclusion of political feasibility, which, of course, is precisely what courts are designed to do. The only solution to this double bind is a long-term one of partisan mutual adjustment in which each side claims its objectives have been met while tacitly making important concessions to the other side (Lindblom 1965).

5. Although it may be an accurate portrayal of the advantages and disadvantages of courts and legislatures, this statement is not strictly true. Courts frequently refuse to decide cases, or decide them on purely procedural grounds, when they raise politically sensitive issues. It is strictly true that these decisions dispose of the cases, but it is not true that they constitute responses to the complaints of the aggrieved.

6. The issue of how courts try to create a climate of support for their decisions is well treated in Yudof (1980).

For the actors involved in the pull-and-tug between court and legislature, there often is no long run, only a seemingly endless series of exasperating, inconclusive short runs. Using the courts to change policy requires a willingness to fight endless tactical skirmishes that often do not add up to a respectable war. The better the two sides are at playing their roles, the less likely is the outcome to constitute a definitive victory for either side. This is the final dilemma of judicial intervention. The competing claims of the courts and the legislature to competence and authority in the making of laws are, in the short term, irreconcilable. In the long term they are reconcilable only by tacit adjustment. Hence, the possibilities for impasse are greater the more effectively the two sets of actors play their roles.[7]

A GATHERING OF FORCES

Legend has it that *Serrano* v. *Priest* grew out of a dinner party conversation in an east Los Angeles barrio between John Serrano, Jr., a social worker, and Derrick A. Bell, Jr., director of the newly formed Western Center on Law and Poverty (WCLP), a federally supported public interest law organization in Los Angeles. Serrano recounted to Bell an exchange he had recently had with his seven-year-old son's elementary school principal. "Your sons are very bright," the principal said to Serrano, "If you want to give them a decent chance in life, take them out of this school." Shortly thereafter, Serrano moved his family from East Los Angeles to the middle class suburb of Whittier (Kirp 1973:83). Serrano's problem was so compelling, the legend goes, that it galvanized Bell and the University of California at Los Angeles (UCLA) law professor Harold Horowitz to initiate legal action at Los Angeles County Superior Court against the California school-financing system.

In fact, the origins of *Serrano* are somewhat murkier. The legal and strategic groundwork for a constitutional challenge to state school-financing systems antedated John Serrano's involvement in

7. In another example of judicial intervention in school-financing policy, the New Jersey Supreme Court closed the schools after the state legislature failed to produce any response to the court's earlier decision invalidating the school-financing system. One could argue that had the legislature been more competent at playing its role the outcome would have been less conclusive and, in many ways, less satisfying to reformers. See Robinson v. Cahill, 303 A.2d 273 (1973), 339 A.2d 193 (1975), and 358 A.2d 457 (1976); as well as Lehne (1978).

the issue by several years. Serrano's case was one of many being pursued more or less independently in courts around the country. Nor is it entirely true that Serrano's complaint initiated the California challenge. The WCLP, according to Bell, was funded by the U.S. Office of Economic Opportunity (later the Community Services Administration) to provide "back-up, legal support, and motivation-by-example" for neighborhood legal services programs throughout the West.[8] Although WCLP had no previous involvement in education issues—its earliest work involved consumer credit and discriminatory treatment of minority group people by law enforcement officers—Bell was intrigued by the opportunity the school finance issue presented. Horowitz had published two law review articles on the subject of discriminatory treatment in the financing of public services (1966; 1968), partly with the backing of the Office of Economic Opportunity. Bell and Horowitz talked about the issue as a promising subject for litigation, and at some point, the exact time is unclear, they decided to proceed with the preparation of a complaint. Horowitz does not recall having met Serrano until well after the decision to proceed with the case. Serrano and his fellow plaintiffs were consulted about their willingness to participate in the case, but in Serrano's words, "after that it was the lawyers' case" (Reinhold 1972: E-26).

Serrano's problem seemed an odd one on which to base a revolutionary assault on the school-financing system of California. After all he had moved his son out of the problem school by the time the suit was filed. Nor was the connection between the principal's indictment of the school and the state's school-financing system necessarily clear. These matters are of little consequence in public law litigation. It was not John Serrano's problem that was driving the litigation, but the ambitions of reform-minded lawyers.

In another sense, Bell and Horowitz could not have found a better exemplar than John Serrano of America's faith in education as an instrument of social equality. Serrano had grown up in East Los Angeles, the son of a shoe repairman and an impoverished refugee from the Mexican revolution. Education was not among the values stressed in his home life. "My parents didn't know the value of an education," he said, "they didn't know how to help me" (Adams 1972:7). His own schooling was dismal: "East LA kids are expected

8. Derrick Bell 31 May 1979: personal communication.

to be dumb, and they usually live up to that expectation" (Adams 1972:7). After a straight-D career in high school and a sporadic bout with junior college athletics, Serrano married and started a family. At this point "I realized that I had to be something more than a meter reader to support my family," and "I really began to get serious about education" (Adams 1972:7). In seven years of hard work, he completed a bachelor's degree in sociology at California State College in Los Angeles, and two years later he completed a master's degree in social work at the top of his class. By the time the California Supreme Court had disposed of *Serrano* v. *Priest*, he had become a psychiatric social worker in an East Los Angeles mental health clinic. When John Serrano spoke about the importance of education for his son, John Anthony, he spoke with knowledge and conviction.

The legend of how *Serrano* got started reinforces the view that important judicial decisions have their origins in the problems of ordinary people—that judicially initiated changes in policy proceed from the claims of individual litigants. In fact, the process works at least as often in the opposite direction: Legal scholars generate theories and then go searching for litigants who match them. This was certainly the case in *Serrano* v. *Priest*. By the time John Serrano met Derrick Bell in 1968, the basic theoretical groundwork for a constitutional assault on state school finance systems had already been laid. Several well-developed, competing theories were waiting to be tested and elaborated; all that was lacking were the plaintiffs, the resources to mount the litigation, and a strategy for bringing the issue before the courts.

In the mid-1960s a number of legal scholars, working independently, began to look on state school-financing systems as a target of opportunity for working out a legal or constitutional definition of equality of educational opportunity. After the U.S. Supreme Court's initial decision in the 1954 school desegregation cases, the idea of equality of educational opportunity began to assume a meaning broader than that of simple racial equality. Reformers began to see the schools as having general responsibility for remedying social inequalities, regardless of their origins (Coleman 1968). This idea was strongly reflected in the dramatic shift in federal policy that came with the passage in 1965 of Title I of the Elementary and Secondary Education Act, which predicated a substantial share of the federal government's support for schools on the proportion of poor children in school districts.

Both school desegregation and compensatory education were a disappointment to reformers. In desegregation, the legal remedies were clear enough, but they were too slowly carried out. In compensatory education, simple arithmetic worked against the aspirations of reformers; the federal government contributed only about 10 percent of local expenditures to the financing of public schools, and compensatory funds were only a fraction of that. State school-financing systems offered an alternative target for reformers interested in equal educational opportunity. The target had several attractive attributes: The bulk of the money spent on schools could be influenced, directly or indirectly, by changing state school-financing systems. The metric of equality was, or at least appeared to be, compellingly simple — money. Instead of talking in abstractions such as racial justice and opportunity, one could express equality in terms of the dollars spent on individual students. Not inconsequentially, school-financing systems presented a formidable challenge to reformers. No significant school finance reforms had occurred in decades. School finance policy was the province of state legislatures, for whom educational reformers had cultivated a deep disdain. Few other issues could match the intellectual and political challenges that school finance promised.

Arthur Wise, a doctoral student in education at the University of Chicago in the mid-1960s, was one of the first scholars to set about constructing the theory necessary for a judicial assault on state school-financing systems. He drew his inspiration and legal support from three areas in which the U.S. Supreme Court under Chief Justice Earl Warren had demonstrated its willingness to initiate substantial reforms: school desegregation, reapportionment, and the rights of persons accused of crimes (Wise 1967). From the criminal justice cases — where, for example, the Supreme Court had ruled that state courts were obliged to provide transcripts to indigent defendants who wanted to appeal their convictions — Wise inferred that the courts had no obligation to remedy an injustice stemming from social inequality, regardless of whether the injustice was the result of intentional state action. From the reapportionment cases — in which the Supreme Court had overturned state systems for apportioning legislative seats — Wise drew the principle that the value of one's vote and by extension the value of any prerequisite of democratic government should not be determined by one's place of residence. From the school desegregation cases, he drew the legal principle that education was a fundamental function of state government and, therefore, must be made available to all children on equal terms. By Wise's reckoning, these three lines of case law reduced to one simple principle: "A child's educational opportunity should be independent of his parents' circumstances and where he happens to live within a state" (1967: xiii).

The legal remedy Wise (1967) proposed was for the U.S. Supreme Court to hold state legislatures responsible for reforming their school finance systems in accordance with his legal principle, just as the Court had held state legislatures accountable for reforming electoral districts on the one man, one vote principle. The standard of compliance for school-financing systems would be a standard of equal dollars per child except where states could prove that interdistrict inequalities were the result of compensatory treatment for disadvantaged children. The federal courts were a logical place to look for a remedy, he argued, because state legislatures could not be expected to confront the difficult redistributional choices involved in school finance reform without judicial prodding, and the federal courts were accustomed to questions of such complexity.

According to the lawyers who were later involved in the school finance cases, Wise's main contribution was not so much his specific legal theory as it was his demonstration that a plausible constitutional argument could be made for invalidating state school-financing systems when they resulted in substantial interdistrict inequalities. Courts make new law by paying deference to old law, and Wise had demonstrated that this could be persuasively done. The *Serrano* lawyers, looking back, saw Wise's book as a landmark of sorts because it focused attention on the constitutional weaknesses of state school finance systems.

Wise's argument did not go unchallenged. Philip Kurland, a distinguished legal scholar and a member of Wise's dissertation committee, published a strong rebuttal that appeared simultaneously with the publication of Wise's book. Kurland's critique began by granting, prematurely it turned out, that the U.S. Supreme Court would accept some version of Wise's theory and emphasized instead what the probable consequences of such a judicial intervention would be. Kurland saw the intervention, first, as a preemption of the power of local government "to choose the ways in which it will assess, collect, and expend funds," adding that "statewide equality is not consistent with local authority" just as "national equality is not consistent with state power" (1968: 589). How far would the Supreme Court be willing to go in undermining the authority of state and local government to bring about equal distribution of resources?

Kurland further questioned the argument on educational grounds. The real problem, he said, was not how to redistribute resources among school districts, but how to make weak school systems as good as strong ones. One could not achieve this objective, he argued, by constraining the ability of good school systems to raise funds. Finally, he maintained that the courts were the wrong forum in which to argue the equity of school finance systems. He said the problem did not admit of a clear, easily understood constitutional rule; the courts did not control the means of enforcing any rule that might result; and public disagreement over any standard that the courts might develop would surely undermine the remedy. The problem, he concluded, should be left for legislative solution (1968). Kurland's argument did not receive much attention at the time it was made, but his words proved prophetic. The U.S. Supreme Court would later borrow heavily from his argument.

At about the same time as Wise was working on his dissertation, Harold Horowitz, the UCLA law professor to whom Derrick Bell took the school finance problem, was developing a similar line of attack. Taking his point of departure, as did Wise, from the school desegregation cases, Horowitz argued that the Fourteenth Amendment of the U.S. Constitution would also support litigation to remedy the failure of school systems "to provide substantially the same services in schools in advantaged and disadvantaged areas," as well as "to adequately compensate for the inadequate educational preparation of culturally deprived children" (1966:1148). Implicit in this position was a theory Horowitz would later argue unsuccessfully with other lawyers in the *Serrano* case: that school-financing systems should be judged on the basis of how well they meet the educational needs of individual children. After this analysis, Horowitz and a student of his, Diana Nietring, took on the more ambitious question of whether the Fourteenth Amendment could be used as a basis for questioning "the provision of governmental services and the distribution of governmental benefits" generally within states (Horowitz and Nietring 1968:787). The gist of their argument was that states could not use the presence of autonomous jurisdictions within their boundaries—school districts, for example—to deflect their constitutional obligation to provide equal benefits.

"Hal Horowitz," a colleague would later say, "is the unsung hero of *Serrano*—the person who, more than anyone else, was responsible for getting the case to court." Associates also have characterized Horowitz as the house intellectual because among the lawyers who worked on the case he had the longest record of legal scholarship on questions of equal protection. More important in the eyes of his colleagues than his legal scholarship, however, was his unusual combination of moral commitment and pragmatism. In contrast to many other legal scholars, Horowitz was more interested in gaining a remedy for his clients than in demonstrating the force of legal theory. Horowitz's pragmatism proved to be the decisive factor in turning the welter of legal theory that developed around the school finance issue into a strategy of litigation.

Encouraging signals were emanating from the federal courts at the time Wise and Horowitz were writing. In 1967, Judge Skelly Wright ruled in *Hobson* v. *Hansen* that the District of Columbia had allowed unconstitutional resource disparities to develop between all-white and all-black schools and that these disparities had to be remedied either by integrating schools and equalizing resources or by providing compensatory education "sufficient to overcome the detriment of segregation" where integration was impossible.[9] In *United States* v. *Jefferson County Board of Education*, the federal courts required remedial education to "overcome the past inadequacies" of a segregated education.[10] These signals meant that the courts might be willing to expand the idea of equal educational opportunity to include both racial integration and the distribution of educational resources.

The strongest statement of this developing logic came from David Kirp, a law student and later director of the Harvard Center for Law and Education. His argument, based on a close reading of judicial decisions in the equal protection area, was, "The state's obligation is satisfied only if each child has an equal chance for an equal educational outcome, regardless of disparities in cost or effort that the state is obliged to make in order to overcome such differences" (1968:636). States, not municipalities, bore the constitutional responsibility "to provide meaningful relief for inequalities of educational opportunity," and although the state might delegate certain powers to political subdivisions, "it cannot free itself of the underlying responsibility for the success of the educational enterprise" (Kirp 1968:660).

Where Wise and Horowitz had been satisfied with a definition of equality that stressed resource inputs, Kirp aspired to have the courts emphasize outcomes, giving preferential treatment to those children

9. 269 F. Supp. 401, 505 (D.D.C. 1967).
10. 372 F.2d 836, 900 (5th Cir. 1966).

with the greatest disadvantages.[11] Where Wise and Horowitz saw compensatory treatment as an allowable inequality, Kirp saw it as the centerpiece of a strategy for producing equal outcomes. All were agreed, however, on the states' responsibility for reform and on the necessity for intervention by the federal judiciary to change the distribution.

The weakness in Kirp's equality-of-outcomes argument, as his colleague David Cohen would later point out, was that empirical evidence on the relationship between school resources and student outcomes was at best indecisive. By Cohen's (1969) reckoning, existing research provided persuasive reason to believe that spending more on compensatory education or altering the racial composition of classrooms would ultimately close the gap between advantaged and disadvantaged students. In one form or another, this argument would frequently recur in the course of *Serrano* litigation.

In 1966 John Coons, a law professor at Northwestern University, began working with two of his students, Stephen Sugarman and William Clune, on an extensive legal, historical, and empirical analysis of school finance inequalities. Coons's motivation came from a study he had done for the U.S. Civil Rights Commission in the early 1960s of funding differences between predominantly white and black schools in Chicago. Thinking back on that study, Coons reflected, "It occurred to me that I was asking the wrong question. The really large differences in expenditures were not between black and white schools in Chicago, but between Chicago schools and suburban schools."[12] This issue set Coons off on an extended investigation of inequalities generated by state school-financing systems.

11. Kirp comments on this statement:

Horowitz and Nietring . . . talk about differential resource allocation to compensate for background disadvantage; in order to know who to compensate, and how much, one would have to attend to differential outcomes: Thus, there is not as substantial a difference between them, on the one hand, and my *Harvard Educational Review* article on the other, as you suggest (David Kirp 1980: personal communication).

12. John Coons 22 August 1979: personal communication. In the Chicago study, Coons makes the following passing reference to the problem of interdistrict inequalities:

May a state surrender educational policy to the municipalities if the inevitable result is discrimination which is more obvious than any existing within any individual school system? The answer for the moment is undoubtedly yes, but the rationale protecting such differentials in the provision of government service is by no means clear. Although the specific factual differentials are not taken up in this study, the author may report the universal opinion that suburban education is superior to that provided in Chicago (Coons 1962: 184).

Using funds from a Russell Sage Foundation grant to the Northwestern Law School for interdisciplinary training in law and social science, Coons, Clune, and Sugarman worked throughout the 1966–67 school year analyzing the historical development of school-financing systems, the distributional effects of various funding formulas, and the legal theory necessary to challenge their constitutionality. By the end of the school year, as Clune and Sugarman left to pursue their careers, they had accumulated, according to Sugarman, an enormous collection of writing from the project.[13] Coons accepted a visiting appointment at the University of California, Berkeley for the following year and arranged for Sugarman to spend the fall of 1967 revising and editing the previous year's work.

The legal argument that developed out of the Coons, Clune, and Sugarman research was different in certain important respects from the arguments developed by other legal scholars. In general terms, it was markedly less ambitious and more calculating than the theories of Wise (1967), H. Horowitz (1966, 1968), and Kirp (1968). Coons, Clune, and Sugarman stated their basic principle in negative terms: "The quality of public education may not be a function of wealth other than the wealth of the state as a whole" (1970: 2). They were fully alert to the advantages of stating the principle this way. It meant that the courts could declare state school-financing systems unconstitutional without proposing a specific alternative to the existing systems and thereby raising complex issues of the state's responsibility toward disadvantaged students or the state's power with regard to local districts. Coons, Clune, and Sugarman were careful to note that the principle neither required nor precluded compensatory treatment. "Discrimination by the state is our sole object," they said, and this "excludes the duty to ameliorate cultural or natural disadvantages" (1970: 9).

Equally important, Coons, Clune, and Sugarman (1970) took a much narrower view than their colleagues of the role of the state with regard to local districts. Wise (1967), H. Horowitz (1966, 1968), and Kirp (1968) were willing to curtail local autonomy substantially to achieve a more equal distribution of resources and outcomes, but Coons, Clune, and Sugarman constructed a legal theory that ingeniously capitalized on local autonomy and tried to harness it to equity. Local funding decisions, they argued, were an important manifesta-

---

13. Stephen Sugarman 22 August 1979: personal communication.

tion of how much local people valued education. Removing local authority meant reducing local incentives to improve education. The problem with local autonomy, or subsidiarity as they called it, was that under existing school finance systems it aggravated expenditure inequalities among districts. If some way could be found to harness subsidiarity to equality, one could imagine a system in which substantial local autonomy would result in greater equality.

This line of reasoning produced the notion of power equalization, which simply meant that local educational expenditures from state and local revenue sources should be distributed in proportion to local districts' willingness to tax themselves for education. Under a power-equalizing system, absolute equality of expenditures would not be produced unless everyone attached equal value to education, but the system would, Coons, Clune, and Sugarman (1970) predicted, substantially reduce inequalities and make the remaining inequalities a function of a legitimate exercise of local autonomy rather than the happenstance of local property values. The basic requirements of power equalization are satisfied, they argued, "when decisions regarding commitment to education are free of local wealth determinants: to make them so, the purchase of education should 'hurt' as much for a poor district as a rich one" (1970: 23).

Coons, Clune, and Sugarman were careful to point out the limits of their argument. It did not, they argued, speak to the relationship between money and student outcomes. For strategic purposes, they were satisfied with a straightforward definition of the quality of education as "the sum of district expenditures per pupil; quality is money" (1970: 25). They explicitly rejected the notion, required by Kirp's argument, that a showing of a relationship between school resources and student outcomes was necessary to prove that equalization would benefit disadvantaged students. "The children of poor districts have a right to equality of treatment, notwithstanding the impotence of schools to solve their problems" (Coons, Clune, and Sugarman 1970: 32).

The appearance of the Coons, Clune, and Sugarman argument, first in a law review article (1969) and then in book form (1970), had a tonic effect on the thinking of school finance lawyers. Kirp and his colleague Mark Yudof said that the argument made previous analysis of equity in school finance "appear almost primitive by comparison" (1971: 621). They took Coons, Clune, and Sugarman to task for emphasizing equalization of tax effort among districts at the expense of equalizing the opportunities of poor children. There could be no assurance, they argued, that power equalization would make school systems, rich or poor, concentrate on the needs of disadvantaged children. The Coons, Clune, and Sugarman argument also received a substantial boost from Frank Michelman (1969), who gave it extensive attention in his annual review of the U.S. Supreme Court's 1968 term. Michelman was likewise critical of the individual effects of district power equalizing but found ample support in the Coons, Clune, and Sugarman argument for his position that the states were required by the Constitution "to protect against certain hazards which are endemic in an unequal society" (1969: 9). These public discussions had one immediate effect: They made Coons, Clune, and Sugarman leading national figures in school finance litigation, a role they played with great enthusiasm and commitment. For two or three years following the publication of their argument, they generated a blizzard of legal briefs before various courts across the country in support of their proposals for school finance reform.

By mid–1968, when California lawyers began work on the *Serrano* case, an impressive collection of legal scholarship had accumulated, outlining the basic constitutional questions and the elements of a legal strategy for challenging state school-financing systems. The Wise (1967), Horowitz, and Kirp studies had been published. The Coons, Clune, and Sugarman book was substantially completed in draft. Out of this literature, two decidedly different positions began to emerge. One, exemplified by H. Horowitz (1968) and Kirp (1968), urged the courts to state positive principles for the reform of school-financing systems. The courts should not only require state legislatures to reform school finance, they argued, but they should also state the specific criteria on which the new systems should be constructed. Equality of outcomes and educational need were the leading criteria.

The second position, articulated by Coons, Clune, and Sugarman (1970) was to urge the courts to adopt a negative or neutral principle, which would allow them to hold the existing system unconstitutional without specifying anything other than the features the court found objectionable. This approach was consistent with a more limited view of judicial intervention and allowed considerable flexibility in the way legislatures could solve the problem. Although Coons and his colleagues preferred legislative solutions based on the principle of power equalization, they stopped short of urging the courts to force such a remedy on the legislatures. All that was necessary, they argued, was for the court to state that school-financing systems could not make educational quality a function of wealth, other than the wealth of the state as a whole. Within this principle, a variety of policy outcomes were possible, they argued. The other disagreements among reformers—the autonomy and legal status of school districts and the relevant body of case law that could be used to justify judicial intervention, for example—were secondary to this general difference of positions.

According to Coons:

> We argued endlessly with Wise on this issue. We were trying to formulate a position consistent with a limited judicial role. He focused more on the policy outcomes he wanted to achieve. We wanted the courts to take a position on what equity did *not* mean—it did not mean wealth discrimination. The worst thing the courts can do is to say to the legislature, "Do this or do that" (3 August 1980: personal communication).

Eventually, the Coons, Clune, and Sugarman position came to be known as fiscal neutrality. "Throughout the writing of the book," Coons recalls, "we were searching for a name that would capture the essential principle" that the quality of education should not be a function of wealth other than the wealth of the state as a whole. "It wasn't until after the book had gone to bed, when we were writing our first *Serrano* brief in 1970, that we hit upon the name 'fiscal neutrality.'"[14] Consequently, although the term later became the rallying cry of reformers, it does not appear in the earlier literature. It was not until after the *Serrano* case began to develop that the full complexity of fiscal neutrality, as a principle justifying judicial intervention, became apparent.

THE RUSH TO COURT

Lawyers were quick to capitalize on the growing scholarly interest in school finance litigation. John Coons tells of being visited late in 1967 by a group of slick corporate lawyers representing the Detroit Public School System, who had seized on the idea of school finance reform as a way of extracting more money from the state of Michigan to remedy the system's acute financial problems.[15] Detroit's

14. John Coons 3 August 1980: personal communication.
15. John Coons 22 August 1979: personal communication.

property wealth was a source of embarrassment because it had a higher than average assessed valuation per capita. The attorneys decided to base their claim on student need, developing the argument that states should be required to distribute school funds on the basis of measures of students' relative disadvantage. The Detroit case died in the state court of appeals.

At about the same time another case was taking shape. In *McInnis* v. *Shapiro*, the plaintiffs were children in the Chicago Public School System, the defendant was the state of Illinois, and the suit was brought in the federal rather than the state courts. Attorneys for the plaintiffs argued that the Illinois school-financing system violated the federal constitution because it failed to provide adequate support for districts with large concentrations of disadvantaged students. Chicago's problem was not a weak property tax base but a heavy concentration of disadvantaged students. If inequalities stemming from economic disadvantage were the target, the plaintiffs' lawyers argued, then the correct remedy was a financing system that took educational need into account in the distribution of funds.

The educational needs argument gave John Coons a great deal of discomfort. He had tried to dissuade the Detroit lawyers from using it, and he watched *McInnis* with great concern. In Coons's words, the needs argument was "OK as policy, but absolutely cuckoo as constitutional law," because of its disdain for the neutral principles position.[16] Educational needs were a legitimate way for legislatures to address the special problems of big cities, he argued, but they provided no basis for a constitutional challenge to school-financing systems. When the three-judge federal district court in Detroit issued its opinion in *McInnis*, Coons's worst fears were borne out. The court rejected the educational needs argument, calling it a "nebulous concept" and arguing that it "provided no discoverable and manageable standards by which a court can determine when the Constitution is satisfied and when it is violated."[17] Furthermore, the court ruled that the inequalities produced by the Illinois school-financing system were a legitimate by-product of local autonomy. Citing "the desirability of a certain degree of local administration and local autonomy," the court said that "effective, efficient administration necessitates decentralization" of school financing.[18] The plain-

---

16. John Coons 22 August 1979: personal communication.
17. McInnis v. Shapiro, 293 F. Supp. 329, 335 (N.D. Ill. 1968).
18. Id. at 336.

tiffs' attorneys appealed the district court decision directly to the Supreme Court.

The mid–1968 district court decision in *McInnis* occurred at a critical juncture in the development of the legal theory of school finance reform. Much of the literature challenging the constitutionality of school-financing systems was either newly published or not yet in print. The intricacies of legal strategy had just barely begun to be discussed. In this context, *McInnis* was a very distressing event for people like Coons who had a lot riding on the courts' willingness to engage the issue. Coons believed that the U.S. Supreme Court would affirm the lower court decision unless it could be convinced that the issue was simply not ready to be decided. With this tactic in mind, Coons, Clune, and Sugarman drafted a bluntly worded amicus brief and submitted it to the U.S. Supreme Court. The brief said that the district court was unaware at the time it decided the case that other cases were in preparation around the country and that a substantial legal literature was developing on the subject. The brief specifically mentions Wise's book (1967) and Kirp's earliest article (1968). Furthermore, the brief argued, the district court "did not exhibit even a rudimentary understanding of the options open to the judiciary in the handling of this problem."[19] Coons, Clune, and Sugarman argued that the Supreme Court should send the case back to the district court for reargument. The Supreme Court ignored their advice, and in early 1969 just as *Serrano* was beginning to work its way through the court system in California, the Court perfunctorily affirmed *McInnis* without saying why.[20]

McInnis could be read two ways. One was that the Supreme Court had simply treated it as a nuisance case and affirmed the district court decision because it did not regard the issue as important enough to decide at that point. The Court did not have a choice of whether to hear the case because it came on appeal from a three-judge district court. Another way of reading *McInnis* was that it expressed the Supreme Court's position on school finance reform— that there was no constitutional basis for a challenge to the inequities produced by state school-financing schemes. Both readings were made, and the Supreme Court's position was not to be clarified for another five years.

19. Coons, Clune, and Sugarman, "Motion for Leave to File Brief of Amici Curiae and Brief of Amici Curiae," McInnis v. Shapiro, 394 U.S. 322 (1969).

20. McInnis v. Ogilvie, 394 U.S. 322 (1969).

SERRANO GOES TO COURT

On 23 August 1968 lawyers representing John Serrano and a dozen or so other named plaintiffs filed a complaint in Los Angeles County Superior Court alleging that substantial disparities existed in per pupil expenditures among school districts within the state and "therefore substantial disparities in the quality and extent . . . of educational opportunities . . . are perpetuated among the several school districts in the state."[21] The complaint asked the court to declare California's school finance scheme inconsistent with the equal protection provisions of both the U.S. and California constitutions and to require the California legislature to "reallocate school funds . . . so as to provide substantially equal opportunities for all children of the state."

The complaint was the work of a small group of lawyers brought together under the auspices of the Western Center on Law and Poverty—Harold Horowitz from UCLA; Derrick Bell from WCLP; and two young attorneys, Sidney Wolinsky and Michael Schapiro, from private law firms in Los Angeles. Horowitz recalls "meeting after meeting" on the drafting of the complaint.[22] Bell remembers being attracted to the school finance issue because it presented "an opportunity to challenge a well-settled legal doctrine" and because "we were all impressed with the absolute difference in per pupil expenditures between the richest and poorest districts in the state."[23] Early discussions centered on documenting inequalities, finding plaintiffs to represent the class of people most adversely affected by the system, and finding a theoretical basis for a constitutional challenge. For documentation, the attorneys simply used the published statistics of the California State Department of Education, compiling a list of comparisons among rich districts and poor districts and demonstrating that poor districts had to tax themselves at a higher rate to raise less money per pupil than rich districts.

It was at this stage that the famous comparison between Beverly Hills and Baldwin Park emerged. Beverly Hills, with a tax rate of less than one-half that of Baldwin Park and less than one-half as many students, was able to spend nearly a million dollars a year more on

---

21. Serrano v. Priest, 557 P.2d 929 (1976), on file at the Western Center on Law and Poverty, Los Angeles, California.

22. Harold Horowitz 9 July 1979: personal communication.

23. Derrick Bell 31 May 1979: personal communication.

its schools, which translated into a per pupil expenditure of nearly 2.5 times that of Baldwin Park.

The job of finding plaintiffs fell to Charles Jones, who used his network of poverty program connections to generate a list of people whose minority group status and place of residence made them good examples of inequities produced by the school-financing system. John Serrano's name went to the top of the list, an insider said, "because we wanted to associate the case with a name that clearly belonged to an ethnic minority and Serrano fit the bill."

The case presented a series of tactical and theoretical problems that challenged the lawyers' ingenuity and pragmatism. In the spring and summer of 1968 when the complaint was being drafted, the *Serrano* lawyers had only the scholarly literature and their own hunches on which to base an argument because the Detroit and *McInnis* cases had not yet been decided. Horowitz describes the drafting as "a group effort" in which "everyone had his own ideas about what should be in the complaint and everyone gave a little."[24] Horowitz's theoretical position, based on his earlier articles, pushed him in the direction of basing the complaint on student needs, the approach that would later be struck down in *McInnis*. His pragmatism, however, won out over his theoretical predispositions. "My position," he said, "was to throw everything we possibly could into the complaint and not to wed ourselves to any specific legal theory."[25] The consequence was what David Kirp has called the "kitchen sink" strategy (1973:98). The complaint, after some twenty drafts, alleged that the school-financing system of the state of California made the quality of education "a function of wealth," "a function of geographical accident," and that it "fails to take account of . . . educational needs," "fails to provide children of equal age, aptitude . . . and ability with . . . equal resources," and that it "perpetuates marked differences in the quality of educational services."[26] What the complaint lacked in theoretical rigor was more than compensated for by its coverage of every conceivable theoretical basis for a challenge. The *Serrano* lawyers were less concerned than the legal scholars about legal doctrine and more concerned about maximizing the possible grounds for constitutional challenge.

24. Harold Horowitz 9 July 1979: personal communication.
25. Harold Horowitz 9 July 1979: personal communication.
26. Serrano v. Priest, 557 P.2d 929 (1976).

The next important tactical question was whom to sue. One possibility was to sue all school districts in the state, save the poorest, but this option was quickly rejected for its logistical difficulties (Kirp 1973). The lawyers decided to sue selected state and county officials on behalf of

> all children in the State of California who are attending free public and elementary schools provided by the State . . . (except children in that school district, the identity of which is presently unknown, which school district affords the greatest educational opportunity of all school districts in California).[27]

This peculiar and clever legalism allowed the lawyers to sue without specifying precisely who would gain and who would lose from a decision in favor of the plaintiffs.

A touchier issue was whether to include Governor Reagan on the list of defendants.[28] Knowing that the issue would eventually have to go to the legislature for resolution and wanting to avoid forcing Reagan to take a position on the issue before it was necessary, the lawyers decided to take the narrowest possible definition of the defendants: the state treasurer, controller, and superintendent of public instruction, and the Los Angeles County tax collector, treasurer, and superintendent of schools. The list of defendants expanded and contracted as the case slowly progressed through the courts, depending on the political climate surrounding school finance reform. In trial court, the defendants were joined by Kenneth Peters, superintendent of the Beverly Hills school system. After the initial state supreme court decision, in 1971, the state superintendent of public instruction, Wilson Riles, switched sides and joined by plaintiffs (by 1980, he had switched back again to join the defendants).

Probably the single most important tactical decision the lawyers made was to sue in the state courts, rather than the federal. They had no way of knowing when they started that *McInnis* would make the federal courts an inhospitable place to argue their case. Their decision to file in Los Angeles Superior Court, rather than federal district court, had an explicit logic behind it. As Horowitz put it, "This was exactly the sort of issue to argue before the California Supreme

27. Serrano v. Priest, 557 P. 2d.

28. According to Horowitz, "At one point we thought of putting Reagan's name at the top of the list, if we could find a leading plaintiff with a name like 'John Good-of-Heart,' but nothing ever came of it" (Harold Horowitz 9 July 1979: personal communication).

Court, because of the Court's eminence and its willingness to consider questions of this magnitude."[29]

They insured that the case would raise both federal and state constitutional issues by basing their complaint on the equal protection clauses of both the U.S. and California constitutions. Although there was no feasible alternative basis, the *Serrano* lawyers were drawn into an extraordinarily complex area of discretionary judicial decisionmaking. The equal protection clause requires a demonstration that either school-financing systems bear no rational relationship to any legitimate state purpose or that education is a sufficiently fundamental interest and school-financing systems involve a suspect classification that justifies special constitutional protection. Standards of judicial decisionmaking on these questions were at the time, and still are, extremely fluid and, therefore, extremely sensitive to differences in decisionmaking style among judges within and between jurisdictions. Sifting evidence on the effects of the existing system to extend existing equal protection reasoning into a new area put enormous demands on both the plaintiffs' lawyers and the judges hearing the case.

The equal protection argument exposed the *Serrano* lawyers to a host of technical problems for which they were initially ill-prepared. One might challenge the suspect classification claim, for example, on the ground that poor children do not necessarily live in poor school districts. All the *Serrano* lawyers were prepared to demonstrate when they filed the complaint was that there was a large disparity in expenditure and tax effort between the richest and poorest districts and that in *some* cases poor children lived in poor districts and rich children lived in rich districts. Did the claim that education was a fundamental interest require the *Serrano* lawyers to demonstrate that unequal educational expenditures produced unequal educational outcomes? If so, they would have been hard pressed to produce definitive evidence on the subject. Did the argument that the school-financing system bore no reasonable relationship to any legitimate state purpose require the *Serrano* lawyers to propose an alternative system that would meet the objections they raised? If so, they would also have great difficulties in producing such a system based on existing literature.

In broader terms, certain political risks were associated with a judicial challenge to the school-financing system. A series of adverse

29. Harold Horowitz 9 July 1979: personal communication.

court decisions, for example, might give the existing inequities a constitutional legitimacy that they did not have before and leave the
Serrano plaintiffs worse off than if they had not challenged the system at all. In addition, at the time the complaint was filed there was
little evidence that a political constituency existed in Sacramento to
press the plaintiffs' interests in the legislature if the court decision
were favorable. Criticisms of the existing system tended to focus on
the total amount of money available for education as a whole rather
than on the proportionate share among districts. Insofar as there was
any support for greater equalization, it came from a handful of dedi-
cated school finance experts and legislators who had great difficulty
finding an attentive audience. This attitude toward the equity issue
meant that the *Serrano* complaint was not seen as particularly important when it was filed. "No one took us very seriously," said one
early participant, "and when I think about it, I understand why. We
didn't have much idea what we were getting ourselves into."

When the complaint was heard in Los Angeles County Superior
Court, representatives of the county attorney and the state attorney
general filed a demurrer, accepting the evidence on inequities contained in the plaintiff's brief and asserting that they raised no constitutional issue. They moved for dismissal of the case without trial. In
January 1969 the superior court accepted the defendants' motion
and dismissed the case. Shortly thereafter, the *Serrano* attorneys—
by now the courtroom work was being handled by Wolinsky and
Shapiro—appealed the decision to the state court of appeals.

It took nearly a year for the state court of appeals to dispose of
Serrano. By the time the appeals court was ready to render a decision
in the case, *McInnis* had moved from district court in Chicago to the
U.S. Supreme Court, which had tacitly affirmed the district court's
decision. This left the state court of appeals an easy way out of the
Serrano appeal. It could simply say that the U.S. Supreme Court's
disposition of *McInnis* was binding on *Serrano* because both cases
involved equal protection arguments and both raised the same issue.
This eventuality had prompted Coons to argue in his amicus brief
before the U.S. Supreme Court that the issue was not ready for decision in *McInnis*.

The failure of the U.S. Supreme Court to send *McInnis* back to
district court for reargument made it possible for any court—state or
federal—to view the district court's disposition of *McInnis* as binding. This is what happened when the state court of appeals dealt with

Serrano. The court made no distinction between the *Serrano* and *McInnis* arguments. The court interpreted the *Serrano* complaint as alleging that "under the equal protection clause the amount of money per pupil may vary only on the basis of the respective educational needs of pupils,"[30] which was the same as the issue presented in *McInnis*. Hence, the court argued, the issue presented in *Serrano* had already been decided in *McInnis*. The inequities complained of by the *Serrano* plaintiffs were not unconstitutional, the court ruled, because they were reasonably related to the legitimate state policy of delegating authority for school financing to local districts and of allowing local districts to demonstrate by their tax rates how much importance they attach to education.

In about a year and a half, the *Serrano* lawyers had succeeded only in producing two court decisions against their clients. It was discouraging and time-consuming work, and the *McInnis* rewards were anything but clear. There was not exactly a groundswell of support developing for school finance reform. There were no signs that the courts would intervene and no signs from Sacramento that school finance reform was high on anyone's legislative agenda.

Between mid–1970 and January 1971, the political and legal environment surrounding school finance began to change perceptibly. One decisive event was the publication, early in 1970, of the Coons, Clune, and Sugarman book, *Private Wealth and Public Education*, which significantly increased the visibility of their argument. Another decisive event was the preparation, between November 1970 and January 1971, of *Public School Finance*, a comprehensive review of California's school-financing system by Alan Post, the state's legislative analyst (1971). Post, a highly respected, very influential insider in Sacramento, anticipated that a state supreme court decision in the school finance area might catch the legislature unprepared. His report was ostensibly to present basic information on the school-financing system for the use of the legislature. Its actual effect was much more far-reaching. By straightforwardly describing the distributional effects of the existing system, it underscored the *Serrano* lawyers' case and lent Post's considerable authority to their cause.

The California Supreme Court granted a hearing in *Serrano* in January 1971 and scheduled oral arguments for that spring. The court's decision to hear the case had a galvanizing effect on the *Serrano* law-

30. Serrano v. Priest, 10 Cal. App. 3d 1110, 1115 (1969).

yers. During this period, Coons and Sugarman spent time briefing Wolinsky and Shapiro, who were preparing the plaintiffs' case, on the details of their argument and on the way evidence should be presented to characterize the operation of the existing system. From these consultations and from long discussions among themselves, the *Serrano* lawyers settled on a strategy for arguing their case before the court.

The appeals court's assertion that *Serrano* was indistinguishable from *McInnis* forced a narrowing of the original kitchen sink strategy in which the *Serrano* lawyers had tried to offer the courts the widest possible range of arguments for intervention. Now the problem was how to provide the court with a rationale for intervening in school finance policy, while assuring the court that it was not required to adjudicate the messy problems raised by *McInnis*. For this purpose, there was no better rationale than the cautious, neutral principles approach advocated by Coons and his colleagues. In Sidney Wolinsky's words,

> The major strategy was to ask for a very restrained principle. . . . We said we were *not* asking for [compensation according to need], only equality. All the Court was asked to do was foreclose one of the thousands of alternatives open to the legislature. They could have vouchers, or could even give extra money to good schools for special programs—as long as a rational choice is made in an educational sense (Reinhold 1972: E-26).

Wolinsky captured the strength of the strategy when he said, "it allowed us to avoid concepts like 'need' and 'educational opportunity'—all those garbage terms that education has become overburdened with" (Reinhold 1972: E-26). Henceforth, the school-financing system would be attacked on the grounds that it made educational quality an artifact of school district property wealth rather than because it failed to meet some positive test, such as educational need.

From a purely strategic standpoint, this shift from the kitchen sink to the neutral principles approach immeasurably strengthened the *Serrano* lawyers' position. It offered the court a way to initiate a major change in policy without having to state, except in abstract terms, what that change should be. It allowed the *Serrano* lawyers to be advocates of both far-reaching reform and judicial restraint. It pushed legal arguments away from discussions of alternatives to the existing system and toward an examination of the undesirable characteristics of that system. Not the least of its advantages was that it allowed the complex issues of school financing to be reduced to the simple, epigrammatic form that lawyers and judges feel most comfortable with.

If the shift in strategy significantly strengthened the *Serrano* lawyers' position, it also concealed certain important ambiguities that would later create a wide gulf between the court and legislature. The first of these had to do with the question of whom reform was intended to benefit. Who precisely were the plaintiffs in *Serrano* and what broader class of interests did they represent? If they won their case, to whom should the legislature address the remedy? The early literature on school finance reform written by Wise (1967), H. Horowitz (1968), and Kirp (1968) had been predicated on the assumption that reform would help poor, disadvantaged students and that the wealth biases of the existing system operated against the interests of this class. Reinforcing this assumption was the fact that the WCLP, with its charge to act as an advocate for the traditionally unrepresented, had taken up the cause.

As early as the drafting of the original complaint, however, the idea of poor, disadvantaged students as the beneficiaries of reform had started to fade. As long as the *Serrano* lawyers pursued the kitchen sink strategy, they left open the possibility that those with the greatest educational needs would be the beneficiaries of reform. With the adoption of the neutral principles strategy, the litigation focused on an abstract attribute of the existing system—the relationship between property values and educational expenditures—rather than on the interests of a specific class or group, defined by social background and opportunities. The notion persisted—and still persists to this day—that *Serrano* was designed to help disadvantaged school children. For such an assertion to be correct, one must make the heroic (and, as it was later discovered, largely incorrect) assumption that poor children live in poor school districts. John Coons argues, in retrospect, that *Serrano* was never intended to help poor children exclusively but rather to attack the constitutionally indefensible connection between property wealth and educational expenditures for all schoolchildren whom it penalized. He admits that the advocates of reform may have given another impression.

> In the 1960s, when we were developing our argument, we were writing for the U.S. Supreme Court, and the Court at that time was going heavily on an equal protection rationale. Strictly as a matter of tactics, we had to move in

that direction. We may have given the impression in some of our rhetoric that we were helping poor children, but our main objective was always to demonstrate the irrationality of wealth-based systems.[31]

The plaintiffs in *Serrano* had never played much of a role in determining the interests at stake in the litigation; in John Serrano's words, it was a "lawyers' case." School finance reform was, from the outset, a collection of legal theories looking for plaintiffs rather than the reverse. With the adoption of the neutral principles strategy, however, the questions of who were the intended beneficiaries of school finance litigation and to whom the legislature should address its remedy receded even further into the background. The *Serrano* lawyers dealt with the dilemma of choosing plaintiffs for public law litigation by pushing it aside. The question was not how broadly or narrowly to define the interests of the intended beneficiaries of the suit as much as it was how to give the court an appealing rationale for intervention in a complex policy issue.

Another source of ambiguity in the neutral principles strategy was the question of how much or what form of equalization would be required by a favorable court decision. The attribute of state school-financing systems that attracted the attention of reformers in the first place was the dramatic difference in expenditures, property wealth, and tax rates from one locality to another. One would assume that school finance litigation had as its objective a marked redistribution of resources from high- to low-spending districts. What Coons and his colleagues meant by a wealth-neutral system was not necessarily one in which expenditures were made more equal although that was a probable outcome. Their interest was in the relationship between tax rates and expenditures, and the objective was to reduce the inverse relationship between tax effort and expenditure that characterized the extremes of the existing system. A wealth-neutral system could be any system in which poor districts were not required to tax themselves any harder than rich districts to achieve the same level of expenditure. Hence, a wealth-neutral system could

31. John Coons 3 August 1980: personal communication. Coons also observes that he and his colleagues were unable to address the relationship between family income and property wealth in any systematic way. As proof that they did not overlook the issue altogether, however, he cites a footnote in their research (1970: 357n) referring to unpublished data estimating that 59 percent of minority students in the state of California reside in districts with assessed valuations per pupil greater than the median for the state.

entail enormous inequalities of expenditure as long as those inequalities were not based on differences in district property wealth.[32]

On this issue, the *Serrano* lawyers—Sidney Wolinsky and, later, John McDermott—parted company with Coons and his colleagues. The *Serrano* lawyers were inclined to treat expenditure inequalities as being at least as important as tax rate inequalities, while arguing that wealth neutrality was the standard against which any system should be judged. This combination of objectives allowed Wolinsky to argue in the same breath that the plaintiffs were asking for equality and that the legislature could give extra money to good schools. Presumably, the result of the suit would be a much narrower distribution of expenditures among districts funded from property wealth, not just a more equitable ratio of tax effort to expenditure. The legislature would also be free to distribute funds to school districts, even good ones, on some educationally relevant basis, as long as it was wealth neutral.

This complex, abstract line of reasoning would later strike many actors in the legislative process as confusing. What, precisely, were they supposed to be paying attention to—tax equity, expenditure equity, or both? The fact that the interests at stake in the suit were not tied down to any identifiable group of people whom legislators could point to as the target of school finance reform made the argument even more difficult to translate into tangible proposals. The aspect of the argument that drove an even deeper wedge between the legislature and the court was the power that the argument concentrated in the hands of lawyers and judges. The neutral principles strategy allowed the lawyers and judges to argue solely in terms of the deficiencies of the existing system, rather than the difficulties of getting from a general statement of those deficiencies to a remedy. The latter task was, after all, the responsibility of the legislature. What the lawyers and judges did not say, however, was that they, not the legislature, would be the final arbiters of whether the legislative remedy was adequate or not. Their judgment on the adequacy of the legislature's response would, of course, be based on the legislature's ability to disentangle and specify such enormously complex abstrac-

---

32. When John Coons was giving oral comments on a draft of this chapter, we asked him what he would think of a school-financing system that duplicated the expenditure inequalities of the existing system but eliminated property wealth as the determinant of those inequalities. His reply was, "Splendid! As long as the result bears some rational relationship to an educational objective" (John Coons 3 August 1980: personal communication).

tions as the relationship between tax equity and expenditure equity. In other words, the neutral principles strategy allowed lawyers and judges to have the best parts of both judicial activism and judicial restraint, leaving the legislature to translate the lawyers' implicit reform objectives into explicit policy.

When oral arguments were actually made before the California Supreme Court, Wolinsky presented the plaintiffs' case, and Coons and Sugarman appeared as amici curiae, representing the Urban Coalition and the National Committee for the Support of Public Schools. The Coons and Sugarman brief was a complete embodiment of the neutral principles strategy. Most if it (thirty-nine of forty-four pages) was devoted to documenting the per pupil expenditure inequalities and tax rate inequities resulting from the existing system and explaining the principle of fiscal neutrality. The remaining five pages dealt sketchily with possible legislative remedies consistent with fiscal neutrality but scrupulously avoided recommending that the court adopt any of them.

The techniques that Coons and Sugarman used to demonstrate the inequities of the existing system were notable. First, they compared the ten richest and ten poorest districts in the state, using assessed valuation per pupil, expenditure per pupil, and tax rate. The message was effective, as the accompanying exhibits show. "Poor districts tax more and spend less," they concluded.[33] From this conclusion they deftly moved to undercut the argument of the state court of appeals that the existing system supported local autonomy.

> Far from being an embodiment of local choice, it is . . . its antithesis. The primary effect of the structure is not the sharing of State power among subordinate geographical units; rather it is the creation of enclaves of widely varying power — some freakishly privileged, others grossly disadvantaged.[34]

Reasoning from extreme cases is a classic device of legal argument, and it was used to good effect. In this instance, however, it concealed some important questions: What about the remaining thousand or so school districts lying between the ten richest and ten poorest? Were the relationships between district wealth and expenditure as clear in the vast and diverse middle as they were at the extremes? What would the analysis have shown if rich and poor districts had been

33. Sugarman and Coons, Amici Curiae Brief at 20, Serrano v. Priest, 487 P.2d 1241 (1971).
34. Id. at 21.

defined in terms of median family income rather than property wealth? Were districts with high property wealth also those with high family income? The brief was mute on these questions.

The second technique Coons and Sugarman used was to represent graphically what would happen under existing law if all school systems taxed themselves at a rate equal to the statewide median. Holding the tax rate constant, of course, accentuated the effect of widely varying property tax bases and showed that wealthy districts could spend on the order of four times the amount that poor districts could under the same rate.[35] Again, the technique effectively demonstrated problems at the extremes, glossed over the problems of the largest number of school districts, and avoided altogether the question of the relationship between family income and property wealth.

The presentation of the data coincided perfectly with the argument behind fiscal neutrality: Property wealth was an arbitrary and inequitable basis by which to determine educational expenditures. For purposes of legal strategy it did not matter that an argument based on extremes might not be useful in understanding the problems involved in constructing a school-financing system that would work for all districts. The extremes of the system captured the attribute that the lawyers wanted to emphasize. Fiscal neutrality, after all, was not designed to point the way to a new school finance system, only to invalidate an existing one.

Coons was also involved in the preparation of another brief which was one of the most politically significant in the *Serrano* litigation. Coons and others approached a number of San Francisco legislators, including Senator George Moscone and Assemblyman Willie Brown, asking them to file a brief in support of the appellants' case. Eventually all six senators and assemblymen from San Francisco joined in a brief, the main argument of which was that the existing system "worsens the plight of our cities, and encourages the growing exodus of more affluent residents to the suburbs which offer them both tax haven and better-supported education" (Kirp 1973:101).

The San Francisco brief was significant in two respects. First, it gave an early showing of political support for reform that might have influenced the court's judgment on the legislature's readiness to confront the issue. Second, and more important, it illustrated how

---

35. Sugarman and Coons, Amici Curiae Brief at 13–18, Serrano v. Priest, 487 P.2d 1241 (1971).

diffuse people's perceptions of school finance reform were when *Serrano* was being argued before the court. In fact, a bit of serious analysis would have raised questions about whether San Francisco stood to gain from a reformed school finance system. By fiscal neutrality standards, San Francisco was a fairly wealthy school system: It had a high assessed valuation per pupil, but it also had high per pupil expenses, which left it in an anomalous position.

In time, San Franciscans would learn to differentiate their interests from those of poor school systems with low assessed valuation per pupil. The fiscal neutrality standard made the stakes of school finance reform sufficiently vague that it remained an attractive cause to all but the very few wealthiest school systems singled out for special attention in the lawyers' arguments. Coons says of the San Francisco brief:

> We explicitly warned San Francisco, "We're asking you to come in because it is good overall, not because it will necessarily help you out." And people like George Moscone were persuaded by that argument. It is true, though, that a lot of people didn't understand the stakes; lawyers are always in a position of wondering how much of the weakness in their own case to show the enemy.

The state of California, at that time represented by State Attorney General Evelle Younger, stuck doggedly to its *McInnis* defense. It did not reply to any of the specific charges because it maintained that, regardless of the magnitude of the inequities, the existing system was a legitimate exercise of state power and could be revised only by legislative initiative. The simplicity of the state's defense was largely predicated on the belief that the California Supreme Court would be sufficiently wary of the political complexities of the school finance issue that it would follow the lead of the court of appeals and interpret *McInnis* as binding.

During oral arguments the state supreme court justices asked pointed but fairly general questions. Wolinsky was asked, "What will happen if you win the suit? Will the schools go out of business?" To which he replied, in the well-developed language of fiscal neutrality, "No, the state legislature may adopt any of a wide variety of alternatives." On the issue of whether education was a fundamental interest deserving of constitutional protection, Wolinsky was asked, "And what about other governmental services—streets, libraries, sewers— are they fundamental too? Do they have to be equalized as well?" To which Wolinsky replied that education was singled out because of its importance to the exercise of basic economic and political rights. To the question of how far the court should go in its scrutiny of school finance, Wolinsky replied, "We ask only that the court set the outer constitutional parameters in which the legislature should be left free to act—so long as it does not discriminate against the poor." Likewise, the justice pressed the state hard on its argument that the system was not constitutionally suspect, asking, "Don't disparities exist? Don't they affect the educational opportunities of children?" (Kirp 1973:101–102). The state's response was exactly as it had been from the time the original complaint had been filed. It acknowledged the disparities but denied they were of any constitutional significance.

The California Supreme Court rendered its decision in *Serrano* on 30 August 1971, exactly three years after the initial complaint. The decision was a vindication of Horowitz's early strategic hunch that the case would fare better in the state than in the federal courts. Justice Sullivan, speaking for himself and five other justices, made an eloquent and tightly reasoned case against the constitutionality of the existing school finance system—a case that accepted all the major tenets of the *Serrano* lawyers' argument. The lone dissent, filed by Justice McComb, was a simple two-sentence restatement of the appeals court's grounds for dismissal, with no significant rebuttal of the court's argument.[36]

The court found the wealth-based nature of the school-financing system constitutionally suspect:

> We think that discrimination on the basis of district wealth is . . . invalid. The commercial and industrial property which augments a district's tax base is distributed unevenly. . . . To allot more educational dollars to the children of one district than to those of another merely because of the fortuitous presence of such property is to make the quality of a child's education dependent upon the location of private commercial and industrial establishments. Surely, this is to rely on the most irrelevant of factors as the basis for educational financing.[37]

The court also established that education was a fundamental interest within the meaning of the equal protection clause, calling it a "distinctive and priceless" benefit that was "essential in maintaining free enterprise democracy" and "unmatched in the extent to which it

36. Serrano v. Priest, 487 P.2d 1241, 1266 (1971).

37. Id. at 1252.

molds the personality of youth."[38] Finally, the court found that the system was not necessary to the accomplishment of a compelling state interest. In a close paraphrase of the Coons and Sugarman brief, the court said,

> So long as the assessed valuation within a district's boundaries is a major determinant of how much it can spend for its schools, only a district with a large tax base will be truly able to decide how much it really cares about education. The poor district cannot freely choose to tax itself into an excellence which its tax rolls cannot provide. Far from being necessary to promote local fiscal choice, the present system actually deprives the less wealthy districts of that option.[39]

Then, in a ringing conclusion, the court declared,

> By our holding today we further the cherished idea of American education that in a democratic society free public schools shall make available to all children equally the abundant gifts of learning.[40]

In passing, the court disposed of *McInnis* with a clever, if not wholly persuasive, device. First, the court argued, the U.S. Supreme Court could not be said to have spoken definitively on the school finance issue in *McInnis* because it had no discretion about whether to hear the case and it had chosen to dispose of the case in a summary judgment without rendering an opinion. Second, the grounds for *Serrano* and *McInnis* were different because the plaintiffs in *Serrano* did not base their claim on an educational need argument. In short, the court concluded, *McInnis* was not binding.[41]

The two most commonly cited sources in the court's opinion were the legislative analyst's report on school finance (1971) and the Coons, Clune, and Sugarman law review article (1969). Consistent with the logic of fiscal neutrality, the court found only that wealth-based inequalities among school districts were unconstitutional. It did not explicitly discuss the relationship between family income and district wealth, nor did it suggest any specific remedies that the legislature might use to address existing inequities.

One story that made the rounds in Sacramento was that Chief Justice Wright asked Legislative Analyst Alan Post, in a private conversa-

38. Id. at 1255–59.
39. Id. at 1260.
40. Id. at 1266.
41. Id. at 1241, 1264–65.

tion, "Will *Serrano* help poor children?" To which Post is supposed to have replied, "Of course." On that basis, Judge Wright is alleged to have thrown his support to the plaintiffs. Whether the story is true or not, the rhetoric of the court's opinion suggests that they thought that by redistributing state funds from wealthy to poor school districts they would be helping poor children achieve a better education.

The fallout from *Serrano* was immediate and extensive. It received widespread attention in the national press. It was the occasion for a nationwide meeting of lawyers from twenty states who were at various stages of school finance litigation (Kirp 1973). Most important, it had an immediate effect on the federal judiciary. Shortly after Coons and Sugarman prepared their *Serrano* brief, lawyers for the plaintiff in a federal court case in Minnesota asked them to prepare a draft opinion for the district court. Their draft followed the general outlines of the fiscal neutrality argument in their *Serrano* brief. When the federal district court handed down its opinion in *Van Duzartz* v. *Hatfield* a few months after *Serrano*, it bore a striking resemblance to the Coons and Sugarman draft, and it cited the California Supreme Court's opinion in *Serrano* as support for its argument.[42] School finance lawyers were optimistic in the aftermath of *Serrano* that they had turned the tide of judicial decisions against the precedent set by *McInnis*. They could now envision taking a case before the U.S. Supreme Court that was clearly distinguished from *McInnis* by virtue of its reliance on fiscal neutrality. The fiscal neutrality argument, its advocates maintained, could change the whole complexion of judicial decisionmaking on school finance because it put the federal courts in a position to initiate nationwide reform without entangling themselves in specific remedies.

In strictly legal terms, the effect of *Serrano* was considerably narrower than the publicity surrounding it suggested. All the California Supreme Court actually resolved by its decision was whether the *Serrano* plaintiffs were entitled to a full hearing in Los Angeles County Superior Court and if so, on what constitutional grounds their case should be tried. Because the original *Serrano* complaint had been dismissed without a trial on the facts of the case, it had to be returned to superior court. Hence, the California Supreme Court's 1971 decision—later called *Serrano I*—was only a preliminary decision. Imme-

42. 334 F. Supp. 870 (D. Minn. 1971).

diately after *Serrano I*, the *Serrano* attorneys began preparing for the complex task of presenting the factual basis for their claim in superior court.

RODRIGUEZ AND SENATE BILL 90 INTERVENE

Before *Serrano* got back to superior court, two important events intervened. The California legislature, with one eye on the Supreme Court's *Serrano I* decision, enacted a general tax and revenue measure, Senate Bill (SB) 90, that made important changes in the school-financing system. In addition, the U.S. Supreme Court delivered a decision in *San Antonio Independent School System* v. *Rodriguez* that changed the entire complexion of school finance litigation.[43] Both of these events precipitated important mid-course changes in the legal strategy behind *Serrano*. Much of the optimism that attended *Serrano I* came as a result of a widely shared feeling that at last some degree of order and predictability had been introduced into school finance litigation. This was not to be. The political and legal environment did not stand still or even slow appreciably in the aftermath of *Serrano I*.

The politics of SB 90 will be treated at length in Chapter 3. For present purposes, the important aspects of the law lie in its equalization provisions. SB 90 did not radically alter the existing school finance system—it maintained the foundation approach, whereby the state guarantees a minimum level of expenditure in each district, although it did increase that level substantially. Insofar as it maintained the foundation approach, SB 90 tended to perpetuate the inequities of the earlier system, because flat grants discriminate against low-wealth districts in favor of high-wealth districts.

The law did introduce an element—the so-called revenue limit— that shifted the distribution of resources in favor of low-wealth districts. For the first time in the history of state school finance policy, the law set a dollar limit on the amount of money school districts could spend per pupil out of funds raised by the basic property tax. The revenue limit was pegged initially on expenditures during the 1972–73 school year and then allowed to increase each following year by a legislatively determined inflation index. The equalization

43. 411 U.S. 1 (1973).

effect of the revenue limit stemmed from the fact that high-wealth districts were given a lower inflation factor than low-wealth districts. Other things being equal, this so-called squeeze factor would produce a convergence in per pupil expenditures over time between rich and poor districts. As one might suspect, however, other things were not equal. SB 90 left in place the voted override provision of the old system, allowing districts to exceed their revenue limits by voting a higher tax rate. Hence, the equalization effects of SB 90 were uncertain. They depended in part on how quickly the squeeze factor would work and in part on the willingness of wealthy districts to vote overrides that compensated for losses due to the squeeze factor. Legislative and executive branch partisans of SB 90 bravely maintained that the law constituted a legitimate, if not sufficient, response to *Serrano I*, but the *Serrano* lawyers were dubious.

SB 90 imposed a significant new burden on the *Serrano* lawyers. Not only were they required to document their original assertion that the school finance system discriminated on the basis of wealth, they now had to establish—to their own satisfaction and the court's—whether SB 90 remedied the system's defects. On the face of it, this complication required a more sophisticated analytic approach than the lawyers had used in the past. They would not simply have to represent the gap between rich and poor districts but would also have to project the effects of SB 90 into the future and estimate how well the squeeze factor would work.

The *Rodriguez* case posed even more serious problems. After *Serrano I*, school finance litigation became an increasingly popular avocation for reform-minded lawyers interested in making their mark. In the year following *Serrano I*, successful challenges were brought in the state courts of Kansas, New Jersey, and Arizona, as well as in the federal courts in Minnesota (Kirp 1977; Berke 1974). The radical decentralization of the American judiciary meant that any lawyer who could read the appellate court reports was in a position to initiate a constitutional challenge to a state school-financing system and have a better than even chance that it would be heard by a state or federal appellate court. In these circumstances, it was impossible to formulate a grand strategy for framing the strongest possible constitutional case for reform. The reform movement, insofar as it existed at all, was a collection of individual legal entrepreneurs, each at least as interested in being associated with the big case as in changing the school-financing system.

Into this welter of opportunists came Arthur Gochman, a San Antonio attorney described by other school finance lawyers as independent, stubborn, and a tough country lawyer. Gochman, interested in getting his case before the U.S. Supreme Court as quickly as possible, settled on the same procedural strategy as the Chicago lawyers had used in *McInnis*. He would take his case to a three-judge federal district court, from which an appeal would move directly to the Supreme Court. This strategy caused considerable discomfort among other school finance lawyers.[44] Between 1969 and 1971 as the momentum for school finance reform was building, the U.S. Supreme Court had undergone a decisive ideological shift with President Nixon's appointment of Chief Justice Warren Burger and Associate Justices Harry Blackmun, Lewis Powell, and William Rehnquist. Taking a case immediately to the Burger court, without first demonstrating the reasonableness and moderation of the case for reform in a number of states was, many lawers felt, an open invitation for a newly appointed conservative Supreme Court to scuttle the reform effort. "Many plaintiffs' attorneys around the country felt that greater gains could be made by chalking up one favorable decision after another in state supreme courts" (Berke 1974: 17). Gochman, however, was not about to be bound by anyone else's judgment. He saw an opportunity to get his case before the U.S. Supreme Court, and he took it.

The three-judge district court for Western Texas took the side of Gochman's clients, Mexican-American school children living in the Edgewood Independent School District, a classic district of low wealth, high tax rate, and low expenditure adjacent to San Antonio.[45] The district court's opinion was little more than a scaled-down rewrite of *Serrano I*. "For poor school districts," the court said, "educational financing in Texas is . . . a tax more spend less system."[46] The court wholeheartedly embraced the fiscal neutrality doctrine, adopting the California Supreme Court's argument:

Unlike the [educational needs] measure offered in *McInnis*, this proposal does not involve the Court in the intricacies of affirmatively requiring that

44. Mark Yudof, who played a role in the *Rodriguez* litigation, said, "A decision to seek a single judge in the *Rodriguez* case might have avoided Supreme Court review" altogether. "I unsuccessfully argued this point with Gochman," he added (15 July 1980: personal communication).

45. Rodriguez v. San Antonio Independent School District, 337 F. Supp. 280 (1973).

46. Id. at 282.

expenditures be made in a certain manner or amount. On the contrary, the state may adopt the financial scheme desired so long as the variations in wealth among the governmentally chosen units do not affect spending for the education of any child.[47]

Gochman introduced one new twist to the fiscal neutrality argument. He enlisted Joel Berke of Syracuse University to do a statistical analysis of wealth disparities in a sample of one hundred Texas districts. Berke's analysis included some data on the relationship between family income and school district wealth in addition to the usual data on the relationship between assessed valuation and per pupil expenditure. Gochman used the family income data in his argument, and the court obligingly made it part of its decision:

> As might be expected, those districts most rich in property also have the highest median family income and the lowest percentage of minority pupils, while the poor property districts are poor in income and predominantly minority in composition.[48]

In other words, a decision based on fiscal neutrality would help poor children. The evidence to support this assertion was lodged in a footnote that used a method of proof already familiar from the Coons and Sugarman *Serrano* brief; it compared the two wealthiest districts in the state with the four poorest, conveniently ignoring the middle of the distribution.

The favorable district court decision confirmed Gochman's optimism about his likelihood of success before the Supreme Court. Other school finance lawyers, however, viewed Gochman's success with increasing alarm. They felt that neither his argument in the lower court nor the court's opinion was strong enough to withstand the hostile scrutiny of the Burger Court. One California lawyer who followed *Rodriguez* carefully said, "Gochman didn't have either the appellate court experience or the theoretical sophistication to handle the case and he was not willing to listen to those who did."

There was a growing sentiment among school finance lawyers that *Rodriguez* was the wrong case at the wrong time. Their consterna-

47. Id. at 284.

48. Id. at 282. Mark Yudof, a professor at the University of Texas Law School and a former coworker of David Kirp at the Harvard Center for Law and Education, assisted Gochman in the preparation of the case. Yudof says of the plaintiffs' strategy before the district court, it "was simple: in order to prevail, the strongest factual showing possible must be made to convince the court of the magnitude of the discrimination against poor and minority children" (Yudof and Morgan 1974:392).

tion increased when, as the October 1972 date for oral arguments approached, the state of Texas enlisted Charles Alan Wright, a University of Texas law professor of awesome reputation who routinely appeared before the Supreme Court on behalf of conservative causes. In a flurry of last minute maneuvering, proreform lawyers tried to get Gochman to turn the responsibility for oral argument over to a lawyer of comparable stature to Wright. Archibald Cox, Harvard law professor and later Watergate special prosecutor, was mentioned as a candidate. Gochman would have none of it. John Coons, seeing the fate of fiscal neutrality hanging in the balance, requested permission to present oral arguments—"my ego was screaming to argue," he said—but was denied.[49]

The confrontation between Gochman and Wright before the Supreme Court was, in the words of an observer, "one of the great legal mismatches of all time."[50] Wright's line of attack was ideally adapted to the temperament of the emerging majority on the Burger Court. The defects of the Texas school-financing system were clear, he conceded, but they must be put against the historical background of steady progress toward a more equal system. History did not show that the state legislature had been insensitive to arguments for reform. Furthermore, he argued, the remedy requested by the plaintiffs was completely out of proportion to the defects of the system. Repairing differences in expenditures did not require upsetting the entire basis for the existing system.

Having drawn the cloak of moderation around him, Wright then proceeded to dismantle the argument that district wealth was a suspect classification and education a fundamental interest within the meaning of the equal protection clause. Strategically, Wright succeeded in turning the tables on the fiscal neutrality argument. The strength of fiscal neutrality had always been that it was a moderate and sensible solution to an obvious inequity. Wright managed to make the doctrine appear radical and immoderate. "If *Rodriguez* were affirmed," he argued, the Court "would be confronted with an avalanche of litigation challenging the distribution of noneducational state and municipal services" (Yudof and Morgan 1974: 400). In

49. John Coons 22 August 1979: personal communication.

50. Yudof argues, however, "I am confident that [critics] are wrong in thinking that some alteration in the timing or a better advocate in oral argument would have changed the result in the case. The suit came five years too late" (Mark Yudof 15 July 1980: personal communication).

addition, he argued, "the principle of fiscal neutrality might spawn any number of legislative responses, most of which were inconsistent with local control of schools, and most or all of which might not benefit poor or minority children" (Yudof and Morgan 1974: 400).

Gochman argued for the plaintiffs that education was "a means of socioeconomic advancement and of inculcating democratic values," "that the Texas financing scheme primarily injured poor children who depended most on public schooling," and "that fiscal neutrality would enhance, rather than diminish, local control of the public schools" (Yudof and Morgan 1974: 400–401).

In questioning, Chief Justice Berger and Associate Justice Rehnquist pressed Gochman on Wright's assertion that adoption of fiscal neutrality would encourage litigation on other public services. Associate Justice Blackmun challenged the plaintiffs' assertion that family income and property wealth were highly correlated. Justices Brennan and White questioned whether district power equalization, one outcome of fiscal neutrality, would not make the quality of children's education a function of the preferences of adults, rather than the needs of children. "Justices Stewart and Powell, widely perceived as the decisive votes, largely remained silent. Justice Marshall was absent for the oral argument, but reserved the right to participate in the final decision" (Yudof and Morgan 1974: 400).

The Supreme Court's decision in *Rodriguez* changed the course of school finance litigation. Justice Powell, speaking for himself, Chief Justice Burger, and Associate Justices Stewart, Blackmun, and Rehnquist (all Nixon appointees, save Stewart), delivered a root-and-branch critique of the carefully nurtured doctrine of fiscal neutrality. The dissenters—Justices White, Douglas, Brennan, and Marshall—mounted a valiant, but unsuccessful, counterattack.[51] The reform lawyers took some encouragement from the fact that the Court was closely divided and that the decision did not preclude further litigation in state courts. The immediate effect was undeniably a severe blow to reformers.

Not the least important part of the Supreme Court's decision was its close examination of the empirical basis for fiscal neutrality. Is it

---

51. According to John Coons, "We discovered two or three years after *Rodriguez*—one of the Supreme Court clerks who worked on the case volunteered it—that the plaintiffs had five votes [enough to turn the decision in their favor] up to the very end of the Court's discussion. Then Justice Stewart switched sides, apparently because he felt that the policy implications of the decision were too large and there were too many imponderables." (3 August 1980: personal communication).

the case, as the district court and the plaintiffs asserted, that family wealth and district wealth are closely enough related that one could argue the existing system discriminates against poor children as well as poor districts? If poor children do not necessarily live in poor districts, then can it be correctly asserted that the school-financing system makes a constitutionally suspect classification? In answering these questions the Court relied upon research, developed quickly after *Serrano I*, that showed a tenuous connection between district wealth and family wealth.[52] Although the relationship was strong at the extremes, it was weak and highly unpredictable in the middle of the distribution. The most telling evidence, however, came from Berke's study performed to support the plaintiffs' case. Here is the Court's summary of that evidence:

> Professor Berke's affidavit is based on a survey of approximately 10 percent of the school districts in Texas. His findings . . . show only that the wealthiest few districts in the sample have the highest family incomes and spend the most on education, and that the several poorest districts have the lowest family incomes and devote the least amount of money to education. For the remainder of the districts—96 districts composing almost 90 percent of the sample—the correlation is inverted, i.e., the districts that spend next to the most on education are populated by families having next to the lowest median family incomes while the districts spending the least have the highest median family incomes. It is evident that, even if the conceptual questions were answered favorably to [the plaintiffs], *no factual basis exists upon which to found a claim of comparative wealth discrimination.*[53]

The Supreme Court had turned Gochman's own evidence against him.

This part of Powell's opinion must have rankled John Coons. As the empirical evidence accumulated on the relationship between family income and district property wealth, Coons had clarified his basic

---

52. The Court cited Note, A Statistical Analysis of School Finance Decisions: On Winning Battles and Losing Wars, 81 *Yale L.J.* 1303 (1972). John Coons characterizes the data analyses in this note as garbage and argues that later analyses done at Berkeley by school finance researcher Norton Grubb "proved the analyses to be suspect" (3 August 1980: personal communication).

Stephen Sugarman recalls, "I can't remember the details but it seems to me that the Court relied importantly on a student note from the *Yale Law Journal*, which, as I recall, the Court received in galleys (perhaps not even through the ordinary processes) and which, in any event, wasn't subject to scrutiny and criticism by the plaintiffs in the normal course. Moreover, I have the impression that subsequent research has shown that the analysis in that article was quite in error even though the point it makes turns out to be true for some other states" (Stephen Sugarman 26 June 1980: personal communication).

53. 411 U.S. at 26–27.

argument to take account of it. In his amicus brief in *Rodriguez*, Coons argued,

> It is true and relevant to the nature of their injury that plaintiffs are poor; pupils from poor families living in poor districts suffer most from the present system. However, the evil here attacked is district poverty—it represents a systematic governmental discrimination affecting children whose families are of all income classes. . . .
>
> Minority persons will be helped or hurt according to the taxable wealth of their district and the new spending systems adopted. As with any neutral constitutional principle, the point is not to reward a particular class or to demonstrate in advance who shall be the beneficiaries.[54]

In other words, Coons would have deflected the argument that a finding of suspect classification depended on a coincidence of low family income and low property wealth by arguing that people who lived in districts having low property wealth were unfairly treated regardless of their income. Low income people living in low-wealth districts were doubly penalized. Gochman and the district court, in Coons's estimation, had walked into a well-laid constitutional trap by appearing to base their case on the correlation between family income and district property wealth. For Coons, the connection was unnecessary and easily avoidable.

Here again, cleverness of legal strategy tended to obscure, rather than illuminate, the basic public policy issue. If fiscal neutrality worked to equalize only district opportunities and not individual opportunities, was it worth all the fuss of a major constitutional confrontation? Justice Powell made more than a purely logical point when he observed that the equal protection clause was intended to protect individuals from discriminatory state action, whereas the fiscal neutrality strategy, which deliberately obscured the definition of the plaintiffs, seemed not to specify a class of individuals as the object of discriminatory policy so much as it did a class of governmental units (Cohen 1974). One can argue, as Coons did, that individuals live within those governmental units, but if their place of residence is all those individuals have in common, why should that entitle them to special treatment under the constitution? Although fiscal neutrality avoided the educational needs trap, it forced its advocates into a progressively more abstract definition of the class

---

54. Coons, Clune, and Sugarman, Motion for Leave to File Brief and Brief for John Serrano, Jr. and John Anthony Serrano as Amici Curiae at 8, 9–10, 411 U.S. 1 (1973).

that stood to benefit from the litigation, a definition that seemed to have little relationship to real people facing real damage from discriminatory state action.[55]

As these ambiguities appeared, even those sympathetic to fiscal neutrality began to question its practical consequences. What exact signal was a legislature supposed to take from a constitutional mandate based on fiscal neutrality? Could the legislature take account of family income disparities in developing a funding system, even when doing so undercut equalization of district wealth? How much equalization would be required in the middle of the distribution, where the relationship between family income and district wealth was the weakest and most unstable? In formulating a remedy, could the legislature take into account the burden imposed on the property tax base of urban areas by municipal services other than education (so-called municipal overburden)? How much better off would disadvantaged children in urban school systems be after the system was reformed? What was the legislature's responsibility to these children under the doctrine of fiscal neutrality?

To questions like these, the advocates of fiscal neutrality gave the same reply they had given from the beginning: The legislature could do anything it chose, so long as it produced a wealth-neutral system that allocated money on rational educational grounds. As the complexities of school finance reform began to unravel, this answer sounded increasingly hollow and fiscal neutrality seemed less and less attractive as a guide for legislative policymaking.

In the narrowest terms, the legal effect of the Supreme Court's adverse decision in *Rodriguez* was twofold: It threw school finance litigation into the state courts, and it foreclosed using the U.S. Constitution's equal protection clause as a basis for a challenge to school finance inequities. For the foreseeable future, school finance reform would be a matter between state courts and state legislatures, not between federal courts and state legislatures. "Constitutional theory continues to be reworked in hopes that a new approach to a presumably more responsive judiciary will unseat *Rodriguez*" (Kirp 1977: 125), but school finance reformers have turned their attention to a state-by-state strategy in which challenges are based on the specific provisions of each state constitution.

55. In oral comments on this point, Coons replied that the answer to the question of whether individuals, or school districts, are the subject of fiscal neutrality litigation "is in the eye of the beholder" (John Coons 3 August 1980: personal communication).

Rodriguez created one especially sticky problem for the *Serrano* lawyers in addition to the general dampening effect it had on the enthusiasm of reformers. The original *Serrano* complaint had been based on the equal protection language of both the state and federal constitution on the presumption that the two clauses meant the same thing. In its *Rodriguez* decision, the U.S. Supreme Court eliminated the use of the U.S. Constitution as a basis for their challenge, leaving the *Serrano* lawyers in the position of having to formulate an argument for why, in this particular instance, the equal protection language of the California Constitution should be interpreted differently from similar language in the U.S. Constitution.

THE JEFFERSON DECISION AND SERRANO II

Serrano went to trial in the Los Angeles Superior Court on 26 December 1972, four years and four months after the filing of the original complaint. The trial consumed more than sixty days of courtroom time, extending over a period of about four months. Judge Bernard Jefferson presided over the trial. A decision was not rendered in the case until 3 September 1974, six years after the filing of the original complaint. In October 1974 the defendants appealed from an adverse decision by Judge Jefferson to the state supreme court. Oral arguments were heard again before the supreme court, and on 30 December 1976, eight years and four months after the original complaint, the court affirmed its earlier decision in *Serrano I* and held that nothing the state legislature had done in the interim had altered the constitutional defects of the state's school-financing system.

During this long period, there were some noteworthy shifts in the cast of characters surrounding *Serrano*. In the aftermath of *Serrano I*, State Superintendent of Public Instruction Wilson Riles and State Controller Houston Flournoy informed State Attorney General Evelle Younger that they would "oppose any effort to appeal the case" from the superior court, "even to the point of hiring their own attorneys." Both Riles and Flournoy said that "they strongly support the concept of equality in school finance and fear that any attempt to appeal the *Serrano* decision will only delay necessary legislative action at the expense of those children who are now in school" (*California Journal*, October 1971:274). By the time the case made it back to the supreme court, the defendants' list had dwindled to five high-wealth school districts and the original Los Angeles County defendants; all the original state defendants had deserted the case. The *Serrano* attorneys took full advantage of the fact that Wilson Riles referred to them as "my lawyers," and the Los Angeles county counsel was referred to out of court as "the attorney for Beverly Hills." At the state level, the political climate surrounding *Serrano* had shifted decisively in favor of the plaintiffs.

As the trial date approached, Wolinsky was joined by another lawyer, John McDermott, to help in preparations for trial. McDermott, who has since become executive director of the Western Center and chief watchdog over the legislature's compliance with the *Serrano* decisions, quickly became a leading figure in the case.

In 1972 before preparations for the trial had started, the Carnegie Corporation and the Ford Foundation had funded a substantial project at the University of California at Berkeley, bringing together five Berkeley professors who had worked on various stages of school finance reform: Charles Benson and James Guthrie, who had recently directed a major study of school finance in New York for the Fleishman Commission; John Coons and Stephen Sugarman, both now law school faculty members; and David Kirp, newly appointed to the Berkeley Public Policy School. The Ford–Carnegie project, funded initially for nearly $900,000 and overall for nearly $3 million, was put under the direction of Robert Mnookin, an experienced analyst, and labeled the Berkeley Childhood and Government Project. Recalling the history of the project, one of its founding members said, "After *Serrano I* the foundations could smell the bacon; they wanted to be associated in some way with the case."

Although the childhood and government project was a broad-gauged research program and later did most of its work on issues unrelated to *Serrano*, the initial infusion of funds had a significant effect on preparations for the trial. Mnookin's staff performed a number of analyses required to demonstrate the equalization effects of SB 90 and to tighten the plaintiffs' case against the inequities of the existing system. In addition, the project provided expert witnesses that the *Serrano* lawyers could use to bolster their case and the research facilities to back them up.

According to John McDermott, however, the decisive technical support for the plaintiffs' case was provided by school finance experts from inside the state government. Paul Holmes, assembly staff consultant, and Ed Harper, the Department of Education's school finance specialist, presented what McDermott calls "the most important analytic data" on the effects of the school-financing system. In addition, the Department of Education "provided expert testimony, data analysis, documents and computer time" and "filed an *amicus* brief on the plaintiffs' behalf in both the trial court and the Supreme Court."[56]

The level of courtroom competence developed by Wolinsky and McDermott, the shifting political climate in the state, and the infusion of analytic resources all added up to a reversal of the mismatch that had occurred before the U.S. Supreme Court in *Rodriguez*. Instead of the defendants having the decisive advantage, it was the plaintiffs who had the advantage in *Serrano*. James Briggs, deputy county counsel for Los Angeles County, handled the case for the defendants. Although he was able to muster some expert testimony and analytic assistance, his backing paled beside the Berkeley Childhood and Government Project and the Department of Education.[57] By the time *Serrano* came to trial the weight of expert opinion, political influence, and the considerable prestige of the California Supreme Court was behind the plaintiffs.

The superior court trial revolved around four major issues: First, the main reason for returning to trial court was to establish whether the facts of the case were as the plaintiffs originally alleged. Second, and closely related to the first, was the issue of whether SB 90 was an adequate remedy in light of *Serrano I*. Third, the *Serrano* lawyers were obliged to demonstrate that wealth-related differences in expenditure affected the quality of education offered by schools. This came to be called the cost-quality issue. And, fourth, both sides were forced to address the issue of whether the U.S. Supreme Court's decision in *Rodriguez* affected the equal protection basis of the plaintiffs' case.

On the first issue, the deputy county counsel clung to the same line of argument the defendants had used since the beginning of the

---

56. John McDermott 27 August 1980: personal communication.

57. John McDermott takes strong exception to the idea that an imbalance in analytic resources, if it existed at all, affected the outcome of the trial. He says, "In the end, Jim lost because his case was bad and right was on the side of the plaintiffs. The evidence was simply overwhelming that there were unequal educational opportunities being afforded school children in this state. . . . In *Serrano*, the result would have been the same if a better defense were presented, though I seriously doubt whether one could have been (John McDermott 27 August 1980: personal communication).

case: Whatever the facts showed about inequities of expenditure and tax effort, the school-financing system was constitutional.

> The people of the State of California . . . have clearly set forth their intent that school districts are to be empowered to raise funds by local taxation, in such amounts as the governing board shall determine, subject only to maximum tax rates to be specified by the legislature. . . . Throughout the history of California this principle has meant that some school districts can raise more money for the support of public schools than other districts. . . . In authorizing this system, [they] were aware that this would result, but, no doubt in the interest of preserving responsiveness to local needs and desires, were willing to pay the price of disparities. The plaintiffs contend that wiser choices are available to the people of California. If the plaintiffs are correct in that respect, no matter how onerous it may be, the sole remedy is with the people of California, to persuade them that the California Constitution should be amended to authorize or require the fiscal system they prefer.[58]

To this argument, the *Serrano* lawyers replied that the state supreme court had already spoken on the issue of what the Constitution required, leaving only the factual question of whether wealth-related disparities existed. The evidence, they continued, indicated indisputably that the system used by the state guaranteed wealth-related disparities and the defendants had produced no counter evidence.

On the question of the effect of SB 90, the deputy county counsel argued:

> Formerly inadequate levels of the foundation program were substantially increased. This means that the criticism made by the California Supreme Court in the *Serrano* decision, that the state's equalization efforts were inadequate, can no longer be applied to California's system. . . . SB 90 increased equalization aid by $454 million, which means a 75.7 percent increase! The districts most advantaged by this increase in equalization are low-wealth districts.

To this argument, Wolinsky and McDermott replied, using extensive analyses prepared by the Berkeley Childhood and Government Project:

> The most significant feature of [SB 90] is that the foundation program financing system is retained in both concept and practical operation, including the authorization to exceed the foundation program by voting tax over-

---

58. Quotations in this and the succeeding two paragraphs are taken from the trial record filed in Serrano v. Priest, 557 P.2d 929 (1976), from the files of the Western Center on Law and Poverty, Los Angeles, California.

rides. . . . The time limit required for the revenue limits of high spending districts to converge with the rising foundation program is about twenty years, assuming no voted overrides. . . . More than two generations of California school children will pass through the school finance system before convergence of revenue limits with the foundation program will occur. . . . Equalization, not convergence, is required by *Serrano*.

The cost-quality issue sparked a lengthy and complicated argument. Coons and Sugarman, who thought the trial should have taken about two days (it eventually consumed sixty days over a six-month period), argued that the issue should be dealt with summarily. "In order to argue that resource differences don't make an educational difference," Coons says,

> the state would have to attack its own system. They would have to say that the system is so bad it doesn't matter how much money you pump into it, you get the same result. That would be a preposterous argument to have to make in court. We always took the position that if you spend public money, there is a presumption that it must be distributed without regard to wealth. Period. Forget the question of effects.

According to McDermott, he and Wolinsky tried "to persuade Judge Jefferson that the cost-quality issue was irrelevant," but Jefferson rejected their argument "and made it clear that he expected us to demonstrate that wealth-created spending disparities resulted in unequal educational opportunities." He did so, McDermott surmises, so that a record of the issue would exist in trial court in the unlikely event that it later proved to be important on appeal. McDermott and Wolinsky sought to avoid "getting into the social science evidence on the impact of school resources on achievement, because, not only was the evidence indeterminate, it was not very reliable or trustworthy." They chose instead, in their initial arguments, to demonstrate "that wealth-created spending disparities result in unequal educational *inputs* or opportunities." Briggs, however, challenged this argument by calling witnesses and presenting evidence for the defense questioning the relationship between school resources and outcomes. This necessitated the plaintiffs' attorneys, in rebuttal, calling their own witnesses to present "a flood of expert testimony on the deficiencies of that social science evidence as well as contrary research that does show a relationship between school resources and achievement." In the end, despite the strong belief by proreform lawyers that evidence on the connection between school resources and achievement was irrelevant, the issue consumed a large amount of courtroom time.[59]

On the issue of the effect of *Rodriguez* on *Serrano I*, the deputy county counsel argued:

> It is clear that the decision of the United States Supreme Court in *Rodriguez* is controlling upon the determination this court is asked to make. While the California Supreme Court in *Serrano* v. *Priest* did the best it could in trying to second guess what the Supreme Court might ultimately do, a comparison of the two cases clearly reflects that the California court guessed wrong. Since the California Supreme Court views as authoritative the United States Supreme Court decision construing provisions of the United States Constitution which are substantially equivalent to provisions of the California Constitution, the California Supreme Court should, even after its strongly worded opinion in *Serrano*, abide by the higher court's interpretation.

To this argument the *Serrano* lawyers replied that the equal protection language of the California Constitution did not necessarily have to be interpreted in exactly the same way as that in the U.S. Constitution, because "fundamental principles of federalism permit states to vary the content of state constitutional rights, at least within federal constitutional limits." In addition, they argued, "the provisions of the federal and California constitutions are not identical in content," the most critical difference being that the California Constitution gives prominent visibility to education as a governmental function, but the U.S. Constitution does not. The plaintiffs' case, they concluded, should be allowed to stand on state constitutional grounds alone.

At the conclusion of the trial, the *Serrano* lawyers recommended a set of elements that might be included in Jefferson's decision. Among these were that the court fix a time limit for legislative compliance and a dollar amount for the maximum disparity between high-spending and low-spending districts.

Judge Jefferson's decision in *Serrano*, rendered first as a memorandum in April 1974 and then as a full statement of findings and conclusions in September 1974, was in all basic respects consistent with the *Serrano* lawyers' argument. The decision's 299 findings restated the essential defects of the school-financing system alleged by Wolinsky and McDermott, before and after SB 90. Lest there be any doubt that he had accepted the plaintiffs' view of the system, Jefferson

59. Quotations from John McDermott 27 August 1980: personal communication.

concluded the findings with the statement that "each and every allegation contained in the plaintiffs' complaint is true"—a remarkable conclusion in light of the complexity and indeterminacy of the case. The decision's 128 conclusions of law likewise restated the *Serrano* lawyers' arguments on each of the major legal issues, in some cases taking language verbatim from their trial brief and recommendations. The decision concluded by setting a six-year deadline for legislative compliance and requiring that the new school-financing system contain differences of no more than $100 per pupil in expenditures financed from property wealth.

Serrano moved directly from Los Angeles Superior Court to the state supreme court, bypassing the state court of appeal, and on 30 December 1976, the state supreme court rendered its decision. There were few surprises in *Serrano II*.[60] One fact that mildly surprised some observers was that in upholding its own prior decision the court could muster only a bare four to three majority. Justice Sullivan again wrote the court's opinion; Justices Wright, Tobriner, and Mosk joined in the opinion. Justices Richardson, Clark, and McComb dissented. Richardson and Clark were recent appointees of Governor Ronald Reagan; McComb was the lone dissenter in *Serrano I*.

In *Serrano II* the scope of argument was more restricted and the issues were much narrower than they had been in *Serrano I*. The court's opinion, in fact, had little to say about substantive issues of school finance, nothing new to add by way of guidance to the legislature, and a great deal to say about rarified issues of constitutional interpretation. Several factors conspired to produce this result: As the case played itself out, the options available to the defendants for appeal became narrower and narrower and more and more technical. The *Serrano II* majority felt that they had already disposed of the major issues with their decision in *Serrano I* and were obliged to deal only with questions that had arisen since the original decision. The basic arguments for and against the plaintiffs' case had been aired so many times in the appeals process that they did not require lengthy rehearsal. As the arguments narrowed, the court's treatment of school finance became more and more perfunctory and detached from the difficult and ambiguous problems underlying the simple doctrine of fiscal neutrality. In the main, *Serrano II* was a defense of

60. 557 P.2d 929 (1976).

the court's original ruling rather than an attempt to elaborate that ruling.

The defendants' appeal was based on three main contentions: that in adopting the fiscal neutrality argument, the superior court had used the wrong standard to evaluate the school finance system; that *Rodriguez* had undercut the court's earlier reliance on the equal protection argument to invalidate the school finance system; and that the equal protection language of the California Constitution was in direct conflict with language expressly requiring the legislature to create a school-financing system based on local property taxes. The court, not surprisingly, disposed of the first contention by saying that "it flies in the face of our holding in *Serrano I* and also of the findings of the trial court."[61] It disposed of the second contention by arguing that the equal protection case could stand on state constitutional grounds alone, without the support of the federal constitution. It characterized the third contention as "utterly devoid of merit"[62] and argued that nothing in the state constitution authorized or required the state legislature to create a school-financing system in which educational opportunity depended on the property wealth of the district in which the student lived. The dissenters focused on the third contention and found the defendants' argument persuasive. The existing school-financing system, they argued, was the result of a careful balancing by the legislature of competing constitutional requirements for equity, local autonomy, and fiscal responsibility.

The majority opinion restated the elements of fiscal neutrality without significantly increasing the doctrine's specificity:

> Although an equal expenditure level per pupil in every district is not educationally sound or desirable because of differences in educational needs, equality of educational opportunity requires that all school districts possess an equal ability in terms of revenue to provide students with substantially equal opportunities for learning. The system before the court fails in this respect, for it gives high-wealth districts a substantial advantage in obtaining higher quality staff, program expansion and variety, beneficial teacher–pupil ratios and class sizes, modern equipment and materials, and high-quality buildings.[63]

61. Id. at 945.
62. Id. at 954.
63. Id. at 939.

The question that would later puzzle many was how one could bridge the gap between an educationally sound and desirable inequality of expenditure and a constitutionally required wealth-neutrality of revenue-raising ability.

The court was offered an opportunity to explore the complexities of this issue when it was confronted with the municipal overburden problem. San Francisco Unified School District, in an amicus brief, asked the court whether its adoption of fiscal neutrality would preclude special legislative attention to urban districts where the property tax base was burdened both by higher educational expenditures and competing government services. Avoiding a detailed discussion of the problem, the court argued that municipal overburden was not peculiar to districts of either high or low property wealth and that the doctrine of fiscal neutrality only addressed the problem of equalizing district capacity to raise funds to meet educational needs, regardless of property wealth. Enigmatically, the court said:

> A fiscally neutral system, if tailored in a responsive and responsible way, would . . . make the individual district's ability to meet its own particular problems connected with providing educational opportunity depend upon factors other than the wealth of the district, and thus dissipate the discrimination which characterizes the system before us.[64]

The court did not directly answer the question that the amici put to it, nor did it say what recourse school systems would have if they happened to find that a fiscally neutral system was neither responsive nor responsible from their point of view.

On another issue—the $100 per pupil expenditure standard for judging wealth neutrality specified in *Serrano I*—the court was inexplicably mute. In its description of the *Jefferson* decision, the court explicitly refers to the six-year deadline but does not mention the $100 standard.[65] It is not clear what the omission means, in strictly legal terms, because the court later says "that the holding of the trial court is grounded solidly and soundly on our earlier decision in *Serrano I*."[66] McDermott continues to argue as if the $100 standard were adopted, and he maintains that it in no way contradicts the basic assumption of fiscal neutrality that the court should not involve itself in the formulation of specific legislative remedies. "It

64. Id. at 947.
65. Id. at 940.
66. Id. at 958.

was a *de minimis* standard designed to measure when property wealth had been sufficiently removed as an influence on school district spending," he says. "In no way was the Court asserting what would be an equitable school financing system."[67] The narrow issue of whether the $100 standard is or is not binding is less important than the broader issue of whether the court, having put itself in the position of sole arbiter of legislative compliance, can also assert that it is not in any way predetermining what the legislature should do. That position would later strike legislative actors as somewhat disingenuous. It is at least conceivable that the court omitted mentioning the $100 standard because it made the dilemmas of judicial intervention a bit too apparent.

The effect of *Serrano II* was, finally, after more than eight years of legal maneuvering, to put the school issue before the legislature. The decision did not end the involvement of the court or the *Serrano* lawyers in school finance policy. The court retained jurisdiction in the case pending legislative compliance. John McDermott assumed the role of watchdog on the legislature's attempts to comply, a role he plays to the present. Insofar as legal doctrine was concerned, the die was cast with *Serrano II*. The legislature had gotten all the guidance it was to get from the court.

CONCLUSION

Viewed strictly from the standpoint of legal strategy, the *Serrano* litigation can be judged as having been something very close to an unqualified success. The *Serrano* lawyers developed a legal theory that justified judicial intervention and defended it successfully through a long and complex process of litigation when the tide of judicial opinion outside the state was running against them. They isolated and focused attention on wealth-related disparities in expenditure in the existing system. They successfully maneuvered themselves and the court into the position of judging the adequacy of the legislature's compliance.

The *Serrano* litigation can be called a success in slightly broader terms as well. Chapter 3 will show how *Serrano I* legitimized the position in state government of a small band of reformers who had pre-

---

67. John McDermott 27 August 1980: personal communication.

viously been unable to gain a foothold. The suit forced prominent political figures to take a position, and in doing so, they galvanized support among state officials for reform. It gave proreform legislators an additional source of leverage over their colleagues. It created a greater sense of urgency that something should be done about the problems of the existing system, although this sense of urgency fluctuated.

Only when the suit is put in a much larger frame of reference—the initiation of broad-scale reform and the dilemmas of judicial inter-vention—do really troubling problems arise. Although there are obvi-ous benefits from the point of view of reformers in relying on the courts to initiate policy, there are also costs. One way of reckoning those costs is in terms of the tendency for lawyers to define reform in terms of legal principles rather than the interests of specific indi-viduals or groups.

Out of strategic necessity and professional judgment, the *Ser-rano* lawyers couched their assault on the existing system in pro-gressively more abstract terms, rather than in terms that made the consequences of that system concrete for real people in real schools. Although the wealth neutrality argument could be made with dev-astating effect at the extreme ends of the distribution (between Beverly Hills and Baldwin Park, for example), it lost most of its explanatory power as a definition of equality of educational oppor-tunity in the vast and indeterminate part of the distribution where most of the children were. Had the basic rationale for the suit been couched in terms other than equality of educational opportunity, this would not have been a serious flaw. To the largest number of individuals who, by virtue of their family background, have the great-est presumptive claim to more equal treatment, wealth neutrality has very little meaning. Individual students in Los Angeles and San Fran-cisco, for example, a large number of whom might be said to deserve more equal treatment, stood to gain nothing directly from the wealth neutrality principle. Los Angeles lies at about the middle of the prop-erty wealth distribution, San Francisco above the median. Individuals take their identity, within the logic of wealth neutrality, from the school district in which they reside.

In the long run, it is impossible to determine what the policy con-sequences of the court's adoption of the wealth neutrality standard will be. Advocates of fiscal neutrality argue that it benefits children with special educational needs because it forces the legislature to specify rational grounds for the distribution of funds rather than the arbitrary ground of property wealth. In order to prove this assertion, however, one would have to know what the legislature would have done in the absence of *Serrano*.

In the shorter term, the main interest of this book is in explaining the outcome of school finance politics in California. As a point of departure for a protracted political battle over school finance policy, it is clear that the *Serrano* lawyers' strategy leaves much to be desired. One of the most thoughtful statements on this issue comes from Derrick Bell, who played an important role in initiating *Serrano*. "*Serrano* represents a kind of suit about which I have since come to have serious doubts," he says. "Because of the way the legal issues were defined and because of the role the plaintiffs played in the case, there was no obvious political constituency to press for legislative action after the Court made its decision."[68] The lack of a political constituency for reform, other than the school finance lawyers themselves and the few committed reformers already inside state government, explains much of the apparent floundering and indecisiveness on the part of the legislature in responding to *Serrano*. Initiating reform is partly an intellectual and partly a political task, but the two parts intersect where the individual interests of those who stand to benefit from reform are defined and galvanized into a political constituency. In the aftermath of *Serrano*, the lawyers would blame the legislature for failing to respond to the crystalline logic of wealth neutrality. At least part of the responsibility for the legislature's alleged lack of responsiveness, however, lies with the lawyers and the legal process itself. Legislatures are political bodies. They are explicitly designed to respond to political incentives and only incidentally to the commands of the courts. Legal doctrines that do not galvanize a political constituency are likely to remain legal doctrines, rather than becoming policy. Wealth neutrality is probably one such doctrine. Within the legal system, it was clever enough. In the larger political system, where reform objectives become policy, it proved to be too clever by half.

One must sympathize with the school finance lawyers' predicament. John McDermott makes a powerful point when he argues for a distinction between reformers and litigators. "Reformers in general," he argues, "are concerned with school finance policy in the total

68. Derrick Bell 31 May 1979: personal communication.

sense," while "the litigators in court . . . were concerned with an exceedingly narrow legal issue that did not require the resolution of endless nonlegal policy issues." "In fact," he adds, "the litigators (and the courts) were foreclosed from addressing those policy issues by the separation of powers doctrine."[69] It is certainly the case that the litigators in *Serrano* became concerned with an exceedingly narrow legal issue, and it is true that the courts are constrained by the separation of powers doctrine in their ability to intervene in the policymaking process. Nonetheless, the reason for intervening in the first place was to change policy, and if that policy is to be changed, litigators (and the courts for that matter) cannot totally dissociate themselves from the political consequences of their actions. The separation of powers doctrine is a useful way to understand the strengths and weaknesses of courts as intervenors in policymaking, but it cannot be used to disown the political motivation behind such public law litigation as *Serrano*. The fact that reformers can be distinguished in practice from litigators is more a testimonial to the incredible complexity of interests spawned by public law litigation than it is a useful normative principle. The object of such public law litigation is to reform policy. If wealth neutrality fails to address the political motivations that make reform possible in the legislative arena, then lawyers and courts share the responsibility with legislators for failures to reform outdated systems of finance.

The *Serrano* litigation left the California Supreme Court and the *Serrano* lawyers in the enviable strategic position of being able to veto any legislative response while never having to specify what an adequate, politically feasible solution would be. The *Serrano* lawyers demonstrated to the court's satisfaction that the legislature had thousands of options available to it in the construction of a wealth-neutral system. Yet the people who do the work of constructing political coalitions around reform proposals quickly discovered that their options were constrained by a political environment the courts could assume away. The options most often referred to in court as examples of the vast array of possibilities available to the legislature were the statewide property tax, district power equalization, educational vouchers, and full state financing of education. As later chapters will demonstrate, these options were subjected to analysis by analytic staff and decisionmakers in the executive and legislative

69. John McDermott 27 August 1980: personal communication.

branches and were all rejected on grounds of political feasibility. This denotes a certain lack of closure between the court and legislature on how reforms are made. After reviewing their options, executive and legislative decisionmakers settled down to making incremental adjustments in the existing system, the one based on the property tax. It is exactly this style of decisionmaking that is most vulnerable to challenge under the wealth neutrality standard.

The policy options proposed by the *Serrano* lawyers have one feature in common: They replace the existing system with one that accurately represents the wealth neutrality principle. By definition, making politically feasible adjustments in the old system would mean that the legislature would always be at a strategic disadvantage relative to the court and *Serrano* lawyers. Because wealth neutrality can be construed by the court to be either absolute or relative (either it means total elimination of wealth as a determinant of expenditure or some reasonable approximation thereto), the court and *Serrano* lawyers can effectively maintain pressure on the legislature as long as they can agree among themselves that this position is desirable. Also, because the *Serrano* litigation is not connected to a coherent political constituency that can decide to terminate litigation when it has extracted sufficient concessions from the political system, the possibilities for judicial intervention are indefinite. In the words of Joseph Remcho, who in 1980 was hired as counsel by the State Department of Education to oppose the *Serrano* lawyers, "He who must specify a remedy loses."[70] This seems a paradoxical result for a legal strategy predicated on judicial restraint and deference to the separation of powers. The following chapters will analyze how this gulf between the legislature and the court affected the formulation of school-financing policy and how coalition politics adapted to the necessity for reform.

70. Joseph Remcho 10 August 1980: personal communication.

3 SENATE BILL 90
The Loss of Innocence

The present plans in use for the apportionment of school funds in fully three-fourths of the states of the union are in need of careful revision.

Ellwood P. Cubberly (1905)

SERRANO I SANCTIONS REFORM

Serrano I changed the rules of the game. The California legislature had always taken an activist role in education generally, and several legislative leaders demonstrated a long-standing interest in school finance reform (Meltsner et al. 1973). Until *Serrano I* came along, efforts to initiate substantial school finance reform had met with little success. Indeed, the 1947 Foundation Plan had been the first and only substantial legislative effort to equalize school finance. As the dean emeritus of California school finance and reform advocate Ronald Cox commented: "Following [1947], all that happened [in the legislature] was a series of fights to keep the ADA [average daily attendance] figures current."[1]

Before *Serrano*, legislative advocates of school finance reform, unable to muster support for their cause, had to satisfy themselves with limited and indirect change. For example, in the mid–1960s Democrat Jesse Unruh, powerful Speaker of the assembly, fastened on

1. Ronald Cox 5 June 1980: personal communication.

school district unification as a way to promote school finance equalization by broadening the tax base available to students in a given
area. Unruh resorted to semantic subterfuge in order to marshall
support for his strategy: "Unruh had everyone in Sacramento arguing administrative efficiency, but that was [a ruse]."[2] Ronald Cox
remembered: "People became for (Unruh's plan) when they realized
it wouldn't hurt anybody."[3] Other legislative leaders—Senators
Rodda and Teale, Assemblymen Greene and Deddeh—proposed statewide property tax measures aimed at reducing the substantial spending differences among California school districts; Senator Collier
introduced a bill requiring the state assumption of 50 percent of public education costs. None of these school finance bills ever reached
the floor of either house (*California Journal*, August 1970).

These legislative efforts received early and authoritative support
from Ronald Cox, then head of the Senate Office of Research, and
A. Alan Post, the respected head of the Legislative Analyst's Office.
Both Cox and Post persistently presented strong arguments and co-
gent evidence urging legislative attention to school finance reform.[4]

Neither evidence nor equity was at issue. None of these influential
individuals succeeded in encouraging serious consideration of school
finance reform because, as John Mockler put it, "Good education
policy is usually bad politics."[5] Legislators concurrently pursue three
interrelated goals: getting reelected, acquiring power, and making
good public policy (see, e.g., Fenno 1973; Uslaner and Weber 1977).
Making good policy and amassing influence in the legislature depend,
of course, on maintaining one's seat. Regardless of one's ideals, advocating school finance reform is politically hazardous.

Other reforms, such as compensatory education or preschool education, can spread benefits throughout the public school system.

2. John Mockler 2 June 1979: personal communication.

3. Ronald Cox 5 June 1980: personal communication.

4. For example, in the 1969/1970 *Analysis of the Budget*, Post anticipated the *Serrano I* decision. He wrote:

> The present system of state and local support for the public schools fails to promote effi-
> cient use of our limited tax resources and, in fact, serves to perpetuate inequities among
> school districts in the amount of local tax effort that is required to support an educa-
> tional program.

Post continued to urge the legislature to consider the proposal suggested in the *Analysis of
the Budget 1968/69*, splitting the assessment roll between residential and nonresidential
property, with the application of a uniform statewide tax upon the nonresidential property
in order to equalize both tax effort and revenues from that portion of the roll.

5. John Mockler 2 June 1979: personal communication.

But school finance reform is bound to create losers, except in the unlikely event of an abundant, unfettered state treasury. Without unlimited resources, equalization—even when it takes the form of leveling up—means some districts gain more than others. As Paul Holmes of the Assembly Education Committee remarked, "Just about every legislator has a [school finance reform] loser in his district." Despite its possible ideological appeal, support for school finance reform conflicts seriously with the political self-interest of elected representatives.

There was no organized constituency of "John Serranos" pressuring California legislators to modify this political calculus. To the contrary, a coalition of wealthy school districts and business and agricultural interests successfully lobbied to oppose the statewide and countywide property tax reforms advanced by school finance experts. In the early 1970s the wealthy school districts—the biggest potential losers in any finance reform measure—banded together to form a new lobbying organization, Schools for Sound Finance. In short, although the large interdistrict discrepancies Ronald Cox and Alan Post enumerated were undeniably inequitable, they did not translate into a coherent political constituency.

In addition to these political obstacles, school finance reform efforts had been stalled by hostile relations between the legislature and the superintendent of public instruction, Max Rafferty.[6] One reform advocate summed up the views of many:

> A major problem in the 1960s with the enactment of school finance reform was that we had Max Rafferty. There was an ongoing battle between Rafferty and the Governor and the Legislature. As a result, the State Department of Education became totally unimportant and anything they said or asked of the legislature was automatically rejected.

Legislators also complained that Rafferty had no clear position on school finance reform. These factors combined to create a vacuum in leadership from the State Department of Education, significantly undermining support for reform.

Against this discouraging history, John B. Mockler and Gerald Hayward, legislative staff advocates of school finance reform, wrote:

> When the California Supreme Court ordered changes in the way California paid for its schools, the simplistic notions of the charge seemed music to the

6. Max Rafferty was superintendent of public instruction from 1963 to 1970.

ears of many who had fought for years for a more effective school finance
system in the state (1978: 387).

The *Serrano I* decision transformed the school finance reform problem from an issue of ideology or political taste to a legal mandate.
The California Supreme Court sanctioned reformers' goals and legitimized their entry into the heretofore unreceptive arena of legislative
politics. Legislative Analyst A. Alan Post, whose previous appeals and
reform proposals were found lacking in political logic, acknowledged,
"We are, in my opinion, indebted to the courts for motivating the
policymakers to seriously study and implement educational finance
reform so long overdue" (1972: 20).

Although the court forced the issue onto the political agenda, it
did not modify the political reckoning that would be used to construct a solution. The court did not propose a remedy for John Serrano's complaint; responsibility was dumped into the lap of the same
political body that had been unable to make substantial change in
the past. Although legitimized by *Serrano I*, reformers remained
a distinct—if more influential—minority. The *Serrano I* decision
did not significantly increase political support for reform; it simply secured a place for school finance reform on the agenda to be
debated by a stubborn governor and a fractious legislature. The *Serrano* decision was just *one* ingredient in the process of negotiation
and compromise that led to Senate Bill (SB) 90, the state's first
response to *Serrano*. Sacramento's 1971 political environment experienced two other important changes without which school finance
reform efforts would probably have amounted to little. The first
was a change in the complexion of gubernatorial–legislative relationships. The second was the election of a new superintendent of public
instruction, Wilson Riles.

Legislative Stalemate and New Cooperation

The *Serrano I* decision found Sacramento in political stalemate. Tax
reform was Governor Reagan's top priority, and his first-term efforts
to pass a tax reform program had been consistently stymied by Democratic legislators. In the last months of his first term, Governor Reagan suffered his most frustrating failure with the narrow defeat of his
tax program embodied in Assembly Bills (AB) 1000 and 1001. In a
late night press conference following this failure, Ronald Reagan pro-

claimed the legislative action a staggering setback to the people of California:

> Tonight the hopes of millions of Californians for tax relief were dashed by the irresponsible action of a small minority of 13 senators who chose to put face-saving considerations—for personal partisan political reasons—ahead of the interests of the people (*California Journal*, August 1979: 238).

Democrats consistently opposed Reagan's tax proposals for several reasons. Central among them was the governor's style of legislative relations. During his first term, Reagan used the power of the governorship largely to veto legislative proposals rather than to bargain. A veteran of Reagan's legislative tax battles remembered,

> The governor felt frustrated in the whole tax area. A central characteristic of Reagan's was that he did not negotiate with the legislature. He liked to feel like he was in the driver's seat simply by saying "no" and vetoing legislation. That made the legislature feel frustrated as well.[7]

Governor Reagan himself acknowledged, "I have not bargained and I don't make deals. Maybe if I did, we'd have a tax package" (*California Journal*, August 1970: 222).

The governor's unwillingness to compromise resulted in an administration tax program that was substantively unacceptable to majority Democrats. Despite their own eagerness to enact tax reform, Democratic legislators refused to support the governor's program on two major points. First, they believed that his proposals emphasized tax relief for asset holders and commercial interests to the detriment of low and middle income wage earners, many of whom did not own property.[8] Second, Democrats in both the senate and the assembly balked at the governor's tax reform proposals because they did not provide new state money for the public schools—additional support many believed was crucial (*California Journal*, May 1970: 134).

7. John Vickerman 18 January 1980: personal communication. Similarly, chronicling the defeat of Reagan's tax program, the *California Journal* observed, "perhaps the most important [reason] was the governor's unwillingness to compromise on any of the major issues [once the package had been put together] or to bargain for support in other ways" (August 1970: 222).

8. For example, in its autopsy of AB 1001, the *California Journal* reported, "Senate Democrats [charged] that the tax increase elements of the program, and particularly the increase in the sales tax from $.05 to $.06, would hit low income families and individuals without giving them back the reductions in property taxes which middle/upper income persons would have received. (August 1970: 222).

The issue of increased state support for public education had been a constant source of friction throughout Reagan's first term. The governor, too, was concerned about California's schools but for very different reasons than were Democratic legislators. The governor had little interest in school finance reform and was strongly opposed to spending more state money on public education. Indeed, battles with educators over these issues characterized Reagan's entire tenure as governor. Many believed he was purposively hurtful. For example, former Governor Edmund Brown, whom Reagan defeated handily in his 1966 bid for a third term, seconded the assessment of outgoing state board of education Vice–President Milton J. Schwarz that Reagan was "the greatest destructive force and enemy of public education in 50 years" (1970:173).

It is arguable whether Ronald Reagan was against public education. He clearly had little sympathy for the purported financial plight of California's schools. He thought there was no fiscal crisis in the schools as educators and many legislators claimed. Governor Reagan believed the schools needed better management, not more dollars. More money, in his view, would be a negative incentive that would only perpetuate inefficient school management (Meltsner, Kast, Kramer, and Nakamura 1973; *California Journal*, May 1970:127 and December 1970:340–341). To further complicate matters, Reagan was steadfastly opposed to joining school support to tax reform, claiming that "tax 'reform' and school financing are separate issues which should be treated separately" (*California Journal*, May 1970: 134).

Legislative stalemate was the result of these substantive differences in reform objectives and the governor's refusal to negotiate or compromise. As Reagan began his second term, Sacramento watchers assessed the differences between the Republican governor and the Democratic legislature as irreconcilable and rated the chance for tax reform or school finance reform as dim:

> Chances of the school financing system being restructured this year are dead, and the fault doesn't lie with the Governor. The legislature is in no mood to enact the kind of tax increase necessary to finance a new school aid system, and undergo a prolonged session to do it in an election year (*Los Angeles Times*, 21 February 1972).

However, these observers underestimated both Reagan's determination to pass a tax relief measure and legislative intention to join tax relief and school aid. Also, Reagan had learned that the negative authority of his first term was inadequate to achieve his goals. As he himself acknowledged, his entertainment career had not prepared him for the give-and-take of legislative politics.[9]

As the incumbent governor campaigned for reelection, he promised: "If you see fit to return us to Sacramento next year, we'll propose, as the first order of business, tax reform" (*Los Angeles Times*, 21 January 1971). With the lessons of AB 1000 and 1001 behind him, Reagan returned to Sacramento in 1971 determined to keep his vow and to participate in the bargaining necessary to make good his word.

New Assembly Speaker Robert Moretti and Senate President pro tem James Mills also returned to Sacramento with a commitment to work toward resolution of the legislative impasse. Moretti believed that the legislature's record of inaction was in many ways as reprehensible as the governor's. He said he "realized that it was the state government as a whole that was on trial" (*California Journal*, November 1974: 363).[10]

Serrano I, then, found Sacramento actors committed to breaking the impasse of Reagan's first term. The governor resigned himself to the necessity of compromise, and legislative leaders hoped to avoid the bitter stalemates of the past.

9. Reagan has commented:

I've learned to read terrible blasts at me by legislators who when they saw me the next day cheerfully said "hello" and visited with me on a friendly basis as if it were part of the game. I suppose to anyone who has never been in politics, not even a lawyer, that you think if anybody says something pretty dastardly about you, they must not like you. I've learned it isn't true (*Cannon* 1969: 300).

10. Noting a new spirit of cooperation, the *California Journal* reported as the new term began in January 1971,

The first official comments from the new legislative leaders indicated a conciliatory approach toward Governor Reagan. Both [Mills and Moretti] expressed a willingness to work with the administration in solving the state's problems, and both refrained from making comments to the press which were openly critical of the Governor. Reagan took up the same theme in his State-of-the-State message and made unprecedented visits to the newly-elected leaders in their offices two floors above the governor's own first-floor suite. Although Reagan denied that the visits signified any change in his approach to the Legislature, previously it was necessary for legislators to come down to his office to meet with him, a practice he followed even when his own party occupied the top legislative post (1971, "Roster of Elected State Officials").

Wilson Riles: A Creation of the Legislature

The second critical Sacramento change concurrent with *Serrano I* was the ouster of Max Rafferty. In the 1970 nonpartisan contest for superintendent of public instruction, to the surprise of most observers, Wilson Riles defeated Reagan-backed incumbent Max Rafferty.[11] Riles's election was a surprise not only because he lacked Max Rafferty's sophisticated and well-financed political operation but also because he was a political unknown. Before his election, Riles was one of two deputies to Superintendent Max Rafferty. According to a former State Department of Education official, "The California legislature created Wilson Riles. They created two deputyships under Max Rafferty on the condition that one of the posts be filled by Wilson Riles."

Riles had won the trust and respect of California legislators as the popular and effective head of the state's compensatory education efforts. By instituting a new deputy's position and assuring that Riles would fill it, the legislature attempted to stop the flimflam attributed to Max Rafferty and cement relations with the department. They hoped that Riles's access to decisions would provide them with reliable information about department operations, something they had not had under Rafferty.

Riles's election contributed critically to legislative willingness to consider an increase in state aid to the public schools or school finance reform. Legislators sympathetic to the educators' cause but unwilling to vote more funds to Rafferty's stewardship were amenable to an increase in state funds supervised by a trusted ally. From the perspective of most legislators, Riles's election replaced a distrusted adversary with a reliable partner.

11. Turner and Vieg (1971:139) explain:

The superintendent of public instruction is the only state executive who is elected on a nonpartisan ballot. He serves as the director of the Department of Education and the secretary and executive officer of the State Board of Education appointed by the governor. This board, in turn, is designated as the governing and policy-determining body of the Department of Education. Thus the superintendent of public instruction, an elected officer, is in the anomalous position of heading a state department whose policies are determined by an appointive board.

As head of the Department of Education, the superintendent regulates and provides professional assistance to all publicly supported schools and colleges of the state except the University of California and the state colleges. He serves ex officio as a member of the Board of Regents of the University of California and of the Board of Trustees of the state colleges.

School finance reformers also gained a valuable ally with Riles's election. Riles, campaigning as an advocate of the children, had made it clear that a top priority was a higher level of state spending for schools (*California Journal*, December 1970:350). Furthermore, he underlined his commitment to equalization. Echoing the language of *Serrano* plaintiffs, Riles asserted, "The quality of every child's education should not depend on where he lives" (*California Journal*, April 1970:112–113).[12]

Generating Reform Alternatives: Political and Technical Pitfalls

This 1971 convergence of *Serrano I*, a conciliatory spirit between the governor and legislative leaders, and the election of Wilson Riles laid the groundwork for consideration of finance reform. The major forces that shaped the state's first response to *Serrano* were Reagan's determination to pass a tax measure and education supporters' determination to get more money for the schools. School finance reform, although sanctioned by *Serrano*, was not center stage.

Buoyed by *Serrano I*, school finance advocates in the senate and the assembly and on the state board of education immediately set to work researching, conferring, and developing their own school finance reform proposals. At the same time, Governor Reagan and Assembly Speaker Moretti, in what political writer Lou Cannon called a "strange alliance," began an extended series of private meetings to develop a tax relief and education support package that would be acceptable to both parties (*California Journal*, November 1974:360). Because legislative leadership—notably Assembly Education Committee Chairman Leroy Greene and Senate Education Committee Chairman Albert Rodda—would insist on a measure that addressed *Serrano*, Governor Reagan directed Department of Finance staff to develop a *Serrano* plan as well.

Although these disparate efforts embodied quite different actors and goals, the participants soon found themselves confronting a common problem: The simplicity of the *Serrano I* decision masked and in fact misconstrued the complexity of the school finance reform problem. Perhaps the only aspect of the school finance reform prob-

12. In this same campaign interview, Max Rafferty commented, "California has the best statewide program of equalization in the United States."

lem that all parties correctly foresaw was its size. By 1971 the tax bases of the richest and poorest school districts differed by a ratio of 14,000:1; the expenditure ratio was approximately 8:1 (see Table 3-1).

These substantial disparities had been publicized in the *Serrano* arguments and underlined for at least the two previous years by the Legislative Analyst's Office. As Mockler and Hayward noted, "The inequality among districts, because of increasing assessed value of property and despite modest increases in the foundation program, were of gargantuan proportions and worsening annually" (1978: 385). The magnitude of these discrepancies made it clear that school finance reform could not be accomplished by tinkering at the margins. Substantial change was required to respond to *Serrano I*. And it would, of course, carry high political and monetary costs. However, the only common conclusions that all participants could draw from this set of facts and the court's mandate for reform were that there was no single or simple solution to *Serrano* and that any solution would be expensive.[13] Substantial change usually requires a measure of clarity about the goals of reform and the nature of the policy problem. *Serrano I* afforded neither.

It soon became obvious that there was little consensus on what goals the court intended school finance reform to address and that the simple baseline data enumerating interdistrict disparities told

Table 3-1. Financial Conditions of Richest and Poorest Districts.

Item	Low	High
Assessed value/ Average Daily Attendance[a]	$75.00	$1,053,000.00
Tax rate[b]	00.39	7.83
Expenditure/ Average Daily Attendance	420.00	3,447.00

a. Assessed value = 0.25 of market value.
b. Tax rates are levied on each $100 of assessed value.
Source: Mockler and Hayward 1978: 386.

13. To this point, one month after the *Serrano I* ruling, Legislative Analyst Alan Post estimated that it might cost as much as $1.5 billion in new revenues to fully comply with the court ruling.

only part of the story. *Serrano I* laid down a principle of wealth neutrality—the quality of a child's education must not be a function of the wealth of his parents and neighbors. Although the court's insistence on greater equalization could be inferred from its opinion, there was substantial uncertainty over who the beneficiaries of equalization were to be. Taxpayers? Students? Or both?

If *Serrano I* were interpreted to mean *taxpayer equity*, then reform measures should equalize the tax efforts' dollar yield, allowing expenditure differences to remain. That is, if two districts chose to tax themselves at the same rate, their return should be the same despite differences in assessed valuation, but districts could spend less by taxing less.[14]

If *student equity* were held to be the heart of the issue, the consequences would be quite different. Either through a substantial increase in the state foundation program or through a Robin Hood measure that would take funds from high-spending districts or some combination of both, each public school student in California should receive the same support from foundation funds. Inequalities in tax rates could be tolerated if the result were equal foundation expenditures.

As the Reagan administration and legislative staff began to develop their plans, confusion over the court-intended goals of school finance reform generated two broad equalization alternatives that could meet the *Serrano* principle of wealth neutrality: expenditures for basic educational programs or capacity to raise revenue.

Full state assumption of local education expenses or replacement of local property taxes with a uniform statewide residential property tax were ways to address the first alternative. The second *Serrano* alternative could be addressed through a policy of district power equalizing (assuring that identical tax rates produced the same revenues), through a statewide property tax, or through a district reorganization policy aimed at tax base equalizing.*

---

14. Dramatic taxpayer inequities existed as Sacramento turned its attention to *Serrano*: "In Alameda County, near Oakland, Emery Unified could spend $2,448 per ADA with a $2.66 tax rate, while its neighbor, Newark Unified, struggled to raise $719 per ADA with a $5.69 tax rate in 1970 to 1971. Just two years earlier, Emery had generated almost $800 less ($1,655 per ADA) with the same tax rate. In the same period, Newark's program grew by less than $100 per ADA" (Mockler and Hayward 1978: 387).

*This discussion draws heavily on Post and Brandsma 1973.

Either alternative or combination of approaches treads upon polit-ically sensitive territory. A policy that pursued expenditure equaliza-tion could greatly reduce the level of spending in politically powerful high-spending districts. Without a substantial commitment of new state funds, high-wealth districts would have to be leveled down. The elected representatives from affected districts would be unlikely to support such a strategy. An equalization policy that leveled up low-wealth districts would require more new state money for education than the administration and many lawmakers would be likely to pro-vide. Strategies that neutralized wealth by raising the tax rates of low-rate districts or by recapturing property tax revenues from dis-tricts with high assessed valuation or high tax rates were contrary to the state's ethos of local control, which held that citizens had the right to set the rate at which they taxed themselves and the priority afforded education in their community.

From the start, the *Serrano* decision generated uncertainty over the nature of the mandate and, consequently, over the nature of the remedy and the appropriate standard of compliance. The simple prin-ciple of wealth neutrality was a political mine field. Planners soon discovered that, regardless of the goal assumed for *Serrano*—taxpayer equity or student equity—the simplicity of the court's decision and the straightforward relationships posited by its underlying theory concealed serious financing complexities. The substantive and politi-cal questions of specifying goals were quickly compounded by tech-nical problems that emerged once planning began.

A central problem for strategists concerned the intended *target* of school finance reform. The *Serrano I* decision implicitly assumed that low-income students would benefit if low-wealth or low-expendi-ture districts were beneficiaries of school finance reform. Once plan-ners examined district data in greater detail, they found that the court's assumption was demonstrably wrong. They found that more than one-half of California's public school students live in districts that would lose money under a pupil expenditure equalization plan and that over 60 percent of the welfare families live in high-wealth districts (Mockler and Hayward 1978). Research subsequent to *Ser-rano I* showed that even Beverly Hills, the archetype high-wealth, high-spending district, had quite a few low-income families. A reduc-tion in the expenditure level of high-spending districts or an increase in the tax rate for low assessed value districts could hurt low-income families—the supposed beneficiaries of John Serrano's class action petition—by reducing the educational services available to them or by increasing their tax burden. Further, planners found that low-spending districts were not always communities of the type that prompted John Serrano's suit. Many were suburban districts with shiny new facilities and few extraordinary expenses beyond a basic education program and were hardly disadvantaged.

Planners also found that a second *Serrano* assumption—a positive relationship between assessed wealth and fiscal capacity—was seriously off the mark (Chambers 1978). For example, the state's urban areas serve many severely poor students and because of commercial interests, have a much higher than average assessed valuation.[15] Consequently, these areas have both special student needs and the ability to spend more on education. Because of the high incidence of students requiring special services, higher per pupil expenditure was not always coincident with a richer, more comprehensive education program. It simply reflected the extra expense of providing appropriate services to a heterogeneous student body with multiple needs. Schools in these districts were by no means rich in the sense assumed by the school finance theories that supported *Serrano I*.

Similarly, planners discovered that higher spending per average daily attendance (ADA) did not always translate cleanly into more *educational* services. Once planners looked closely at school district budgets, they saw that high ADA subsumed many noneducational expenses. For example, further research showed that "of the 35 highest spending unified districts, 27 were small rural districts with extremely high costs of operation due to sparsity and energy costs" (Mockler and Hayward 1978:388). The small Sierra Nevada district of Truckee, for example, must own and operate its own snow plows because the school's access road is not on county land. In addition, extreme winter temperatures require the district to heat school buildings on a twenty-four-hour basis to prevent frozen pipes and other subzero damage. Largely as a result of these noneducational but essential costs, the Truckee Unified School District spends well above the state average per pupil expenditure.

Close looks at district budgets showed other factors that contribute to higher than average expenditures but reflect district peculiarities rather than a taste for program embellishment. For example,

15. All of the big five California districts—San Diego, Long Beach, Los Angeles, Oakland, and San Francisco—were either at or above the average assessed-valuation per pupil.

teacher turnover and a fairly low living cost reduce the portion of district budgets allocated to teachers' salaries in small rural communities. Urban areas must provide higher starting salaries, and longer teacher tenure means many of the district's staff occupy top range on the salary scale. These fixed costs mean that large high-spending districts often have fewer discretionary funds available in their budgets than many lower spending districts.

Finally, planners found that the state of the art of schooling provided scant guidance. Strategists pursuing both broad alternatives were stymied as they discovered that no one knew what education dollars bought and there was no consensus on an appropriate level of spending for a quality education program. "Since nobody really knows what an 'effective and efficient' education is, it seems almost impossible to determine how much it should cost" (Benson et al. 1974:55).

As legislative and administrative planners set to work on *Serrano I*, the simple charge that had seemed music to the ears of reformers became cacophony. There were no clear goals or benefits that reformers could stitch into a banner to mobilize school finance reform movement. Worse, the straightforward relationship between right and remedy implicitly assumed by the court's findings turned out to be wrong. The simplicity of the court mandate was an illusion; as a result, any response to *Serrano I* would confront imposing political and technical obstacles.

Reformers' Response

Hoping that time was finally ripe for change, reform advocates in both houses introduced school finance proposals soon after the legislature reconvened for the 1972 session. They all sought to remedy *Serrano's* political pitfalls and technical problems with dollars. Senator Ralph Collier, a Democrat from Yreka, launched the legislative school finance reform drive on 24 January 1972 with a proposal for a multibillion dollar tax program that he said would solve California's school finance problem. Collier's bill proposed to replace the sales tax with a 5 percent gross receipts tax that would wipe out the need for local property tax and support full state assumption of public education costs. Collier's bill also proposed to consolidate the state's smaller school districts with the big districts as a matter of administrative efficiency. Collier, called the dean of the state legislature, termed his proposal a "response to *Serrano*" and said the main purpose of his bill was "to get people thinking about big money bills, particularly in the Senate Select Committee on School District Finance" (*Los Angeles Times*, 25 January 1972). On the next day, 25 January 1972, Assemblyman Leroy Greene introduced a measure that proposed a uniform statewide property tax of $2.53 per $100 of assessed valuation and increased state aid for public education by $584 million. Introducing his bill, Assemblyman Greene asserted that "it would meet *Serrano*" (*Los Angeles Times*, 26 January 1972).

At the same time, the state board of education convened a special board advisory committee composed of tax experts, businessmen, farm leaders, labor officials, educators, minority leaders, and Reagan administration representatives. The advisory committee was charged with the design of a reform plan to meet *Serrano*.

In March the committee submitted the product of their deliberation, a plan that called for a statewide property tax of $2.50 per $100 of assessed valuation (*Los Angeles Times*, 10 March 1972). State board members then conferred with Superintendent of Public Instruction Wilson Riles to put together a proposal for legislative consideration. The *Los Angeles Times* gave the result of these conferences front-page attention:

> Two landmark school reform proposals were approved by the State Board of Education calling for education programs for four year olds and school financing by statewide property tax. These measures represent two of the most far-reaching changes in the history of state public education and are top priorities of Wilson Riles (*Los Angeles Times*, 15 April 1972).

The bill moved to the legislature in May 1972, carried jointly by long-time reform advocates Democratic Senator Stephen Teale and Republican Assemblyman Dixon Arnett (*Los Angeles Times*, 10 May 1972). This bill was soon joined by yet another proposal to reform school finance through statewide property tax, sponsored by reform advocate Senator Albert Rodda. Before the 1972 legislative session was halfway over, legislative advocates had proposed four major and expensive school finance reform measures.

A statewide property tax was a strategy common to these reform measures. It seemed to be the most straightforward path to taxpayer equity—all property in the state would be taxed at the same rate. Student equity could be addressed as the state dispersed these tax revenues. Assessing the political feasibility of school finance reform, Arnold Meltsner argued in 1972 that a statewide property tax was the most likely legislative response to *Serrano*. Meltsner's surveys of school superintendents and legislators showed substantial support for this approach: Adoption of a statewide property tax as a school finance reform measure received approval from 65 percent of the superintendents surveyed and 50 percent of the legislators. Superintendents from small or wealthy districts were disproportionately opposed to the proposal (Meltsner et al. 1973).

The notion of a statewide property tax also received authoritative backing in Sacramento. School finance experts Cox and Post had long advocated a statewide property tax as a strategy for equalization (Meltsner et al. 1973; Legislative Analyst 1969–70; Legislative Analyst 1970–71; Post and Brandsma 1973). In addition, Governor Reagan's own 1972 Commission on Educational Reform recommended a statewide property tax as the best equalization measure. Even State Controller Houston Flournoy, a codefendant in the *Serrano* suit, urged this strategy as "the only way to meet *Serrano*" (*Los Angeles Times*, 25 July 1972). Staunch reform advocate Assembly Education Committee Chairman Leroy Greene said: "A statewide [property] tax is apparently the only practical, legal way to finance schools in California" (Meltsner and Nakamura 1974:229).

Despite this influential support and its promise to solve *Serrano* once and for all, the statewide property tax notion was quickly discarded for lack of political practicability. The idea was strongly opposed by the Reagan administration and by many legislators for a number of reasons. One was a technical problem: Local assessment practices varied enormously. A statewide system assumed uniform assessment practices. There was little consensus among experts about how district assessment practices could be fairly standardized throughout the state.

The statewide property tax also raised equity problems of a different sort. Imposition of a uniform statewide tax would have raised tax rates in many high assessed valuation areas. For example, Kern County's rate, traditionally kept low by the presence of oil companies, would have escalated more than 200 percent because of the extremely high assessed value of its commercial property. More politically important, Beverly Hills's rate would have doubled, and San Francisco's tax rate would be boosted by over 50 percent. Under a statewide property tax plan, property taxes would have increased substantially in at least 25 percent of the state's school districts, including the most influential.[16]

In addition, because a statewide property tax would recapture tax revenue from high assessed valuation districts for distribution to low assessed valuation districts, many opponents argued that the scheme would constitute taxation without representation. This, opponents contended, was taxpayer inequity of another kind—curtailing the ability of some taxpayers to determine how their tax dollars were spent.

The Reagan administration staunchly opposed a statewide property tax scheme for yet another reason. It would have moved the state into the traditional purview of local governments—the collection and disbursement of property taxes. The Reagan administration argued that this constituted an inappropriate and unacceptable encroachment on local control.

For all of these reasons, the first serious efforts to meet *Serrano* were rejected out of hand by the administration and the legislature. Kenneth Hall remembers that, "although the concept was widely debated, statewide property tax politically was never considered as a way to equalize expenditures. Everyone, both the administration and the legislature, agreed that it was not practical."[17]

As their proposals foundered on the shoals of political practicability, so did reformers' hopes that *Serrano I* would lead to major school finance reform. *Serrano I*, they discovered, provided sanction for reform but did not generate a constituency. Further, reformers' efforts to mobilize support were obstructed by confusion about the goals, the inherent political costs, and the technical complexity of

16. One solution to this dilemma was suggested in 1969 and again in 1970 by Alan Post—a split-roll assessment in which a uniform statewide tax to fund basic education would be levied on nonresidential property. Under this scheme, commercial property would be taxed at a different rate from residential property. According to the Legislative Analyst's Office, this proposal has a number of advantages. First, it would neutralize the tax differences dependent on location, which might assist urban areas in attracting new industry. Second, Post believed that a variation in residential property tax rates would allow homeowners to cast votes reflecting their different priorities concerning education, thereby upholding the tenets of local control. This proposal never received serious legislative attention because disadvantages were perceived to outweigh the advantages. For one, a uniform tax rate might attract industry to some areas but might also move it from others. Second, because Section I of Article XIII of the California Constitution requires all property to be taxed at the same rate, a split-roll strategy would require a constitutional amendment. Few expected it to succeed.

17. Kenneth Hall 22 January 1980: personal communication.

reform. If the reformers' proposals failed to receive serious attention from the administration or the legislature, they did serve notice—as Senator Collier had hoped—that new state dollars would be needed to address *Serrano* and that the issues of tax relief and school finance reform were inextricably bound.

The Reagan-Moretti Compromise: Senate Bill 90

"SB 90 was a dishonest covenant, secretly arrived at," charged a veteran of Sacramento school finance struggles, referring to the closed-door sessions during which Reagan and Moretti fashioned a compromise. As the legislative proposals for reform were developed and then quietly died in committees, the governor and the assembly speaker began meeting privately to work out a measure that would provide fiscal relief and address school finance concerns.[18]

After the failure of his first term, Reagan understood that compromise would be necessary if he was to have a bill. He did not want to engage in open bargaining and staff debate typical of the legislative process. The governor believed he could depend on Republican support for any proposal he advanced; he counted on the influence of the assembly Speaker, whose position is termed the second most powerful in Sacramento, to deliver the necessary Democratic votes.

The agenda for compromise between Governor Reagan and Speaker Moretti involved issues central to their quite different political philosophies. Four major questions needed to be resolved if a compromise measure were to result:

- How to provide property tax relief
- How to get more money to the schools
- How to address *Serrano*
- How to pay for it all

18. Moretti's proposal to exclude staff members from meetings with the governor was regarded with apprehension by both Reagan's aides and Moretti's lieutenants. But, as Lou Cannon explains:

> The meetings took place anyway, largely because the individual pride of Moretti and of Reagan did not permit either to shrink from the challenge (of resolving the legislative stalemate). In one sense, it can be said that neither the Governor nor the Speaker was as politically skilled—some would even say as intelligent—as their predecessors in the Brown-Unruh era had been. But they understood more (*California Journal*, November 1974: 363).

AB 1000 and 1001, the governor's tax bills defeated in the fiscal hours of the 1970 legislative session, were resurrected as the vehicle for the compromise. Three of the four central issues upon which agreement had to be reached turned on questions of social philosophy—the extent to which state aid to the schools would be increased, the beneficiaries of a tax relief measure, and the nature of a tax shift to fund the package. Reagan and Moretti had made their positions on these issues clear in the series of proposals aborted in Reagan's first term. What remained, then, was identification of quid pro quo compromises on each issue.

The *Serrano* question, as Reagan and Moretti soon discovered, involved more than points of social philosophy. The issue of school finance reform involved technical problems that required expert assistance. Neither the Legislative Analyst's Office nor legislative school finance staff was called upon to help. They were excluded in part because Reagan believed that the finance experts simply wanted more for the schools (see also Meltsner and Nakamura 1974). Another major reason was that Reagan did not want to cede his central role in developing the proposal. The Reagan-controlled State Department of Finance was called in. As Kenneth Hall, then deputy finance Director and architect of the governor's program, commented, "The Governor wanted to have the technical capacity to compete with 'outside experts' and to justify his major school finance policy decisions."[19] Hall undertook a crash course in the technicalities of school finance and set to work developing a *Serrano* component for the Reagan–Moretti proposal.

Hall soon discovered that he had neither well-developed finance reform models to guide his efforts nor adequate data upon which to base his estimates. John Mockler, then a member of the assembly staff and subsequently legislative liaison for the Department of Education, remarked that the absence of district level information made many of the subsequent calculations "guesstimates" at best:

> There was very little data upon which to base the formulas or analyses. The best thing we could tell people in terms of effects on their districts (once the compromise was introduced to the legislature) was that it's bigger than a breadbasket and smaller than an elephant.[20]

19. Kenneth Hall 22 January 1980: personal communication.
20. John Mockler 2 June 1979: personal communication.

According to Hall, revenue limits, the *Serrano* measure subsequently adopted, was the only equalization measure ever considered by Department of Finance staff. The origins of the concept are somewhat vague although it came from state technicians rather than from any of the national networks. Hall remembers: "We had heard rumors that another state had used revenue limits to equalize expenditures. So we started working on it for California. But we didn't follow the model of another state; we worked out the specifics totally on our own." Revenue limits put a lid on spending in all school districts and, through differential inflation adjustments (the squeeze factor), slowly moved high-spending and low-spending districts together. In the long run, this modified leveling up strategy was expected to yield expenditure equity without unnecessarily damaging programs in high expenditure districts. Also, it was calculated in the familiar terms of dollars per average daily attendance (ADA) and thus could be grafted onto the existing system. Hall notes,

> All the old formulas—the foundation plan and so on—were written in terms of ADA. Plus Post relied on ADA in his reports and McDermott used the same methodology in the *Serrano* complaint. So when *Serrano* hit, revenue limits were preordained—nothing else was discussed.[21]

Revenue limits also were consistent with the governor's goals. First, they agreed with his objective of limiting education spending. Second, because limits did not embody recapture mechanisms or full state assumption, this strategy was seen as least harmful to Reagan's local control principles. The governor's protection of local control also led to the retention of voted overrides whereby voters could authorize their district to exceed their revenue limits.[22] With Hall's revenue limit plan, the basic structure of the Reagan–Moretti school finance component was in place.

The increased support for public education contained in the compromise was less than education supporters wanted and more than the governor thought was necessary, but it had crucial strategic value for him. Reagan's first-term legislative battles had taught him the importance of securing a broad base of support prior to legislative debate. They also had taught him something about logrolling. He hoped to secure support necessary for passage by devising a package that was sufficiently attractive to legislative education advocates to

21. Kenneth Hall 22 January 1980: personal communication.
22. Kenneth Hall 22 January 1980: personal communication.

still other concerns. In particular, Reagan's original tax program had emphasized rate control for the counties, an unpopular strategy. According to Hall, the governor's first-term tax program "got killed in Senate Revenue and Taxation Committee because the counties came unglued." As a result of this defeat, Hall remembers recommending a change in emphasis for the resuscitated AB 1000 and 1001: "Let's make rate control a secondary issue and make school finance primary. We can use the school finance component to run over opposition from the counties."[23] Or, as another participant remarked: "Basically, [the Reagan–Moretti compromise] was a deal between Moretti and the right wing. Moretti cut his deal with Reagan. Schools were just a way to put it together."[24]

An ingredient still missing from this coalition-building strategy was the support of Superintendent Wilson Riles. John Mockler said, "Reagan had found out that Riles could put together a hell of a coalition that could have exerted lots of pressure." For example, a May gathering of representatives from thirteen education interest groups—a meeting Riles called a "crisis summit conference"—had not gone unnoticed by the administration. Consequently, the governor moved "to find something for the education types to coalesce around."[25]

The result was a $25 million side payment to Wilson Riles, funding for his top priority, the Early Childhood Education (ECE) program. As one observer put it: "Riles was brought in by Reagan's promise for ECE. It was a quid pro quo for his accepting revenue limits." Consequently, in July, Riles formally announced his backing of AB 1000. He commented: "It's not perfect but no compromise pleases everybody." Riles also conceded that the Reagan–Moretti proposal "does not fully answer the court's demands . . . but it does take a major step" toward school finance reform (*Los Angeles Times*, 19 July 1972).[26]

23. Kenneth Hall 22 January 1980: personal communication.

24. John Mockler 2 June 1979: personal communication.

25. John Mockler 2 June 1979: personal communication.

26. Moretti showed similar resignation in announcing his support of the bill. The *Los Angeles Times* reports: "A Moretti spokesman said the Speaker is not jumping up and down and turning cartwheels but feels this (AB 1000–1001) goes about as far as possible this year" (1 July 1972).

Legislative Legerdemain

With the support of Wilson Riles and Moretti's sponsorship, the compromise tax and school finance reform package was ready for its debut in the Senate Finance Committee. One lobbyist described what followed next as the "Perils of Pauline" (Meltsner and Nakamura 1974:280). Once again, the senate proved the fatal stumbling block for the governor's package. After hours of bitter debate, the Reagan–Moretti package was pushed to a vote in the Senate Finance Committee; supporters hoped that, once it was extricated from the committee, the measure would pass on the senate floor.

To the anguish of supporters and the anger of the governor, AB 1000 was killed in committee by a vote of six to seven. The governor's ire was compounded by the fact that the losing vote was a Republican, Fresno Senator Howard Way, and the issue was county rate controls. The California county lobby began mounting a vigorous campaign against the bill in July. Daniel G. Grant, president of the County Supervisors Association, condemned the bill as "arbitrary" and "crippling to local government" (*Los Angeles Times*, 19 July 1972). Senator Way, who was not a vocal education supporter, agreed with the county's position and refused to support the governor's package.[27]

In a move that represented legislative legerdemain of the highest order, Senate Finance Committee leaders quickly substituted a $900 million bill carried by Democratic Senator Ralph C. Dills of Los Angeles, Senate Bill (SB) 90. Supported by the California Teachers Association (CTA), it was a straightforward education revenue measure, providing a generous increase in state support for the schools but no *Serrano* components or tax rate controls. SB 90 was hurriedly amended to include the sale tax increase included in the Reagan–Moretti compromise as a way to pay for it all and was sent off to the Assembly Ways and Means Committee.

"It appeared that an atmosphere of 'legislation by exhaustion' was beginning to set in" (Aufderheide 1974: 49). Legislators postponed

---

27. Bill Hauck, formerly Moretti's policy advisor and now with California Research Consultants, said: "The counties had the same gripes as the cities. They were being mandated to do things [such as welfare services] that no one was paying for. Jack Merelman [then Executive Director of the Supervisors Association] was a good man and made [the counties] strong during the SB 90 negotiations" (Bill Hauck 16 January 1980: personal communication).

their scheduled summer recess to make a last-ditch effort at passing a bill acceptable to legislators and the governor. Once in the Assembly Ways and Means Committee, Dills's SB 90 was gutted through "some imaginative parliamentary footwork," and the original Reagan–Morletti compromise package was substituted (Aufderheide 1974:50). The Committee voted fourteen to three to send SB 90 to the assembly floor, where it passed.

When the measure reached the senate floor in the beginning of August, the county issue once again obstructed passage. SB 90 received a favorable vote of twenty-three to fourteen, just short of the two-thirds approval needed for appropriation. On August 8 "an exhuasted legislature recessed with Speaker Moretti predicting that the legislature would return from recess on November 8 for a 'bitter, difficult and unhappy' windup" (Aufderheide 1974: 50).

With the future of his program uncertain, Governor Reagan began "going after the dirty dozen in the Senate. The legislature was called back early from recess and some heavy dealing and trading began to take place."[28] Governor Reagan threatened to campaign against recalcitrant legislators in their districts and to grant a one-time income tax cut of up to $450 million if the legislature would not pass the compromise property tax measure when it reconvened. The education community was also alarmed by the legislative stalemate. The July 1 budget deadline had passed and their funding future appeared bleak. The CTA began to pour money into key campaigns for the senate and the assembly. One participant remembers that, for example, a Republican senator was given $50,000 to pay off campaign debts.

Ronald Reagan also initiated new bargaining for support and made what Kenneth Hall called "his most difficult compromise of all."[29] Willie Brown, the influential chairman of the Assembly Ways and Means Committee and Democrat from high-spending San Francisco, believed that the bill's *Serrano* features would hurt his district. In exchange for Brown's support, the governor agreed to add an urban factor to SB 90. A participant remembers:

> A phony thing called Education for Disadvantaged Youth (EDY) was written up for Willie Brown. The governor said we could give Willie $10 million; that was raised to $20 million. But in the Ways and Means Committee hearings,

28. John Mockler 2 June 1979: personal communication.
29. Kenneth Hall 22 January 1980: personal communication.

Willie Brown screamed [that San Francisco would be hurt by revenue limits] and so it was raised to $40 million. Then the conference committee got nervous that Willie was going to walk, so the EDY funding was raised to $80 million; I began to get nervous—they were allocating all this money on a hokey formula. Then new problems arose with the formula because it excluded San Diego and Long Beach. So we added another $2 million for "security protection and vandalism protection" to bring in San Diego and Long Beach. Never before in California history had so much money [$82 million] gone into a special program.

Kenneth Hall said that this compromise with Willie Brown was particularly irksome for Reagan because the money would go to San Francisco:

> The Governor was not particularly a fan of San Francisco. He thought San Francisco exemplified the problem of high input [to the school district] and low output. In fact, no district in the state had been more broadly criticized [for inefficiency] at that time. Reagan thought the urban factor [EDY] would just be more money down a rat hole.[30]

But with his bill as ransom, and on the advice of Speaker Moretti, Reagan gave Willie Brown his urban factor.[31]

The day after the November 7 election, the legislature reconvened for a final, exhausting month to try to resolve the SB 90 deadlock. During this final period in the 1972 legislative session, political pressure and infighting escalated:

> Reagan . . . threatened to take his own initiative package to the voters if the legislature did not pass SB 90. Speaker Moretti, with his hat in the ring for the 1974 Democratic gubernatorial nomination, countered that if the Governor were to take an initiative to the people, *he* would take *his* version to the people also and let them choose between the two plans (Aufderheide 1974: 51, emphasis in original).

For the first time, the education interest groups banded together to change "no" votes. With the exception of the California Federation of Teachers (CFT), represented by Mary Bergan, all of the educational interest groups aggressively backed SB 90.[32]

30. Kenneth Hall 22 January 1980: personal communication.

31. Ironically, once SB 90 passed the senate and was returned to the assembly, Willie Brown did not vote for it. John Mockler recalls: "Reagan flipped. Moretti replied that 'I didn't say he would vote for it, I just said he would walk if you didn't put in the extra money" (John Mockler 2 June 1979: personal communication).

32. Bergan believed that the bill did not give enough money to the schools and that the revenue limits would hurt districts in the long run. Members of the CTA, the Association of

Participants agree that pressure from education interest groups finally broke the SB 90 deadlock. Bill Lambert, UTLA lobbyist, after hours of closeted conversation, finally succeeded in getting the swing vote number twenty-seven from Democratic Senator David Roberti.[33] The twenty-eighth and twenty-ninth votes followed upon Roberti's switch.

Kenneth Hall remembers Assembly Speaker Robert Moretti waking him with a jubilant late night telephone call: "You'll never believe it, but we did it" (1973:1). Senate Bill 90, against most odds, had finally squeaked off the senate floor. Its last-minute passage broke the four-year legislative deadlock that had prevented both Governor Reagan and the legislators from achieving their substantively different tax reform objectives. The next day, 1 December 1972, the California legislature enacted the largest dollar increase ever given to public schools in the state's history and the most expensive piece of legislation enacted by any state.

SB 90 was primarily a tax bill, with more money for public education thrown in as a way to bind Democratic support. The measure was ambitious and wide ranging. Except for a small band of reformers, *Serrano* concerns were at best secondary as the Reagan–Moretti compromise was developed. The bill's weak equalization strategies received serious legislative attention only when they necessitated a sidepayment to San Francisco's Willie Brown. Legislative leaders and their staff, who had wrestled with school finance equalization measures for years, were not invited to participate in constructing the state's first *Serrano* response. Nonetheless, SB 90's equalization measures established the structure that would shape subsequent legislative school finance reform efforts. Major components included:

- An increase in state equalization aid for low-wealth districts
- Revenue limits on district taxing ability

California School Administrators (ACSA), the California School Boards Association (CSBA), and the United Teachers of Los Angeles (UTLA) exchanged strategies and cooperated on contacting legislators' constituents to apply pressure and buttonhole individual senators and assemblymen. The CTA took particularly aggressive action and organized a successful march on the capitol that, according to a participant, "left legislators screaming 'get those teachers out of my office'" (Paul Holmes 22 January 1980: personal communication). Aufderheide notes, "An interesting and curious example of 'politics makes strange bedfellows' was the appearance of conservative Ronald Reagan before a group of demonstrating teacher-pickets on the Capitol steps telling them they were 'doing the right thing'" (1974:51).

33. The nature of Lambert's deal with Roberti has never been explained. Most participants, however, agree with the assessment of a legislative staffer who said: "I don't know what [Roberti] got, but he probably got plenty!"

- A squeeze factor for differentially adjusting state aid increases, local assessment rates, and inflation allowances
- Funds for reducing tax rates in high-tax, low-wealth districts

Kenneth Hall, who has been called the architect of SB 90, claimed that the bill "revolutionized school finance" (1973: 4). In his January 1973 State-of-the-State Address, Governor Reagan announced to the legislature:

> For the first time in four years we can speak of tax reform and school finance in the past tense. The legislation you passed and I signed a few weeks ago fulfills our joint pledge to provide California's homeowners some of the tax relief they deserve. This legislation means the greatest single-year increase in state school funding ever provided. The program we enacted simplifies an outmoded school-aid formula and assures sufficient financial resources to give all students in California a quality education, no matter where they live (Meltsner and Nakamura 1974: 280).

1972's REFORM — 1973's FIASCO

SB 90 was a strategic masterpiece. The bill was crafted to capitalize upon the existing array of key participant objectives and to exploit the minimum consensus necessary for passage. Designers reasoned that many actors would settle for less than they hoped for, as long as this resolution did not foreclose future options. Meltsner and Nakamura (1974) describe SB 90 as a move in which no one is worse off than before, and most parties are better off. Riles got his Early Childhood Education program; Willie Brown and the big five districts got their urban factor; Reagan and California taxpayers got tax rate controls, revenue limits, and property tax relief; Moretti, legislative education supporters, and the school districts got a large increase in state aid to public education; low-wealth districts got increased aid; wealthy districts did not suffer loss; school finance reform advocates got an equalization measure that at least did not conflict with *Serrano*.

Scarcely one year after its passage, however, SB 90 began to unravel. It became an inferior strategy — almost all parties, notably taxpayers and school districts, were hurt as several crucial assumptions underlying the bill turned out to be wrong. As early as February 1973, the *California Journal* pointed out:

[SB 90], which is already beginning to cause the headaches that many of its opponents (mainly in the Senate) warned of, now seems to have been one of the least carefully considered pieces of major legislation to have been passed by the Legislature (at the Governor's urging) in many years. Not only did it raise taxes well beyond what was needed to balance the budget for several years to come, it has created serious problems for both state and local government and will not provide the kind of property tax relief for many homeowners that was promised (1973: 46).

SB 90, one year later, was widely seen as a fiscal Frankenstein—a tax blunder and a financial disaster for California's school districts (*California Journal*, August 1973:261).

Taxpayers shouldered the burden of a one-cent sales tax increase that was levied to balance SB 90's property tax relief features. Miscalculation of the state's economic position meant that a massive surplus of $1 billion accumulated. Although the surplus was acknowledged well before 1 July 1973, the date the new sales tax became law, the tax went into effect anyway because Reagan and Moretti could not agree on a way to rescind the measure. The *California Journal* reports:

Both the Governor and Moretti . . . blamed each other for the breakdown of the governmental process. Moretti said that the vetoed bill (Moretti's proposal to withdraw the sales tax increase) gave the Governor "98 percent of what he asked for," and blamed Reagan's "intransigence" for the public's plight. And, in vetoing the bill, Reagan said Californians "should remember that it was one man, Robert Moretti, who made that increase necessary." . . . Mail and telephone calls to their offices showed that the general (public) attitude was "a plague on both your houses" (August 1973:261).

In addition to problems caused by the unnecessary sales tax, Reagan's greatest triumph, property tax relief, soon turned to ashes as the assessed valuation of California residential property took off. The tax relief features of SB 90 were quickly outdated as homes in the state began to double and triple in value; this growth was duly noted by very efficient assessment practices. Consequently, homeowners had little to thank the governor for as they received their 1974 property tax bills.

Technical defects in the school finance features of the bill, exacerbated by unexpected trends, created urgent problems for the state's school districts. Imposition of ADA–based revenue limits coincided with the beginning of student enrollment decline. As a result, many districts—particularly large urban districts—faced severe budget deficits unless the original SB 90 allocation formulas were modified. Enrollment was not declining in convenient classroom units, allowing districts to reduce staff proportionately. Thus, state funds declined with the ADA, while expenses remained the same. Many Sacramento school finance experts blamed the educators for not foreseeing the problem of enrollment decline. One said: "School people always live about 20 years behind reality. School people remembered a time of growth so everyone bought into revenue limits."[34] Another commented, "There's a perversity about educators. They always seem to vote for things that are not in their best interests."[35] A third observed, "School people have a marvelous ability to get on the wrong side of the power curve."[36]

Many argue that school people should have expected student enrollment decline, but almost all participants agree that nobody foresaw a second SB 90 problem that almost bankrupted many districts—inflation. For example, Kenneth Hall confidently told a 1973 meeting of the California School Boards Association: "The annual program increases will make it possible for school districts to keep up with the consumer price index and not have to reduce their educational services because of cost of living" (Hall 1973:3). Hall now says, "The inflation factor in California had always been 2 percent or 3 percent—no one could have predicted that in just a year it would take off and start hitting 8 percent and 9 percent."[37] Follow-up bill AB 1267, sponsored by Assemblyman Joe A. Gonsalves, chairman of the Assembly Revenue and Taxation Committee, was rushed through to moderate the most serious problems with SB 90. According to former senate staff school finance expert Gerald Hayward, "If AB 1267 had never passed, SB 90 would have been a disaster of the highest order."[38]

Why did school people work so hard for the passage of a bill that would hurt them so badly? In part, they were victims of circumstance—no one expected the dramatic rise in inflation. The major reason for their vigorous support was their immediate anxiety over the financial plight of the schools. This anxiety made school people

34. Gerald Hayward 22 September 1978: personal communication.
35. John Mockler 2 June 1979: personal communication.
36. Paul Holmes 22 January 1980: personal communication.
37. Kenneth Hall 22 January 1980: personal communication.

both blind to the problems of SB 90 and inclined to bank on short-run gains. As a result, they compromised the power they had. Gerald Hayward remembers:

> The schools were hungry and afraid that if they held out they would get less rather than more. Not a single legislative staff person recommended that SB 90 be passed. We tried to talk the education lobby into holding out by saying, "Reagan needs you worse than you need him," but they were scared. They were anxious and they sold out.[39]

John Mockler, then an assembly staff assistant said:

> [Schoolmen] were hoping that when Reagan left in two years, a liberal governor would be elected who would be for the schools.
>
> [Referring to subsequent governor Jerry Brown.] Have you ever seen a liberal Jesuit?[40]

Education lobbyists agree that they exchanged short-term gains (a substantial increase in the state foundation) for possible longer term costs. Most education interest group members believed it was either SB 90 or nothing. Jim Donnally, CTA representative, remembers:

> Prior to SB 90, school districts were totally relying on voters to pass overrides to increase the district budget. The phenomenon of "slippage" [in which the state's relative contribution as determined by the minimum foundation grant goes down] was becoming more and more apparent. More and more school districts were becoming basic aid districts [because the local property values had become sufficiently high to cut off state assistance in addition to the basic $125 grant received by all districts]. The state's portion was becoming "peanuts." SB 90, consequently, was seen as free money from the state. We did not believe then that we could have gotten more. The speaker [Moretti] is powerful man in town. The fact that his bill, AB 1000, died was evidence to make the CTA believe that SB 90 was the only game in town.[41]

The educators gained from SB 90 in other ways. William Lucas, Los Angeles Unified School District lobbyist, recalls, "When the dust cleared, the school districts found they had been screwed by SB 90. That realization is what drew the education coalition together and was the birth of coalition politics in California education."[42] John

38. Gerald Hayward 22 September 1978: personal communication.
39. Gerald Hayward 22 September 1978: personal communication.
40. John Mockler 2 June 1979: personal communication.
41. Jim Donnally 22 January 1980: personal communication.
42. William Lucas 2 August 1979: personal communication.

Mockler dubbed passage of SB 90 as the "loss of innocence" for school districts.[43]

According to Lucas and others, education interest groups learned important lessons from the saga of SB 90. They learned that legislative attitudes toward education had changed. They discovered that the interests of public education were no longer assured a receptive ear in the legislature or seen as pure and beyond scrutiny. As Lucas put it,

> Attitudes in the legislature changed around the mid–sixties. Before that, a school district could simply go to the legislature and make a case for the kiddies. All they had to say was "we need more money for the kids." Then, with the uproar of the sixties, all that changed. The legislature began to ask, "How is the money going to help the kiddies? What's the evidence?"[44]

SB 90 also taught education interest groups that the nature of the issues had changed. No longer was it simply a straightforward question of more money for the schools. *Serrano I* transformed financing issues into complex technical questions requiring expertise and much more comprehensive information than had been necessary before. As John Mockler and others have pointed out, "One reason the CTA and other education groups went for SB 90 and revenue limits was that they didn't understand it."[45]

In their fractionization and lack of organization and expertise, California educators were no different from education interest groups across the country (see, e.g., Kirst 1970). In most states in the early 1970s, organizational disarray and naivete were the educators' prominent political characteristics. To this point, Lucas observes that before the passage of SB 90, school districts and other education interest groups did not recognize these legislative changes and the consequent need for educators to support a professional, integrated lobbying effort. Thus they were ill-equipped to compete with other demands for legislative attention and to play a major role in the development of school finance bills.

According to Lucas, at the time SB 90 was debated and passed, education lobbying efforts were small time and uncoordinated. Most of the big districts had representatives in Sacramento, but they were part-time and expert in matters of old-style political diplomacy

---

43. John Mockler 2 June 1979: personal communication.
44. William Lucas 2 August 1979: personal communication.
45. John Mockler 2 June 1979: personal communication.

rather than the technicalities of school finance. Lucas remembers that Los Angeles, Sacramento, Oakland, and Long Beach representatives shared a desk; San Francisco had a small adjacent office. Furthermore, Lucas adds, the effectiveness of this somewhat haphazard lobbying arrangement was diluted because district lobbyists in Sacramento represented management. "We were always across the table from the CTA; we never presented an integrated [educators'] position on anything."[46] All of this changed as educators learned the lessons of SB 90.

SENATE BILL 90 FAILS JUDICIAL TEST

SB 90 failed to provide the promised tax relief, and it failed to ameliorate the financial condition of California's public schools. On 11 April 1974, it failed to meet the test of wealth neutrality laid down in *Serrano I*. Judge Jefferson of the Los Angeles Superior Court found the state's school finance system to be unconstitutional even though it had been greatly modified by SB 90. The court concluded:

> It is an inescapable fact that under SB 90 and AB 1267 the high-wealth districts, with far greater funds available per pupil than are available to the low-wealth districts, have the distinct advantage of being able to pay for and select the better trained, better educated and more experienced teachers, the ability to maintain smaller class sizes by employing more teachers, the ability to offer a wider selection of courses per day, the ability to keep the educational plants in tiptop shape. These are the kinds of items that go into the making of a high quality education program that benefits the children of a school district that has a relatively high level of expenditures flowing from high assessed valuations of property. . . . Pupils in low-wealth school districts are thus being denied the quality of education and uniformity of treatment called for by the *Serrano* court in order for the state's public school financing system to comply with the demands of the equal protection of the laws provision of the California Constitution (as quoted in Post 1974).

The court found that these disparities would not be very much decreased by SB 90's financing mechanisms. It pointed out that although the revenue limits of richer districts rise at a slower rate than those of foundation program districts (which means that the foundation program districts could approach but never equal the

46. William Lucas 2 August 1979: personal communication.

higher spending districts), the gap between them did not close fast enough. For example, an elementary district with a 1973–74 revenue limit of $1,065 (which would be $300 more than that of a foundation program district at $765) would have a 1977–78 revenue limit of $1,201. In 1977 to 1978 the foundation program district would move up to $947; however, this lags $254 behind the high-spending district after the operation of SB 90 for five years. Thus, the difference in revenue was reduced by only $46, or 15 percent of the original $300 amount. By projecting this example to 1982 to 1983, which is the tenth year the bill would have been in effect, the revenue difference would still have been over $200. This simply was not fast enough for the court. Also, districts could exceed their revenue limits with voter-approved overrides, thereby mitigating the intended squeeze effect.

Judge Jefferson's decision came as no surprise to most Sacramento actors and probably not even to members of the Reagan administration, which had been chided early on for its *Serrano* response. For example, school finance reform lawyer John Coons, Superintendent Wilson Riles, and Legislative Analyst Alan Post all agreed that the governor's proposals obviously did not comply with the court mandate (*Los Angeles Times*, 19 May 1972). The ambiguity of the *Serrano I* decision allowed the Reagan administration a particular interpretation of the court decision. In response to the doubts of these reformers, an administrative spokesman argued: "No one has claimed that the *Serrano* decision dictated full equalization. We feel the *Serrano* decision requires that a low-wealth district must have a basic educational program, not (necessarily) the same as a high-wealth district" (*Los Angeles Times*, 19 May 1972).

A number of observers thought that the *Serrano* measures included in SB 90 embodied more than a difference in interpretation of the court mandate and that they represented a political strategy on the part of the Reagan administration. For example, California State Board of Education President Michael Kirst, who aligned the Reagan administration with the antireformers, said, "They used a footdragging strategy. They thought if they passed one half-assed bill after another, the whole issue would stay in the courts almost indefinitely and the *Serrano* issues would not have to be addressed."[47]

47. Michael Kirst 19 September 1978: personal communication.

Senator George Moscone used even harsher language in his response to Ronald Reagan's State-of-the-State Address:

> The Governor puts behind us, apparently for all time, the problems of school finance. He indicates that the new school aid formulas "give all students in California a quality education, no matter where they live." That kind of high-handed overview is an empty promise, devoid of the facts. . . . The new school finance formulas, it is generally agreed, do not move toward solution of the inequality of financing education in the various districts in California. The Governor seems to admit that *Serrano* v. *Priest* will not be his to handle, that his successor in office will have to cope with that one. If, before he leaves office, the courts hand down a decision that is unpopular either financially or legally, the Governor has left himself a way clear for a favorite target: criticism of the courts when their decisions counter his. In response to the Governor's stated belief that all students can now get a quality education, I would only ask the parents of our students to reflect on what kind of instruction their children now receive in school (*California Journal*, February 1973:69).

Legislative Analyst Alan Post buttressed Senator Moscone's position; even if legislators did not support *Serrano* principles, they were aware that SB 90 did not meet the court mandate:

> At the time SB 90 was moving through the legislature, I pointed out that although the bill would provide a massive increase in state support for schools, and would narrow the differences between rich and poor districts, it would *not* meet the fiscal neutrality principle of *Serrano* as established by the Supreme Court (1974, emphasis in the original).

Paul Holmes, principal consultant to the Assembly Committee on Education, characterized the view of most Sacramento school finance hawks: "The SB 90 equalization measure was a joke."[48]

LESSONS OF SENATE BILL 90

One month after *Serrano I* was handed down, school finance reform advocate Denis Doyle predicted: "*Serrano* v. *Priest* will undoubtedly be regarded as the most significant education decision of the decade. It is rivaled in importance only by *Brown* v. *Board of Education*, but unlike *Brown*, its effects may be rapid and dramatic" (*California Journal*, September 1971:237). However, the response to *Serrano*

---

48. Paul Holmes 22 January 1980: personal communication.

contained in SB 90 fell far short of Doyle's expectations and the
hopes of reformers. Doyle and other school finance reform advocates expected that the *Serrano I* decision would significantly alter
the chances for reform and through its sanction of reform objectives remove many of the obstacles that had blocked school finance
change. As reformers soon learned, these expectations were based on
incorrect assumptions (or wishful thinking) about the etiology of
reform, the nature of political systems, and the role of the courts in
effecting change.

Reform is not a discrete occurrence or an isolated event. It is
embedded in a broader organizational and political environment.
Except in cases of revolution, it results from traditional processes of
bargaining, negotiation, and compromise. In crucial respects the outcome of a reform proposal is a dual product. It reflects not only the
objectives of reformers but also the characteristics of the political
system and its established goals. The *Serrano I* court did not impose
a solution upon California's legislature; it explicitly acknowledged
the boundary separating legislative and judicial authorities. Therefore, although the court decision modified the legislative agenda and
secured an audience for school finance reform proposals, that was
the only aspect of the problem it changed. It did not alter the underlying political forces that would constrain legislative response, nor
did it generate a politically consequential constituency for reform.
As a result, the legislative response to *Serrano I* was determined by
features of the Sacramento political arena: Governor Reagan's fiscal
objectives and misgivings about the efficiency of the public schools,
the demands of powerful urban legislators, legislative and administrative commitment to tenets of local control, the condition of the
state's treasury, and Reagan's determination to end the legislative
stalemate. *Serrano* concerns took a back seat.

Reformers' ambitions were also compromised by the breadth of
the coalition necessary to pass SB 90. SB 90 was not primarily a
school finance reform bill; it was a tax relief measure. As Hayward
put it: "The tax issue wagged the school finance dog."[49] The school
finance components were seen—particularly by members of the Reagan administration—as part of a logrolling strategy. SB 90 was a
Christmas tree measure designed to secure broad and diverse support.

49. Gerald Hayward 22 September 1978: personal communication.

As the consensus necessary for passage broadened, the specificity and comprehensiveness of particular objectives diminished. In the absence of agreement on particular legislative objectives, highly ambitious or concrete components threatened to undermine support for the package as a whole. Thus, the eagerness of Reagan and Moretti to pass a bill and the governor's general disinterest in school finance reform led them to what could be called a minimalist position. They sought consensus on a broad, short-term response rather than on a well-specified, long-term solution, only one component of which addressed *Serrano*. This strategy was aided and abetted by confusion about the court's intent, inadequate information about the nature of the problem and the effects of alternative remedies, and the enormous complexity of the issue. In neither tax reform nor school finance reform did the bill go as far as proponents hoped. The crucial tradeoff for this minimalist response was express open-endedness. If SB 90 did not meet the objectives of reformers, neither did it foreclose future options.

California's first response to the *Serrano* mandate was quite different from what the court or reformers expected. As the bill's school finance components were put together, the strategic issue was not how to meet *Serrano* but how to be consistent with it in order not to alienate legislative reform advocates. Change advocates hoped for an untenably radical departure from established norms and prevailing political beliefs. But political systems are adaptive, self-regulating, and self-transforming; abrupt change threatens their stability. SB 90 taught reformers that California's state government was even more impervious to reform than they had believed and that reform goals required a different strategy.

Without *Serrano I*, an SB 90 would probably not have addressed issues of expenditure equalization at all. However, in contrast to the rapid and dramatic renovation reformers expected, the legislative response, enmeshed in the broader context, was one of marginal adjustment. The system acted in character. In the view of Riles, Moretti, administration officials, and other political leaders, SB 90 was as far-reaching a reform as the existing political consensus would support (Meltsner and Nakamura 1974).

Although it was little appreciated at the time, California's first response to *Serrano I* was an important step for reformers. Indeed it can be argued that SB 90 was the best possible legislative rejoinder.

At least four options are available to a political system reacting to an externally generated demand, such as a court mandate:

- Compliance
- Denial or authoritative resistance
- Cooptation
- Incremental adjustment

Full compliance was not a feasible response given the many conflicting goals, the complex political and technical considerations, established school finance policies, and the condition of the state treasury. The court did not have the power necessary to force the radical change required by full compliance.

Authoritative resistance or denial, in which a political system acts to fend off external pressures simply by ignoring them or instituting countervailing pressures of their own (such as a court suit), also was not possible because Sacramento had influential support for reform goals. Codefendants in the *Serrano I* case, Superintendent of Public Instruction Wilson Riles and State Controller Houston Flournoy, publicly subscribed to the plaintiff's brief. Long-time legislative school finance reform advocates, such as Senator Albert Rodda and Assemblyman Leroy Greene, occupied powerful positions.

Because of this well-positioned advocacy, the third response was not possible either. Cooptation, in which external injunctions are captured almost indefinitely through a series of pro forma and ineffective responses, could have derailed school finance reform efforts for years. (As one district official quipped concerning his district's response to a desegregation order: "Never underestimate the power of a dragged foot.")

There was enough sympathy for the reform objectives to generate a cautious and limited response not inconsistent with *Serrano*. SB 90 put a reform system in place—in particular, revenue limits and a squeeze factor—that future tinkering could move toward compliance. These features had political significance that was little appreciated at the time. They made it possible for the state to assert control directly over school district spending, rather than indirectly through tax rate adjustments. Thus SB 90's equalization mechanisms made it politically possible to pursue convergence of foundation expenditures as a policy goal. The short-run equalization and political effects were modest. However, SB 90 established a crucial precedent for the notion of differential treatment of wealthy and poor districts, thereby foreclosing debate on a principle central to equalization. The process of developing and passing the Reagan–Moretti compromise provided both reformers and the education community with pragmatic lessons that would serve them well in the subsequent reform effort, Assembly Bill 65.

4 ASSEMBLY BILL 65
Reform after a Fashion

About two years out, a lot of school systems just plain fell off the table.[1]

Such was the assessment of Gerald Hayward, senate school finance expert, in the aftermath of Senate Bill (SB) 90. As time passed and the effects of SB 90 became clearer, California school people were increasingly alarmed and chagrined. What had been billed as a once-and-for-all solution to California's school-financing problems had turned into a fiscal nightmare. Education interest groups in Sacramento were sadder but wiser, more skeptical, and slowly becoming more sophisticated.

The aftereffects of SB 90 were due largely to the bizarre economic situation facing California and the nation in late 1974 and early 1975. It was during this period that the term "stagflation" became part of the national vocabulary. Inflation in California was racing at a record 12 percent, but unemployment was also up. Projected demands on the state treasury for unemployment insurance and medical benefits for the poor were high. At the same time, the state's major revenue sources, with the exception of corporation taxes, were producing substantial surpluses over what had been expected. State officials viewed these contradictory trends with barely concealed bewilderment, first predicting economic disaster and then turning

1. Gerald Hayward 21 September 1978: personal communication.

113

their attention to the revenue windfall produced by soaring inflation. Taxpayers too were bewildered, watching their property taxes
climb with increasing real estate values at a faster rate than their
income.

Rising costs, increasing public resistance to tax overrides, and
SB 90's revenue limits had the schools in a bind. Teacher contract
settlements and other school district costs reflected increased inflation. In March of 1975 voters in sixty-three California school districts refused to authorize tax overrides to cover increased costs (*Los
Angeles Times*, 7 March 1975). SB 90 revenue limits allowed a maximum 6 percent increase in expenditures, running against an inflation
rate of twice that. Furthermore, the foundation system of state funding had a perverse effect when property values were inflating. The
state's share of educational expenditures was determined by applying
a computational tax rate to the district tax base and subtracting this
product from a fixed per pupil foundation expenditure. With increasing local property values, the state's share of educational expenditures declined. As total district expenditures increased, the net effect
was to shift a larger and larger proportion of educational expenditures to local tax bases. In 1974 an unexpected 11.7 percent increase
in local assessed valuation shifted at least $14 million from the state
to the local tax base (*Los Angeles Times*, 5 August 1975). This came
to be called slippage. Local districts were facing increasing costs, but
the state's share was declining.

When a tax override proposal failed in Los Angeles in May 1975,
the school district announced plans to trim $41 million from its
$1.1 billion budget, laying off 1,200 employees, shortening the
school day, and cutting out a number of special programs (*California Journal*, August 1975:280). A survey by the California School
Boards Association (CSBA) of 312 school districts, enrolling 75 percent of the students in California, showed expected layoffs of 4,000
to 5,000 employees and program cuts of $37 to $50 million in the
next school year (*California Journal*, August 1975:280). Similar predictions of fiscal crisis had preceded the passage of SB 90. The magnitude of the crisis was no clearer in 1975 than it had been earlier,
but the complaints of school people were difficult for legislators to
ignore.

January 1975 saw a new governor and a new legislature installed
in Sacramento. Governor Edmund G. Brown, Jr. took office with
a legislature that had Democratic majorities in both houses for the

first time in five years. The senate was twenty-five to fifteen and the assembly fifty-five to twenty-five Democrat to Republican. These proportions were important because two-thirds majorities were required in both houses to dispose of fiscal matters; the majorities meant that effective cooperation between the governor and the legislative leadership could produce substantial changes. The big question was how well Jerry Brown would work with the legislative leadership.

School finance reform was not at the top of the legislative agenda. *Serrano* attorney John McDermott had gone to the state supreme court in January 1975 to ask for an immediate hearing on the *Jefferson* decision, bypassing the state court of appeals. McDermott reasoned that the legislature would not act without a final supreme court ruling and that the six-year deadline imposed by the *Jefferson* decision could not be met if the usual appeals process were followed. McDermott's motion was granted (*Los Angeles Times*, 8 January 1975). In the short term, this move relieved what little pressure there was on the legislature from the *Jefferson* decision to produce a *Serrano* solution. The period between January 1975 and January 1977 when *Serrano II* was rendered saw little attention to school finance reform and a great deal of attention to the fiscal plight of schools. In an effort to galvanize legislative action, the state board of education convened a citizen's committee, which recommended a uniform statewide property tax to cover basic school expenditures and a power-equalized system of redistribution for revenues raised by locally voted overrides. Estimates of the proposal's costs ranged from $1 billion to $3 billion, which may explain why it was largely ignored by legislative leadership (*Los Angeles Times*, 18 November 1974 and 29 November 1974).

When the legislature convened in January 1975, Senate President pro tem James Mills (D–San Diego) called *Serrano* compliance the legislature's "Number 1 priority," but quickly added, "I'm not confident we're going to be able to do it this year. That would cost a substantial amount of money. A major income tax increase would be necessary. So I guess we won't get it" (*Los Angeles Times*, 7 January 1975). Assembly Speaker Leo McCarthy said, "The legislature's first priority should be to help the California economy. Many extremely important programs will have to be deferred this year because they cost a lot of money. They will have to give way to legislation that produces jobs and reduces suffering" (*Los Angeles Times*,

7 January 1975). The message was clear. The legislature would attend first to the immediate problems posed by the state's economy and then, if it had the resources, to the problems posed by *Serrano*.

Governor Brown took Sacramento by storm. He threw himself into last-minute revisions of the fiscal year 1976 budget, which had been prepared by his predecessor, Ronald Reagan. His style in budgetary matters was the opposite of Reagan's. Instead of delegating budget decisions to the Department of Finance and line agencies of state government, Brown personally reviewed and decided each issue. Word quickly spread through Sacramento that Brown would be his own finance director (*California Journal*, August 1975:279). Brown's budget reflected his campaign promise of no tax increases. It put a tight lid on state expenditures and produced a surplus of $313 million as a hedge against expected deficits in future years (*California Journal*, August 1975:277). Immediately after signing the budget, Brown issued instructions to state agency heads:

> I intend to take every step possible to avoid a general tax increase in fiscal year 1976–77. Accordingly, new programs which cost money require corresponding reduction in other programs (*California Journal*, August 1975:288).

He directed the Department of Finance to "challenge vigorously" departmental proposals that "do not show results" (*California Journal*, August 1975:278). From initial indications, Brown promised to be a tougher fiscal conservative than Reagan.

The unpredictable state of the California economy, the arrival of a new governor and legislature, and the state supreme court's pending *Serrano II* decision all meant that legislative action on school finance reform would be slow. A long warm-up period of two years preceded Assembly Bill (AB) 65, a bill hailed by many as the most ambitious reform of school finance and governance ever undertaken by a state. In the seeming inaction and piecemeal decisionmaking that preceded AB 65, important things were happening. The governor and the legislature were testing mettle, the education lobby was assimilating the hard lessons that accompanied its loss of innocence, and the analytic machinery of the executive and legislative branches began to focus with increasing sophistication on the problem of devising a politically feasible solution to *Serrano*. Taken together, these were the beginnings of the reform coalition that would shape AB 65.

WARM-UP—SENATE BILL 220, SENATE BILL 1641, AND RISE

Brown did not have long to wait for an opportunity to demonstrate his fiscal conservatism. Senator Ralph Dills (D–Gardena), with the backing of the California Teachers' Association (CTA), introduced a bill in February 1975 to provide a $75 million cost-of-living increase to tide financially troubled school systems through the remainder of the 1974–75 school year. Dills called the proposal a very minimal response to the fiscal crisis. Brown responded immediately by opposing the Dills bill and noting that there were many competing priorities for the taxpayers' dollar and a need for schools to readjust programs in line with declining enrollments. Senate Finance Committee Chairman Anthony Bielenson (D–Los Angeles) seconded Brown's opposition, asking whether dumping millions of dollars into the coffers of school systems in the remaining months of the school year would really improve education (*Los Angeles Times*, 25 February 1975).

The Dills proposal provoked disarray among educational interest groups and sparked the first public conflict between educators and Governor Brown. The CSBA opposed the Dills bill, arguing that it was designed to get more money on the table for teachers' salary negotiations next year. The CTA snapped back that their interest was in the total school program, not in teachers' salary increases (*Los Angeles Times*, 27 February 1975). CTA president Bryan Stevens lashed out at Brown's opposition to the Dills bill, accusing Brown of acting irresponsibly, deceitfully, and callously (*Los Angeles Times*, 7 March 1975). Later, the CTA accused Brown of a breach of promise to education in the state (*Los Angeles Times*, 1 April 1975). The CTA's outrage over Brown's position might have had something to do with the fact that they had contributed $25,000 to his campaign and thought they deserved somewhat more sympathetic treatment. Brown responded in kind to CTA criticism, asking, "Do you really think that another $100 million would make it possible for children to read and write better?" Reiterating a campaign theme, he continued,

> Expectations are inflated. People are not facing economic reality in this state or in this country. . . . It will ill serve anyone if I kidded people into thinking there are more cookies in the jar than I actually see. . . . Mindless pouring of

money into the multiplicity of pipelines does not add up to a solution. . . . Once you've said that [taxes will not be increased], a tremendous number of decisions make themselves (*Los Angeles Times*, 7 March 1975).

Brown's exhortations to fiscal austerity might have been greeted with more equanimity by education lobbyists had they not been delivered two days after local voters defeated tax overrides in sixty-three California school districts. The Dills proposal was defeated by an eight to three vote in the Senate Finance Committee. Attention shifted to Senator Albert Rodda's SB 220, a bill to grant school systems fiscal relief in the following school year.

SB 220 was understood by all involved to be a short-run, bandaid proposal. It did very little to augment SB 90's equalization provisions. It raised the foundation level somewhat beyond that provided by SB 90, producing a slight leveling up effect for low-spending districts. This effect was offset to some degree by a one-year reduction in the squeeze factor for wealthy districts. The main purpose of the bill was to channel an additional $115 million through existing basic support and categorical programs.

Negotiations between the legislature and the governor over provisions of SB 220 grew more intense as the end of the fiscal year approached. The legislature was scheduled to recess on June 30 after it had dealt with the state budget. In the final days before the recess, the governor and the legislative leadership reached an agreement: Rodda's SB 220 would move from conference committee to the floor of both houses with a $115 million price tag. The governor would not oppose the bill in either house but would retain the option of using his veto powers to trim it to $88 million. The legislature would have the advantage of approving a generous school support bill, and the governor would have an opportunity to make good on his campaign promise of fiscal austerity (*Los Angeles Times*, 28 June, 29 June, and 1 July 1975). As the bill went to the floor, however, the agreement fell apart. It failed to get the needed two-thirds majority in each house; the senate voted twenty-four to eleven in favor, three votes short, and the Assembly voted fifty-three to twelve in favor, one vote short (*Los Angeles Times*, 29 June 1975).

A key factor in the defeat of SB 220 was CTA and CSBA opposition. In the rush to clear the bill out before recess, the legislative leadership had made a number of changes to accommodate Governor Brown: a 20 percent reduction in funding for adult and summer programs, a provision allowing the governor to shift some of the bill's cost to local property taxes, and hortatory language discouraging the use of new funds for teachers' salary increases. CTA and CSBA lobbyists, who had earlier been divided on the Dills bill, were united in their dislike for these amendments. "As the amendments came in," CTA representative Leonard Kreidt said, "it finally got so bad we pulled off and opposed the bill" (*Los Angeles Times*, 3 July 1975). CTA and CSBA opposition in the waning moments of the session was sufficient to sway the few votes needed to stall the bill. The legislature recessed on June 30 without resolving the school-funding issue.

During the recess, CTA reconsidered its position. Afraid that continued opposition would result in further cuts, CTA lobbyist Cal Rossi said, "It's the only game in town," and supported SB 220 (*Los Angeles Times*, 9 July 1975). CSBA maintained its opposition. The California Parent–Teacher Association announced its support of SB 220 during the recess. The education lobby was not giving the legislature a uniform set of signals.

When the legislature returned, it was operating under a tight deadline. School systems were preparing their final budgets in August for the coming school year without firm commitments of state money. This pressure, coupled with CTA's support, was sufficient to break loose SB 220 within one week after the legislature reconvened. Both houses passed the bill with the required two-thirds majorities (*Los Angeles Times*, 5 August 1975). The bill was sent to Governor Brown for signature, and as expected, he used his item veto power to eliminate $37 million. The exercise of the item veto required that the bill be returned to both houses for votes to determine whether the vetoes would be upheld or overturned.

During the debate over SB 220, Brown changed his position slightly from simply opposing increases in school expenditures to the stance that schools should receive new funding only if they were willing to undertake substantial reform designed to improve their performance. This no reform/no money position became Brown's hallmark in the ensuing debates over school funding (*Los Angeles Times*, 9 July 1975). During the summer recess the *Los Angeles Times* criticized Brown editorially, calling his remarks during SB 220 negotiations "scathing and abstract" and accusing him of having no clear proposals to back up his position. The *Los Angeles Times* called on Brown "to match his criticism of the schools with positive recommendations for their improvement" (1 August 1975). Brown used the item veto of SB 220 as an occasion for sketching a broad, five-point educational reform plan that would respond to his critics. The plan called for more attention to survival skills in the school curriculum, more flexibility in state requirements, greater local control of educational decisionmaking, school finance reform in response to *Serrano*, and a revision of the state's higher education master plan to reflect more modest goals. His tone was critical. He characterized summer school and adult education programs as designed to capture state dollars rather than meet educational needs on a priority basis. He suggested that salary policies should be reviewed because they "encourage teachers to leave the classroom or to take endless courses of dubious value" (*Los Angeles Times*, 15 August 1975). Three weeks later, Brown's two appointees to the state board of education—Michael Kirst, a Stanford education professor, and John Pincus, a Rand Corporation executive—gave a more detailed explanation of Brown's five-point program (*Los Angeles Times*, 7 September 1975). These statements left educators unsatisfied, and the education lobby in Sacramento adopted an arm's length posture toward the governor.

Brown's veto message did not sit well with the senate either. On 18 August 1975 a coalition of sixteen senate Democrats and twelve Republicans bolted their leadership and voted to override Brown's item vetoes, throwing the carefully contrived prerecess compromise off the track. The vetoes could not be overturned, however, without the concurrence of both houses. Assembly Speaker Leo McCarthy restated his own support of the governor's position but predicted a tight floor fight (*Los Angeles Times*, 19 August 1975). Brown personally lobbied the assembly with a persistence and attention to detail that had not characterized his previous relations with the legislature. Assemblyman Vincent Thomas (D–San Pedro) refused to return Brown's phone calls, citing the governor's arrogance and disdain for legislators. Brown persisted, finally reaching Thomas through an intermediary, U.S. Congressman Augustus Hawkins. Thomas chatted cordially with Brown and then voted to override the governor's vetoes (*Los Angeles Times*, 22 August 1975). Ultimately, however, the governor's lobbying paid off. The assembly upheld the item vetoes by a wide margin. SB 220 became law.

The performances of the governor, the legislature, and the education lobby on SB 220 did not inspire confidence in the future of school finance reform. The legislature's attention was focused on the short-term fiscal crisis, not the longer term problem of *Serrano*. The governor's record in dealing with the legislature and the education lobby was erratic at best. He had bargained skillfully with the legislature to produce the original SB 220 compromise, which gave the legislature credit for passing a generous bill and allowed him to demonstrate his fiscal conservatism by using the item veto. As the compromise began to fall apart, he became more strident in his criticism of the legislature and the education lobby, which in turn generated opposition. In the critical votes to sustain or override the item vetoes, he failed to maintain support in the senate but succeeded in the assembly. His position of no reform/no money did little to improve his standing with either the legislature or the education lobby.

The performance of the education lobby was likewise erratic. Early divisions between the CTA and CSBA over the Dills bill and their postrecess split over SB 220 underscored the differences rather than the commonalities within the education lobby. When the CTA and CSBA did agree, it was only on their opposition to the final SB 220 compromise, which could not have endeared them to the legislative leadership. In the aftermath of SB 220, there were few positive signs that a broad-based coalition would emerge to support a major reform of the school-financing system.

The legislature did not turn its attention to school funding again until the end of the following fiscal year, June and July of 1976. Inflation had not abated. Local support for voted tax overrides had not increased appreciably. Once again school systems came to the legislature asking for short-term fiscal relief. By May of 1976, it had before it a variety of proposals. Assemblyman Leroy Greene (D–Sacramento), veteran of many school finance reform battles and chairman of the Assembly Education Committee, wrote a bill that would have substituted countywide property taxes for school district taxes. That would have pooled the property wealth of districts within county boundaries, raising the tax rate for high-wealth, low-tax districts, lowering or stabilizing the tax rate for low-wealth, high-tax districts, and equalizing basic aid within counties. Greene predicted that his proposal would result in 80 percent equalization statewide, and some estimates suggested that it would redistribute about $200 million from high-wealth to low-wealth districts (*Los Angeles Times*, 26 June 1976). Insiders gave Greene's proposal little chance of passage because it invited strong opposition from districts with above-average wealth within counties and because it seemed highly unlikely to generate the required two-thirds majority in both houses.

Senator Jerry Smith (D–Saratoga) modeled a bill after the state board of education's statewide property tax proposal. The Smith proposal would have instituted the statewide property tax incrementally over a five-year period, indexed the state's share of the foundation program to inflation, and applied a squeeze factor to districts with revenue limits above 150 percent of the foundation. Objections to Smith's proposal were much the same as those to Greene's—the number of districts that stood to lose was sufficient to jeopardize the two-thirds majority needed for passage. The Smith proposal was endorsed by the CSBA and the newly formed Association of Low-Wealth School Districts.

Senator Ralph Dills sponsored a CTA–backed bill that would have maintained the SB 90 system, raised foundation levels by about 40 percent, and speeded up the convergence between low-wealth and high-wealth districts. The Dills proposal was the most expensive of all those introduced, by a factor of five or six times, and for that reason alone was not regarded as politically feasible.

The most pragmatically designed proposal was Senator Albert Rodda's, which provided for a flat dollar increase of $61 per pupil in the foundation program over and above what districts would have received under SB 90 and for power-equalized tax overrides for districts with revenue limits above 150 percent of the foundation. Each of all these proposals, unlike SB 220, tried in some way to address *Serrano* in addition to providing fiscal relief.

Rodda's bill, SB 1641, became the focus of legislative attention. It passed the senate unamended and went to the assembly in mid-June. As the assembly went to work on it, important and long-standing differences between the two houses began to manifest themselves. The senate in general and Rodda in particular had consistently taken a critical view of categorical funding and a moderate view on equalization. The senate resisted attempts to channel state support through the categorical programs—Early Childhood Education (ECE), Educationally Disadvantaged Youth (EDY), and Bilingual Education, for example—and preferred instead to fund education through the basic aid system. In the words of one legislative staff member,

> Rodda came away from his own experience as a classroom teacher with a very old-fashioned view that the state should give money to local districts with as few strings attached as possible and let the people at the school building level make the important decisions about how it would be used.

Rodda and his senate colleagues favored equalization but tended to look more sympathetically on the claims of high-wealth and high-expenditure districts. As it was passed by the senate, SB 1641 was consistent with Rodda's predisposition to an across-the-board increase in basic aid and a modest attempt to correct the extremes in expenditures produced by property wealth.

The assembly counted among its members strong *Serrano* hawks and advocates of categorical programs. Greene's countywide property tax proposal was one in a long line of equalization proposals he had written. Most of the categorical programs passed by the legislature were initiated by assembly members who tended to view school reform as a major objective of state policy and to champion the causes of specific minority constituencies.

What the assembly did to SB 1641 illustrates these differences with the senate. First, with Rodda's approval, the Assembly Ways and Means Committee added additional funding for adult education and the inflation-plagued State Teachers' Retirement System. Because both the senate and the assembly wanted to keep the cost of the bill in the neighborhood of $250 million, these additions meant that Rodda's initial $61 per average daily attendance (ADA) increase in the foundation program had to be reduced to $45 per ADA. The Assembly Ways and Means Committee then added several other amendments representing special interests of assembly members: Greene's countywide property tax; additional funds for bilingual education, special education, and education for the disadvantaged; and funding for a newly passed in-service training program for teachers sponsored by Gary Hart (D–Santa Barbara).

The net effect of these amendments was to further reduce the foundation program increases from $45 to $27 per ADA, less than one-half the $61 increase that Rodda had originally proposed. The bill that left the Assembly Ways and Means Committee represented the assembly's preference for stronger equalization measures and more categorical aid. On the assembly floor, Greene's countywide property tax proposal was defeated, as many observers had predicted it would be, and the remainder of the bill was passed by the required two-thirds majority.

The stage was set for a confrontation between the senate and assembly in conference committee, but it never occurred. While SB 1641 was in conference, the remainder of the state budget was being debated on the floor of the assembly. Assemblyman Ken Meade (D–Oakland), who had announced that he would not run for reelection, had joined a unanimous Republican minority, giving them the bare number of votes necessary to deny the Democrats a two-thirds majority in opposing the budget bill until after the school aid bill had been passed. The assembly Republicans also wanted the original senate version of SB 1641 reported out of conference, and Meade joined them in this demand.

Meade, who was characterized by his assembly colleagues as "combative, unconventional, and otherwise obstreperous," had managed to acquire considerable notoriety during his brief tenure in the assembly. Among his escapades were a fist-fight with another assemblyman landing Meade in the hospital, a refusal to honor the assembly's unwritten dress code to wear a jacket and necktie, and a brief scrape with state authorities over his wife's use of a state-leased car for a trip to the Midwest (*Los Angeles Times*, 26 June 1976).

Meade played his pivotal role to the hilt, enjoying the attention lavished on him by the press and other legislators. In the end he agreed to support the state budget bill in exchange for an addition of $7.7 million to the EDY program that would be targeted on heavily impacted districts, of which Oakland was one. In retrospect, legislative staff members and lobbyists remember SB 1641 as "the time Ken Meade held up the state budget until he got more money for Oakland."[2] A State Department of Education official said at the time that "Ken Meade may have been worth $200 million" to education in general (*Los Angeles Times*, 3 July 1976).

In its final form, SB 1641 represented a compromise of senate and assembly positions. The assembly's increases in categorical programs were pared back to $14.6 million for EDY (including the $7.1 million necessary to fund the Meade amendment) and $11.3 million for special education. The foundation increase was raised to $37 per ADA from the assembly's $27, in line with the state's preference for more basic support. Inflation adjustments for adult education and teachers' retirement were maintained.

SB 1641 also included Rodda's proposal to power-equalize voted overrides in districts with revenue limits at 150 percent of the foundation level. On its face, this provision did not appear to be of much significance; it provoked little comment at the time. It was consistent

2. John Mockler 6 February 1979: personal communication.

with the senate's position of moderating the extremes of the system, and it affected very few districts. Over the long term, however, it turned out to be an important increment in school finance reform. For the first time it established a legislative precedent for a state recapture of revenues raised by high-wealth districts. The provision was a product of unobtrusive staff work by Rodda's aide, Gerald Hayward, and understated political maneuvering by Rodda himself. It hardly raised a ripple in the education lobby, but it would later serve as the basis for a key provision in AB 65.

Another important development in SB 1641 was the emergence of increased cooperation in the education lobby. After SB 220, a few education lobbyists took the initiative in pulling together divergent groups around the common concern of more money for schools. Mary Bergan, representing the California Federation of Teachers (CFT), said, "We found in SB 220 that our internal conflicts hurt us; with SB 1641 we made a deliberate effort to pull together."[3] A loose collection of education groups was formed under the banner of "The SB 1641 Mobilization Committee." Bergan prevailed on Assembly-man Howard Berman (D–Beverly Hills) to arrange for a room in the capitol that the committee could use as a base of operations. She also used the CFT's Sacramento office to print and circulate flyers to local school people soliciting their support. The flavor of the mobilization committee's strategy is represented by a memo from Bergan to local CFT members at the time SB 1641 was being considered by the assembly:

> It is of the utmost importance that heavy, in-person lobbying efforts on SB 1641 continue ... until the legislature recesses. ... Every organization supporting the bill is asking its members and their families and friends to be in Sacramento this week to demonstrate their support for SB 1641. ... Only relentless pressure on the Legislature and Governor Brown will give us a school finance bill that really does something to ease the financial crisis of California schools.

As SB 1641 moved from Assembly Ways and Means Committee to the assembly floor, the mobilization committee circulated a memo calling for restoration of the bill to Rodda's original proposal, eliminating the assembly's categorical additions and Greene's countywide property tax proposal. The memo called Greene's proposal "a partial response to *Serrano*," but "political death" for the bill in the Senate.

3. Mary Bergan 7 May 1980: personal communication.

The signatories of the memo included representatives of the Association of California School Administrators (ACSA), CTA, CSBA, the Association of Low-Wealth School Districts, the United Teachers of Los Angeles (UTLA), and the school systems of San Francisco, Los Angeles, Oakland, San Diego, Los Angeles County, and Riverside County. The key actors in the Mobilization Committee—Mary Bergan (CFT), Ron Prescott (Los Angeles Unified School District), Bill Lambert (UTLA)—would later become the core of the Tuesday Night Group, the education coalition that formed to shape AB 65.

The formation of the mobilization committee represented a formal acknowledgment of an idea that had been steadily gaining acceptance among education lobbyists in Sacramento: The important glue that binds educational interest groups together in Sacramento is more money for schools. Interest groups with divergent objectives should at least be able to collaborate on the basic issue of school funding. Conflicts of the kind that occurred between CSBA and CTA on SB 220 ought to be avoided. A broad-based coalition of educational interest groups would, at a minimum, provide a forum for the resolution of these conflicts before they became public. Announcing the passage of SB 1641 in its June 19 newsletter, the mobilization committee called it "probably one of the best school finance measures approved by the California legislature," and lauded its constituents by saying, "Your presence, your letters, your telegrams, your commitment, underscored the needs of the California schools. And the legislature and the governor had to respond."

Another feature that distinguished the SB 1641 debate from the SB 220 debate was the low profile maintained by Governor Brown. In contrast to his hard-nosed examination of SB 220, Brown did not bargain over the contents of SB 1641. He deleted only a token $14 million from the $270 million bill before signing it. Brown's fiscal 1977 budget contained expenditure increases of 16.5 percent and a surplus of $600 million. The average annual expenditure increase for Brown's two gubernatorial predecessors was 12 percent (*Los Angeles Times*, 3 July 1976). Brown's determination to hold state spending down seemed to be temporarily fading. One explanation for the contrast between his positions on SB 220 and SB 1641 is that during the spring of 1976 he was running in presidential primaries across the country and had neither the time nor the inclination to engage in state legislative politics. When he did return from his presidential foray, he resumed his former posture of strict scrutiny of new expenditures.

After the summer recess of August of 1976, the legislature directed its attention to an ambitious secondary school reform bill developed by Wilson Riles and his staff at the State Department of Education. The RISE bill (Reform in Intermediate and Secondary Education) was an extension of Riles' ECE strategy into junior highs and high schools, and it was the result of a two-year discussion of secondary school reform by a prestigious statewide commission appointed by Riles. The bill called for participating districts to convene school site councils (one-half students and parents, one-half teachers and administrators) to develop a plan that included individual learning plans for students and schoolwide performance standards and to initiate broad community involvement. The bill authorized expenditures of $300,000 in 1977, $4.7 million in 1978, $14.2 million in 1979, $27.4 million in 1980, and $35.2 million in 1981. Legislative Analyst Alan Post observed that even at that level of expenditure only about 20 percent of the eligible schools could be served and added that the cost of the bill could well exceed $200 million per year by the 1980s. RISE passed the senate by a narrow margin (twenty-two to sixteen) in June 1976 and the assembly by a wide margin (fifty-nine to ten) in late August. Riles called the legislature's action proof "that our legislators realize it's not enough to wring our hands and criticize our junior and senior high schools—we must take action to make them better. RISE does this in a practical, workable way" (*Los Angeles Times*, 26 August 1976).

In early September, Governor Brown vetoed the RISE bill, effectively killing it because the narrowness of the vote in the senate precluded an override. Brown dismissed the RISE reform measures by saying, "If [educators] like these particular suggestions, they can implement them with the money we've already given them." He invoked fiscal austerity, arguing, "If educators don't want to draw the line [on expenditures], I'll do it for them" (*Los Angeles Times*, 26 August 1976). When he vetoed the RISE bill, Brown signed a competency testing bill, written by Assemblyman Gary Hart, which actually cost more in the first year ($399,000) than RISE. Brown said that the Hart bill would accomplish the same purpose as RISE at a much lower cost. Hart, a RISE supporter, quickly disowned Brown's statement.

According to his staff, Riles was at first dumbfounded and then furious at the governor's action. RISE had been the result of more than two years of careful staff work and consensus building. "Brown didn't consult with Wilson at any point before the veto," a staff member said, "and Wilson assumed that Brown would talk to him personally about any difficulties he had with the bill. Instead, he had a staff person from the Department of Finance call Wilson on the telephone a few hours before the veto was announced." In an unusual display of public anger, Riles called a press conference in which he called the governor's action "unconscionable," the governor's invocation of the Hart bill as a substitute for RISE he labeled "nonsense," and the governor's fiscal position he called "penny-wise and pound-foolish" (*Los Angeles Times*, 11 September 1976).

In addition to widening the rift between Riles and the governor, the RISE veto further undermined Brown's position with the education lobby. The lobby had been lukewarm in its support of RISE, but Riles had done his political homework and had managed to neutralize opposition in the lobby and capitalize on modest support. When Brown vetoed RISE, a number of education lobbyists were not as upset with the outcome as they were with the fact that, again, Brown seemed to go out of his way to take potshots at education, a posture reminiscent of Brown's predecessor Ronald Reagan. The governor did little to allay this feeling when, immediately after the RISE veto, he announced the state had been too generous with the schools in SB 220 and SB 1641. "Enough is enough," the governor said. "This was a generous year for education. Next year we will really put on the brakes" (*Los Angeles Times*, 6 October 1976).

In December 1976 the California Supreme Court delivered its decision in *Serrano II*, removing the final excuse for legislative delay. At a Los Angeles press conference, John McDermott, *Serrano* attorney, and John Serrano celebrated the court's decision and castigated the legislature for its inaction. "By and large," Serrano said, "the people we have sitting in Sacramento don't have the guts it takes to change the tax structure so that every person is paying their share." Ruben Cordova, assistant superintendent of Beverly Hills Unified School District, called the decision "a cruel hoax" on disadvantaged children. "Most of the poor and minority members actually live in districts that have above the state average in wealth," he said. Betty Jones, a school board member from Lawndale and president of the Association of Low-Wealth School Districts, said, "Finally all children in California will have access to an equal education regardless of the district in which they happen to reside" (*Los Angeles Times*, 31 December 1976).

In Sacramento, Leroy Greene and Albert Rodda were subdued in their response to the decision. Greene publicly doubted that the legislature could meet the court's 1980 deadline. "We will make a try," he said, "but the political problems involved are horrendous. We can find solutions that are technically correct and also would work but, politically, you're walking through a minefield." Rodda said, "It's going to be very difficult to comply with a court decision in that period of time," adding that compliance would probably require a tax increase (*Los Angeles Times*, 3 December 1976).

Serrano II did not take Sacramento by surprise. In the months between the passage of SB 1641 and the court's decision, considerable backstairs work was being done to find a politically feasible way to comply with *Serrano*. In mid-July before SB 1641 had passed, Dave Doerr and Betsy Hauck, Assembly Revenue and Tax Committee staff members, informed committee chairman Willie Brown that they were in touch with other committee staff and staff members from the Department of Finance and Department of Education in order to "pull the interested parties together in a joint effort, building on what had been done, insuring cross-fertilization of ideas and minimizing duplication of effort." They recommended that the legislature delay holding hearings on the school finance question until some clear proposals had been worked out at the staff level. Assemblyman Brown endorsed their plan, scribbling at the bottom of their memo, "As usual, I agree with you. Interim hearings in the abstract are usually [worthless]."[4]

By mid-August, shortly after the passage of SB 1641, Leroy Greene and Willie Brown, in their capacity as chairmen of the Education and Revenue and Taxation Committees, had formally convened a task force to address the school finance issue. The task force eventually involved all legislative staff who had anything to do with school finance—including Hauck and Doerr from revenue and tax, James Murdoch and Paul Holmes from Greene's education committee, Catherine Minicucci and Martin Helmke from the Senate Office of Research, Gerald Hayward from the Senate Finance Committee—

4. Memo from Dave Doerr and Betsy Hauck to Willie Brown, Jr., "School Finance," 16 July 1976.

and representatives from the Legislative Analyst's Office, the Department of Finance, the Department of Education, and the state board of education. The task force was charged to "develop whatever data base and simulation models are necessary so that alternative proposals may be analyzed," and "develop alternative proposals for consideration in January including information showing the impact of such proposals on different types of taxpayers and school districts."[5]

The task force convened in late August and broke into smaller groups to examine a range of alternative solutions, including full state assumption, vouchers, district power equalizing, split assessment of business and residential property, and a constitutional amendment validating the current system. It met regularly, every two weeks or so until December 1976 when it issued a succinct report assessing four main options: full state assumption, coupled with an elimination of property taxes as a basis for education funding; countywide property tax; split assessment with a statewide business property tax to be used for the foundation program and local residential taxes for expenditures over the foundation; and a freeze on property taxes in high-wealth districts coupled with state recapture of revenues generated by those districts in excess of their revenue limits (*Serrano/Priest* Task Force 1977).

The task force's staff work was important in two respects: It subjected a broad range of options to discussion, even those that raised serious legal and political problems such as a constitutional amendment validating the existing system. It also cemented working relationships among the various units of state government that had an interest in the school finance issue. The routine meetings and discussions set a tone of staff-to-staff cooperation that would later prove to be important.

Among the issues that puzzled those working on the legislative response to *Serrano* was whether the decision was about tax equity or expenditure equity or both. In its narrowest terms, fiscal neutrality focused on whether the property tax system returned equal revenue for equal effort. That seemed to be the gist of Coons, Clune, and Sugarman's (1970) argument. However, the rhetoric surrounding *Serrano* suggested that the state should do something to remedy expenditure inequities among districts. Why else would the *Serrano* lawyers

5. Memo from Leroy Greene and Willie Brown to Committee Staff, "*Serrano v. Priest* Issues," 17 August 1976.

choose their plaintiffs from low-expenditure districts? The problem posed for legislative staff was that the two objectives were mutually exclusive and often contradictory. John Mockler, an aide to Wilson Riles at the time, and Gerald Hayward, Senate Education Committee staff member, put the matter this way:

> Was the goal of narrowing of noncategorical expenditure differences, or wealth-related noncategorical expenditure differences? If the latter, one could imagine a scheme with dramatic expenditure differences but with tax rates proportional to any given expenditure level as meeting the mandate; or even more dramatic, a system with no expenditure differences but with tax rate disparities as *not* meeting the mandate. Was it a student equity suit, a taxpayer equity suit, or both? The legislature itself was divided over the appropriate interpretations. . . . Obviously, uncertainty about the nature of the mandate led to uncertainty over the appropriate remedy and over the appropriate compliance standard (Mockler and Hayward 1978:389).

This, of course, was exactly the issue that had divided the reform lawyers from the time of the initial complaint to the final decision in *Serrano*. The lawyers could never agree whether the real plaintiffs were taxpayers or school children, or what to do if the interests of the two groups were not compatible. In the courts, this issue was never fully aired because the defendants' lawyers did not exploit it and the courts did not see it as their responsibility to grapple with the practical consequences of their decision. In the legislature, however, the issue created a difficult problem of coalition politics. It produced two broad divisions among legislators—those who stood to gain or lose from tax equity and those who stood to gain or lose from expenditure equity. Because the two divisions did not relate to each other in any straightforward way, legislators had no simple decision rule for figuring out whether they should be for or against a given reform proposal. Also, the greater the number of divisions among legislators, the less likely it is that they will agree, and the more difficult it is to form a winning coalition.

While the joint legislative–executive task force was at work, Governor Brown had begun his own independent school finance reform effort. In July 1976 he drafted Charles Gocke, a veteran staff member in the Department of Finance, giving him instructions to develop a response to *Serrano*. In Gocke's words, Brown said, "Solve *Serrano*. I want a proposal by January 1." Gocke convened a four-member working group within the Department of Finance, calling it the Educational Systems Unit, and told them, "Let's go academic on this. I want all the options. No restrictions. Wipe the slate clean."[6] The Educational Systems Unit's work dovetailed with the work of the legislative–executive task force in the early stages of assessing options. Both groups worked from the same basic list of alternatives, and the Educational Systems Unit was represented in task force discussions. Gocke's group took the initial list of sixteen options developed by the task force and broke it into two categories: full compliance options, including full state assumption, district power-equalization, and vouchers; and partial compliance options, including full state assumption of teachers' salaries and countywide property taxes. From these options, Gocke and his staff developed five plans, two of which they classified as in full compliance with *Serrano*, the remaining three they classified as in partial compliance.

The first plan collapsed the foundation program and all categorical programs into a single state block grant and power-equalized all locally raised revenues. The second plan proposed a statewide property tax with district power-equalization for all revenues raised above the foundation level. The third plan substituted a countywide foundation system for the district-based system and eliminated state basic aid. The fourth plan applied a statewide property tax to all increases in assessed valuation after 1976 to 1977 and distributed the proceeds of that tax by an equalization formula. The fifth plan proposed a guaranteed yield for locally raised revenues above the foundation, designed so as to reduce tax rates in low-wealth districts while giving them an inflation-adjusted increase in expenditures (Department of Finance 1978).

These packages were presented to the governor and underwent considerable discussion and revision. Governor Brown also brainstormed with academic experts and with representatives of the State Department of Education. As Brown's January 1 deadline approached, staff work on his school finance proposal gave increasing emphasis to developing his proposal and less to the broad staff-to-staff cooperation that had characterized early discussions.

The staff work that went on between July and December 1976 left the legislature and governor fairly well prepared for the commencement of a new legislative session in January 1977. No startling breakthroughs were expected or produced, but all options were framed and discussed, and the precedent for close staff-to-staff work-

6. Charles Gocke 22 September 1978: personal communication.

ing relationships was established. As Assemblyman Leroy Greene said in the aftermath of *Serrano II*, the major problems were not technical but political. Wide-ranging discussions of options were useful to a point, but ultimately education finance reform was less a matter of framing technically correct solutions than it was of building a politically feasible solution that would bind together a broad coalition of educational interests.

ELEMENTS OF THE REFORM COALITION

Everyone involved in the school finance issue knew that the piecemeal approach that had characterized SB 220 and SB 1641 would not be adequate as a response to *Serrano II*. A major change in policy was required. It is in the nature of coalition politics, however, that the key actors never understand in advance how to achieve a major shift in policy or exactly what combination of elements will bind together a winning coalition. No one controls the play; everyone's position depends to a substantial degree on everyone else's. The creation of a reform coalition depends upon both the tactical skill of the players and their willingness to cooperate. The elements of the school finance reform coalition in California were the governor, the legislature, Wilson Riles and the State Department of Education, and the education lobby. Each had its own history, its own peculiar set of strengths and weaknesses, and its own political agenda.

Governor Brown

Governor Jerry Brown was probably the biggest unknown in the coalition. His erratic and unpredictable performance irked both his allies and his enemies, but his record in Sacramento showed him to be a formidable political force when he wanted to be. He impressed Sacramento insiders initially as a tough adversary—"a detail man," "an inquisitive academician who rarely accepts the conventional wisdom," and "a tireless investigator who is turning elements of the state bureaucracy upside down." His early symbolic gestures toward fiscal austerity were effective if somewhat eccentric. He refused to ride in a limousine, he kept a modest apartment across the street from the capitol rather than living in the newly constructed governor's mansion, he returned all gifts, he opposed higher salaries for state officials, he removed paper shredders from state offices, he banned state-issued briefcases, and he refused to use a signature machine to sign his mail (although he did concede that it was necessary for signing university diplomas) (Salzman 1975:140). His legislative record outside education was impressive. He successfully initiated legislation ending the state oil depletion allowance, reducing penalties for possession of marijuana, legalizing all sexual conduct between consenting adults, and making collective bargaining possible for farm labor (*Los Angeles Times*, 28 June 1975).

In the spring of 1976, however, his image as a tough political actor in Sacramento began to fade. In the words of one person who observed Brown's education decisions closely during this period,

> He had an incredibly short attention span; his work style was to focus on an issue only when it was important and then to do virtually nothing else. In 1975 [SB 220] he was very focused and very effective. In 1976 [SB 1641] he was terrible. We all got madder than hell at him. I still don't think he knows why he vetoed RISE.

One of those who grew increasingly impatient with Brown was John Pincus, head of the Rand Corporation's Education and Human Resources Program and a Brown appointee to the state board of education. In August 1976, shortly before he resigned from the state board, Pincus wrote a stinging critique of Brown's education record. "The Brown administration," he said, "was caught off base" by SB 1641.

> The governor spent all spring campaigning for higher office, he had no staff to work on school policy, and neither the State Department of Finance, which works on the governor's budget, nor his chief lieutenants in the legislature received any clear signal on reform policies because there was no one around to provide the signals (1976a).

Pincus called Brown's performance on SB 1641 "a fiasco" and attributed it to "the governor's inexperience as a policymaker." Brown's greatest strength, Pincus argued, "is as a critical interpreter who perceives and gives voice to citizens' unrest." By his abdication of a strong policymaking role, Pincus said that Brown had allowed Wilson Riles and the education lobby to dominate decisionmaking. "What is missing," Pincus argued, "is the interplay of competing solutions, . . . different sets of priorities, to be resolved by the familiar process of collaboration and dissent. This is the challenge that the governor is free to accept, to reject, or to avoid" (Pincus 1976a). Brown, in other words, stood to lose considerable influence if he did not become a more serious and effective participant in the coalition politics of education.

Brown's engagement of Gocke and the Department of Finance staff in July of 1976 demonstrated his growing seriousness about the reform question. No one disputed that the governor was a critical actor in the formation of a reform coalition. He exercised significant control over the financial resources necessary for reform through both his initiating power in the budgetary process and his item veto power. He could materially improve or jeopardize the prospects of reform simply by clarifying his no reform/no money position. Substantial equalization of school financing would require a leveling up strategy in order to be politically feasible; the position of low-spending, low-wealth districts could not be improved purely at the expense of high-spending, high-wealth districts. Would Brown be willing to endorse the additional funds necessary to level up? What would he accept as satisfactory evidence of school reform if reform was to be a precondition of increased funding? How much attention would he focus on the school finance issue? How seriously would he bargain with the elements of the reform coalition?

Wilson Riles

Riles was, in temperament and action, the exact opposite of Brown. Elected in 1970 after serving several years as the State Department of Education's compensatory education chief, Riles had carefully gone about constructing a politically supportive environment for himself inside and outside of the department. In 1971 he made substantial changes in the organization and staffing, simplifying the department's structure and placing administrators with compatible interests in newly created positions. In 1974 he created a Governmental Affairs Unit within the department and staffed it with people who had a sophisticated knowledge of legislative politics, notably John Mockler from Willie Brown's staff. With the Early Childhood Education (ECE) program, he made his reputation as a reformer.

ECE provided Riles with something more than visibility as a reformer. It gave him a readily mobilized political constituency in the school-site councils mandated by the law. Riles's closest lieutenant and political confidante, Marion Joseph, nurtured contacts with ECE supporters across the state and used these contacts to bring increasingly effective pressure on the legislature. Riles was also instrumental in forming the Education Congress of California, a loose confederation of education groups. "In education, when you want to get something done," Riles said, "you need as many allies as you can get. I work for allies" (Madigan 1975:25).

Riles came to office with a rough blueprint for school reform that entailed more emphasis on individualized instruction, greater parent and teacher participation in school-level decisions, and increased attention to math, reading, and English skills. ECE and RISE were manifestations of this blueprint.

> Riles counted on gaining the support of educators by having them play a part in program planning, and he depended on effective lobbying to win legislative support. It was an ambitious and risky move: ambitious, because no state had ever tried with a small investment to completely restructure school districts' activities; risky, because school districts might veto it or, even if adopted the program might not work (Pincus 1976b).

On the school reform issue, Riles had one important advantage over all the other actors: He knew what he wanted and could conceive of a variety of ways of getting it. Brown used the school reform issue largely as a rhetorical device, deflecting requests for increased funding with demands for reform, but Riles had in mind specific outcomes for which he was willing to wait until the opportune time.

Riles's strategy went beyond the institutional reform. In 1975 he secured state board of education endorsement for a three-point plan to guide state educational policy: (1) a foundation program covering the basic costs of education, designed on the principle of equal yield for equal effort; (2) a battery of programs addressed to the needs of special student populations—disadvantaged, handicapped, and bilingual, for example; and (3) a program of institutional reform and renewal based on the principles of ECE and RISE. Later, the plan was adapted to include allowances for differential costs on local districts. From Riles's perspective, any reform legislation that included each of the three major elements could be seen as progress; the more progress, the better.

The three-point strategy had several obvious advantages: It was simple and easy to state, it fit in well with existing state programs, and it emphasized the interrelationship of all the state's education support programs. The strategy also had political advantages that were not quite so obvious. Each of the elements was designed to appeal to a major educational constituency and to hold all the major pieces of the education lobby in a broad coalition. A well-funded foundation program would satisfy the demands of teachers and administrators for general, unrestricted support to maintain local programs and keep teachers' salaries at a decent level. A battery of targeted categorical programs would satisfy many minority and special interest groups—blacks, Chicanos, special education parents, and so forth. Most important for Riles, a program of reform and renewal would support innovation, underwrite the formation of locally based parent groups that could be mobilized for political support in Sacramento, and assure that a certain portion of the local district's budget was kept off the bargaining table, which meant that it could not be used for across-the-board teacher salary increases. By insisting that each of the three parts of the strategy be linked and by carefully building and nurturing a broad-based coalition, Riles allowed himself freedom to advocate substantial reform of the schools while satisfying established professional interest groups.

The verdict on Riles's philosophy, administrative competence, and political skill is far from unanimous. Even his own staff admit that at certain key points they have made serious tactical errors. "After the RISE veto," one staff member said,

> Wilson understood that he had made a tactical error identifying himself so closely with the bill. We made too much of Wilson's sponsorship of RISE; he was over at the legislature every day. We wanted to get away from the idea that the department initiated everything—away from the "we–they" thing. We made a conscious decision to avoid the RISE situation the next time around and give other people as much credit as possible. Wilson said, "The important thing is to get the program, not the credit."

Members of the education lobby who have observed Riles's actions closely deliver a mixed verdict. Mary Bergan, lobbyist for the AFL–CIO–affiliated California Federation of Teachers (CFT), said,

> It all gets down to what people want the state superintendent to be. If he is to provide some educational leadership, then you are going to have to accept that the programs he proposes are based on certain assumptions as to what is good and bad. On the one hand, people expect the superintendent to be some great leader and, on the other hand, whenever there is any threat to local control they go absolutely bananas (Madigan 1975:23).

One lobbyist, after summarizing Riles's attempts to bring competing education groups together, concluded harshly, "Wilson couldn't lead the education lobby out of a paper bag."

Riles also made his share of enemies in the legislature and local school districts through his advocacy of institutional reform. As local school systems gained more and more experience with ECE, some of them began to chafe at what they viewed as increasingly heavy-handed state intervention in local schools. One urban superintendent said,

> They [the State Department of Education] are accepting less and less what faculty and community wish. They are making changes without input from us. We thought that was one of the innovative dimensions of the program. We also thought we were dealing with the "whole" child. But now they have tied class expectancy into grade equivalent [test scores]. This doesn't embrace the ungraded, individualized concept (Madigan 1975: 24).

In the fall of 1976, State Department of Education evaluations of ECE revealed that the program was having equivocal effects: Schools that had been in the program one year showed modest achievement gains, those that had been in the program two years showed slight declines, students with the lowest entering test scores seemed to be doing worse than those with higher scores, and anecdotal evidence indicated dissatisfaction with the department's increasingly tight oversight procedures and administrative control. When the Senate Education Committee, chaired by Albert Rodda, held oversight hearings in October 1976, it heard testimony from local administrators who were generally supportive of the program but critical of the department's paperwork demands. It also heard from a group of Stanford University evaluators who were generally critical of the effect of the department's administration on local district operations. It heard from staff of the legislative analyst, underscoring the lack of strong evidence on positive student effects. Legislative staff and senators were unimpressed with the department's response to these criticisms. One staff member said:

> The Department's response was very evasive and defensive; it rubbed everyone the wrong way, even supporters of the program. During the hearings we began to get the sense that Riles was in trouble on ECE, that his support was eroding.

Another staff member said:

> Riles's standard response to criticism seemed to be to trot out a lot of loyal supporters of the program — mostly school-site council members and teachers — who would deliver these great testimonials, "I just glow from head to toe with ECE." They didn't speak directly to the questions that were being raised about the effectiveness of the program and their administration of it.

Coming immediately after SB 1641 and immediately before the state supreme court's decision in *Serrano II*, these hearings created serious political problems for Riles. Criticisms of ECE undermined both his comprehensive reform strategy and his political standing with the legislature. The criticisms also fueled the underlying split between the assembly and senate on the value of categorical, reform-oriented programs. Assembly members and staff were basically sympathetic and supportive both of Riles and of such reformist programs as ECE and RISE; senators and their staff were skeptical at best and unsparingly critical at worst. If school reform efforts became a subject of controversy between the two houses, it could well scuttle any comprehensive reform effort.

Riles's position in any reform coalition would hinge on his ability to see progress toward his reform objectives and to protect his earlier gains. His resources included a broad-based, loyal political constituency, a strong legislative staff, and a longer time horizon than most other potential members of a reform coalition.

The Legislature

The California legislature stands apart from other state legislatures in its institutional complexity and sophistication. The state's history of legislative reform dates back at least to 1941 when the legislature established the Joint Legislative Budget Committee and the Office of the Legislative Analyst to serve as staff to the committee. Alan Post, who became legislative analyst in 1948 and held that office for nearly 30 years, developed a national reputation for thoroughness and analytic skill. In 1951 California preceded most other states in providing permanent office space and secretarial assistance for legislators. In 1955 the legislature's staff capacity was further enhanced with the creation of the Joint Legislative Audit Committee and the Office of the Legislative Auditor General. Together with the legislative analyst, that gave the legislature an independent capability to scrutinize agency budget requests and expenditures enjoyed by no other state legislature.

With Jesse Unruh's election as Speaker of the assembly in 1961, the legislature started another period of extensive institutional growth and reform. Unruh personally took a national and statewide leadership role in support of a full-time, well-staffed, professional state legislature. It was not an easy position to defend against critics who argued that Unruh was motivated mainly by a desire to make state politics a more lucrative profession and to enhance his own position as Big Daddy of the assembly. To these criticisms, Unruh replied that in the days of Artie Samish, a famous California lobbyist who allegedly owned most of the legislature, politics was a very lucrative business, and the way to guard against corruption was to make professionals of the legislators.

In 1961 Unruh managed to get home district office staff and increased committee staff for the legislature in addition to their small existing state office staff. The distribution of committee leadership positions assured that more than one-third of the assembly and all of the senate would have more than the minimum allotted staff. In 1966 Unruh spearheaded a successful constitutional amendment campaign for annual legislative sessions, replacing the old system of general sessions and budget sessions of strictly limited duration in odd and even years. Between 1960 and 1970, the years roughly corresponding to Unruh's leadership, the staff of the legislature roughly doubled. By 1971 the assembly had a total professional staff of 217, the senate 135, the legislative analyst 49, and the legislative auditor 41 (Wyner 1973).

At least two possible advantages accrued to legislators as a result of these reforms. Better staffing in Sacramento and the home districts increased the incumbent's advantage and reduced turnover, allowing legislators to become specialists in such policy areas as education. Senator Rodda and Assemblyman Greene are both good examples of the advantages of incumbency. Increased staffing also allowed staff members themselves to develop expertise; the major staff positions in education are occupied by people with several years experience. The leading staff who worked on AB 65, for example, had all been working on school finance legislation since before SB 90.

Although incumbency and stability of staffing can undermine competence and reinforce complacency, in the field of education this did not seem to be the case. As the staff work of the joint legislative–

executive task force illustrates, the legislature was able to mobilize awesome staff resources around the school finance issue: James Murdoch and Paul Holmes from the Assembly Education Committee, Gerald Hayward from the Senate Education Committee, Hal Geiogue and Steve Rhoads from the Legislative Analyst's Office, Dave Doerr from the Senate Revenue and Tax Committee, and Martin Helmke and Catherine Minicucci from the Senate Office of Research were all regular attendees at task force meetings.

Beyond the obvious advantages of size and continuity of staffing lie other, less visible advantages. One lesson that staff members took away from the SB 90 experience was the importance of accurate data in the formulation and selling of legislative proposals. John Mockler, legislative staff to Assemblyman Willie Brown and later to Wilson Riles, said about SB 90, "When legislators would ask us, 'What does this bill do for my district?' we'd get out this one little print-out and thumb through it, as if we knew what we were doing, and then say (with raised eyebrows), 'You're gonna do OK.' "[7]

In the aftermath of SB 90, the data issue became more important because very few school districts really did do OK under SB 90 and school finance reform proposals promised to be difficult to sell to legislators. Legislative staff began to discuss the need for a common data base that could be used to estimate the effect of various proposals. The memorandum establishing the joint legislative–executive task force stated the creation of such a data base as one of the major objectives of that group.

James Murdoch remembers that sometime early in 1976, during a meeting between staff and legislators to discuss reform options, the staff began to argue about the assumptions underlying estimates of the effects of various proposals. "The legislators said, 'We're not interested in hearing you argue about assumptions. We want to know about effects. Go away and don't come back until you agree on the data.' "[8] In February 1976 negotiations began between the legislature, the Department of Education, and the Department of Finance, and by December of that year, Catherine Minicucci was able to announce to legislators that the system was up and running.[9]

7. John Mockler 6 February 1979: personal communication.

8. James Murdoch 21 September 1978: personal communication.

9. Interim Hearing on *Serrano* v. *Priest* 1 before the Senate Revenue and Tax Committee, 1976 Cal. Stat. 42.

The system is managed by an executive committee composed of representatives of each of the participating bodies and by a technical committee composed of the data specialists from each body. The system allows equal access for all participants and protects the confidentiality of computer runs on tentative proposals. The pooling of data analysis capability in this way removes the dependence of the legislature on executive branch estimates yet allows all parties to school finance decisions to share in the state's basic data on enrollment, tax bases, and revenue estimates. Joint administration of the system means that little time is wasted cross-checking differing assumptions in arguments over competing proposals. Although staff members will still say that you can prove anything you want to with those numbers and that the estimates are notoriously shaky, they will also testify that the system has made their jobs immeasurably easier and generally improved legislators' ability to assess the effects of competing proposals on their districts.

By any standard of reckoning, the California legislature was well equipped to confront a major school finance reform. Level of staffing, continuity, and expertise of both staff and members plus access to information were all major strengths that had a great effect on the way the legislature tackled the issue.

Coalition building within the legislature was a function of long-established differences between the assembly and the senate and the strength of leadership in the two houses. The assembly–senate split on the categorical or general funding issue is well illustrated by the debate on SB 1641. Beyond this split, however, are several other differences between the two houses that affect their ability to handle legislation. One legislative staff member characterized the differences between the two houses as follows:

> The Assembly has always been the activist house—lots of bills, younger members who want to make a name for themselves. In education, the Assembly has traditionally believed in categorical programs because of the widely held belief that schools don't do well by disadvantaged kids and, more recently, a strong feeling that state money should be kept off the bargaining table where it goes directly into teachers' salary increases. Also, the Assembly has a much stronger leadership. The Speaker controls all the important housekeeping functions of the Assembly—appointments and rules—and really runs the place. Whatever the Speaker says goes. In the Senate, power is much more diffuse, members are much more inclined to question the addition of new

programs, and in education they are more inclined to say, "Give the money to the school systems and let them decide how to spend it."

The same staff member continued:

> The differences between the two houses are as much a matter of personalities as issues and structure. There are real differences in style between the members; we've had enough run-ins on specific issues over the years to establish some real personality conflicts. Senator Rodda would like a less complicated society—no parental involvement, fewer programs, respect for the teaching profession, and deference to locally elected officials. A lot of Assembly members think this position is outmoded and get very impatient with Rodda. Negotiations sometimes get a little heated.

Coalition building in the legislature consisted of mobilizing the considerable analytic resources legislators had at their disposal and meshing the disparate personalities, institutional styles, and policy preferences of the two houses. Individual legislators representing very diverse constituencies had to be convinced that the legislature's response to *Serrano* was the best or the least worst solution for their constituents. On this point the staff's analytic work would be critical, framing options, probing their political feasibility, and projecting their effects on the distribution of funds among districts. The business of meshing the two houses was a matter of legislative leadership and bargaining skill among the principal legislative actors. Legislators who were specialists in education had to be given a reason to claim ownership in a reform proposal; they had to see their influence and their point of view expressed in the final product. Those who were not education specialists had to be satisfied that their electoral interests and policy preferences were adequately addressed.

The Education Lobby

Before SB 90, the education lobby was, for all practical purposes, the California Teachers Association (CTA). Oscar Anderson, CTA's veteran lobbyist, was more than just a special interest group representative. He was the leading spokesman for the education community on finance matters and the major source of expert advice outside of the State Department of Education for legislators. One of Anderson's last acts before his death was to appear on the senate floor as a technical advisor to Senator Dills during the debate on SB 90.

In the late 1960s and early 1970s, several major changes began to occur in the education lobby. Following the lead of its national parent organization, the National Education Association (NEA), the CTA became more politically active and adopted a hard labor– management distinction that eliminated school administrators from its membership. The education lobby became split three ways among teachers (CTA), administrators (ACSA), and governing boards (CSBA). Before the break-up, CTA was considered by many observers to be the single most powerful professional interest group in the state (Owens, Constantini, and Wechsler 1970).

After the break-up, the verdict was much the same, but the political environment was considerably more complex. As the erratic performance of the education lobby in SB 220 demonstrated, even when organizations are politically powerful in their own right, fragmentation can be a serious liability. The CTA, even in its newly conceived role as militant defender of teachers and political power-broker, has to play smart coalition politics to achieve its objectives. In addition, the CTA's membership position in the state is not totally secure. The largest single local teachers' organization, United Teachers of Los Angeles (UTLA), has its own independent organization and its own Sacramento representative. The CTA's main competition, the AFL–CIO–affiliated California Federation of Teachers (CFT), has a small local membership but an extraordinarily strong presence in Sacramento. The CTA's ability to speak for teachers in legislative politics is hedged by the UTLA and CFT.

Another important change in the education lobby was the appearance in Sacramento of lobbyists from the major local school systems. First the big five—San Diego, Long Beach, Los Angeles, Oakland, and San Francisco—sent lobbyists regularly to the capitol, and then the large county school districts and smaller cities began to follow their lead. These lobbyists communicate district needs to their local legislative delegation, keep tabs on legislative decisions for their superintendents, expedite the district's business with the State Department of Education, and work with other school system lobbyists on common legislative interests. The special attention accorded urban school districts in the Educationally Disadvantaged Youth program and the urban aid factor added as a result of Assemblyman Ken Meade's holdout on SB 1641 were testimonial to the increasing influence of their lobbyists in Sacramento.

As the legislature confronted *Serrano*, the education lobby was transforming itself from a simple, unified force into a sprawling and complex collection of special interests. The individual influence of Oscar Anderson, based on a combination of political understanding and technical expertise, was multiplied and fragmented several times as representatives of statewide organizations and local districts established their presence in Sacramento. Power and access to important decisions were up for grabs. Certain key actors began to emerge: Cal Rossi from the CTA, Mary Bergan from the CFT, Ron Prescott from the Los Angeles Unified School District, Bill Lambert from UTLA, Gordon Winton from ACSA, Joe Brooks from the CSBA, Mike Dillon from the low-wealth districts, and Ken Hall (former Reagan Department of Finance staff member) from the high-wealth districts. The period from SB 90 to SB 220 to SB 1641 was, in effect, a shakedown cruise for the newly expanded education lobby, a time when lobbyists established their positions and discovered how to work in a more complex and demanding political environment.

Lobbyists have a good deal more in common with each other than their disparate constituencies suggest. Their success depends on access to influentials, on the reliability of the information they purvey to legislators, on their ability to read the political environment accurately and explain it to people who are not in it every day, and on their ability to bargain skillfully. Education lobbyists in Sacramento also share more mundane problems. A large proportion of them are commuters to Sacramento, leaving their residences, their families, and their workplaces for weeks at a time and working out of temporary quarters close to the capitol. One lobbyist who lives in Sacramento said:

> They spend a lot of time together because they really have nothing else to do. It's as much a social thing as anything else. They trade political scuttlebutt, compare notes, test each other, and reinforce their own importance. It gets old after a while for those of us who live here. We're home doing Little League and Cub Scouts, and they're in a bar somewhere shooting the bull.

Whether for social support or mutual political benefit, lobbyists tend to stick together.

Out of the SB 1641 mobilization committee grew a loose network of interests that was initially called the Tuesday Night Conspiracy and later the Tuesday Night Group. The group came together under the encouragement of Ron Prescott, lobbyist for the Los Angeles school system, and involved the big five urban school districts, the UTLA, the CFT, the CTA, the CSBA, and ACSA. The name of the group was appropriate in the sense that it was originally defined only in terms of its meeting time and place—Tuesday night in the Sacramento offices of the Los Angeles Unified School District. The lobbyists were aware of the necessity for collaboration, based on their experience with SB 220 and SB 1641, but wary of it for several reasons.

Prescott said, "We worried about the reaction of citizens and legislators. As soon as you form an organization, it begins to look self-serving and greedy."[10] Others were somewhat suspicious of Prescott's motives for forming the group. "The whole thing looked like an effort by L.A. to dominate the lobby," said one lobbyist. "We were, and to some degree still are, leery of L.A.'s role in the group." Still others were dubious about the ability of individual lobbyists to work effectively with each other. Because they are solely accountable to the membership and governing boards of their organizations, lobbyists are very limited in the amount of bargaining they can do with each other. If a group of lobbyists were to take a position, it would be questionable whether they could bind their membership to that position and even more questionable whether they could maintain themselves in Sacramento for very long. Lobbyists had to be very careful in agreeing to collaborate that they did not compromise their primary responsibility to their memberships.

Overall, the necessity for concerted action was strong enough to overcome the disadvantages of collaboration. As one lobbyist put it, "All of us were doing our own thing until we discovered that we could all lose. Then we started to compromise." UTLA representative Bill Lambert said, "Previous to the Tuesday night club everybody filled the air with finance bills, like shooting buckshot into the air" (Luther 1980). The effect of the group, he continued, was to find areas where the education lobby could agree.

Members of the group deliberately kept its structure informal. There were no written rules, no dues, no membership policies, and no formal leadership rules. The group would convene itself regularly at the scheduled time and begin discussing major legislative actions affecting education. Out of these discussions grew a set of informal agreements that defined the group's structure and processes. The

10. Ron Prescott 5 May 1980: personal communication.

most basic agreement was that no participant in the group could be expected to bind his or her membership to any proposal. "Where we could get agreement from our membership, we worked with the group. Where we couldn't, we agreed to disagree," said one participant.

The second basic article was that the group would focus only on those issues on which it could get broad agreement. School finance, because it meant more money for all educational constituencies, was one such issue. Labor–management relations, which would have divided the group, was excluded from discussion.

A third basic article, as Prescott put it, was "don't surprise any-one."[11] All positions, agreements, and disagreements were to be thor-oughly aired in discussions, and once the consensus position was reached, members were expected to behave consistently with their stated position. "The operative term for the group was trust," said Prescott, "and few violated the rule. When they did, they were told."

A fourth basic article was that members who supported the con-sensus position would represent it as the position of the group as a whole, rather than taking credit themselves. This enabled the group to present a united front on consensus issues and to share the work of lobbying individual legislators. "Each of us has our friends in the legislature," one lobbyist said, "and we discovered that if we pooled our contacts we could cover almost the whole legislature."

Maintaining and nurturing the group was a difficult and subtle chore. "We had to make sure that there were opportunities for indi-vidual lobbyists within the group to surface. They have to go back to their organizations and say, 'Here's what I've done for you,'" said Prescott. As the group became known, first inside and then outside Sacramento, size became a problem. The core group grew from six or eight to twenty-five or thirty and beyond. Smaller districts and organizations would send representatives to Sacramento on Tuesday afternoon just to be able to say that they were part of the Tuesday Night Group. The major lobbyists were, and still are, split on how to handle the size problem. Prescott said:

> I understand that some members are uncomfortable with the number of peo-
> ple coming to meetings. I don't think you exclude them. You accommodate
> them. The problem with all the newcomers is that they don't understand the
> "rules of the game" and they don't understand all the tacit agreements that

11. Ron Prescott 5 May 1980: personal communication.

have evolved over the years within the core group. The problem, then, is to educate them fast. We can't waste a whole meeting debating something we reached agreement on years ago.[12]

Some original participants in the group, weary of personality conflicts and the size problem, have recently begun to pull away from regular participation. "Lambert (the UTLA representative) takes a 'with us or against us' attitude toward the group," said one regular member, "and a lot of us feel it's inconsistent with the group's original purpose." "As the group increases in size," another member said, "it gets less useful as a place to thrash out differences."

The pulling together of the disparate pieces of the education lobby under the umbrella of the Tuesday Night Group was one of the critical events in the construction of a reform coalition. It solved a major political problem that had dogged reformers in California and other states: how to keep competing educational interests from destroying each other on issues of mutual benefit.

Informational Groups

Two important pieces of the reform coalition were outside Sacramento. One was the Education Congress of California (ECC) and the other was California Coalition for Fair School Finance (CCFSF). Both groups brought together a broad array of people, some of whom are only peripherally concerned with education finance—the League of Women Voters, the American Association of University Women, and the Parent–Teacher Association, among others. ECC grew from an early objective of Wilson Riles to bring a broad-based constituency of groups together to support public education. Under the volunteer direction of University of California at Berkeley education staff member Elaine Boyce, it now serves as the major conduit for information from Sacramento to the local level.

CCFSF grew out of the volunteer efforts of a handful of women who were concerned about public awareness of the *Serrano* issue. Two of its founders, Barbara Levin and Barbara Miller, both active in citizen efforts, thought of the coalition as a way of reaching what they called "the shampoo crowd"—ordinary citizens who stood to gain or lose a great deal from school finance reform but who did not

12. Ron Prescott 5 May 1980: personal communication.

ordinarily participate in political activities. With the support of the League of Women Voters Education Fund and the State Commission on Arts and Humanities, they developed a television spot and a large quantity of informational materials on *Serrano*. They also held several meetings. They found that most of the people who attended the meetings and requested their information were not the shampoo crowd but local educators. "We discovered that we were filling a need that the State Department of Education had neglected," they said, "getting basic information on school finance to local people."[13]

Because of the broadness of their constituency and the sources of their support, ECC and CCFSF are nonpolitical organizations. They played no active role in mobilizing support or lobbying on education finance, but they had a considerable effect nonetheless on the political environment in which school finance reform proposals were considered. They alerted local school people and citizens to the stakes involved in school finance reform and served as sources of information on legislative decisions. The ECC also provided major decisionmakers in Sacramento—Greene, Rodda, Riles, and the staff that supported them—with ready access to a public forum to discuss legislative business, and it provided a wider group of professionals and citizens with a place to see and question state decisionmakers.

The role of such informational groups as ECC and CCFSF is difficult to measure because their objective is public awareness rather than political influence. The level of activity of these two groups and their success in reaching large numbers of people are a testimonial to the general level of sophistication in mobilizing and disseminating information that characterized reform politics in California.

THE MAKING OF ASSEMBLY BILL 65

Governor Brown was first off the mark in responding to the *Serrano II* decision. On 31 December 1976, the day after the supreme court's decision, Brown held a press conference to announce that within a week or ten days he would unveil "a reasonable response" to *Serrano* (*Los Angeles Times*, 1 January 1977). He hinted that his proposal would involve some leveling up of low-expenditure districts and some reallocation of funds between categorical programs and the

---

13. Barbara Levin 21 August 1979: personal communication.

foundation program. Two other topics of discussion at the press conference were the state's budget surplus and homeowner property tax relief. California's economy had started to boom. By July 1976 the finance department was predicting an $800 million surplus. A large proportion of this windfall was a result of inflating property values, which meant that homeowners were feeling the bite of increased property taxes. The California Taxpayers Association called attention to this problem (Salzman 1976b).

Brown proposed a $480 million circuit breaker property tax rebate for families whose property taxes rose above a certain proportion of their income. Beyond this proposal, however, Brown was guarding the surplus, aware that the cost of compliance with *Serrano* might require a substantial share of it. The political risks of using the surplus to level up school districts instead of reducing property taxes were not clear, but political commentators were warning that there were danger signals in the air, one of which was the possibility of property tax revolt (Salzman 1976c).

Brown's approach to the legislature with his reform proposal proved he could be politically skillful when the occasion required it. On January 5 he called a conference with legislative leadership in which he presented the broad outlines of the plan emerging from Gocke's staff work in the Department of Finance. His presentation to the legislators emphasized the total cost of the proposal—$300 in the first year; $350, $600, $800 million in the three subsequent years; and $1.2 billion in the fifth year—and that it could be financed without tax increases. One person invited to the legislative briefing was Wilson Riles. A Riles staff member recalled:

> Wilson arrived in the governor's office—the press was there, the TV lights were on, and it was clear it was going to be a big deal. Brown did a very smart thing. He motioned to Wilson and said, "Hey Wilson, come on up here and sit with me." Wilson really had no choice but do do it, and became identified with the governor's plan. He shouldn't have done it, though.

Brown's attitude toward Riles before the conference had been a good deal less cordial. A Department of Finance staff member who worked on the governor's proposal said, "Riles wasn't called in until after the plan was developed. The governor was explicit in saying, 'When we have a plan, then I'll start sharing information.'" An assembly staff member who watched the conference unfold concluded, "The governor hijacked his entire proposal from Riles. It was essentially the plan that Riles had been pushing for years, with some typical Jerry Brown fiscal magic in it. To his credit, he stole the initiative from everyone."

The legislators' response was mixed. Paul Priolo (R–Malibu), minority floor leader in the assembly, took advantage of the occasion to embrace the governor's position that the proposal should be financed without a tax increase:

> I commend the governor, doggone it. I raised hell with him for two years just talking and never doing anything. Now he's doing something to follow up on that rhetoric, and I think it's incumbent on Republicans and me as minority leader to support him when he is doing something.
>
> The other thing he said . . . which was just terrific was, "I don't want to leave the legacy of former governors Goodwin Knight and Pat Brown and have a massive deficit when I go out of office, but I don't want to increase taxes because we are second only to New York in the U.S. So we're going to have to learn to operate within the limit of the taxes that we have now. . . ."
>
> Today Brown talked more Republican than Democratic. I felt *deja vu*. I've heard Governor Reagan talk that way before (*Los Angeles Times*, 5 January 1977).

Assemblyman Greene and Senator Rodda, the leading education figures, were noncommittal, restating their earlier theme that the political problems of constructing a solution were enormous and the money required substantial. According to a Department of Finance staff member, the governor's staff spent the weeks following the announcement trying to generate commitments to sponsor the legislation from key legislators, including Rodda and Greene. Rodda demurred, a senate aide said, "because he didn't want to be in cahoots with Jerry Brown and the Department of Finance," and resolved to develop his own bill. Greene began to negotiate. An assembly staff member recalled, "After the January announcement we started to meet almost daily with the Department of Finance people. It was clear from the start to us, although we didn't let on, that Greene would sponsor the bill. We wanted concessions, and we got them."

Reactions outside the legislature to Brown's proposal were also mixed. The CTA described it as "totally inadequate" because it did not provide large enough increases in the foundation program and it did not give sufficient attention to "the special problems of urban school systems, regardless of their wealth" (*Los Angeles Times*, 7 January 1977). Other parts of the education lobby adopted a wait-and-see attitude, foregoing public comment. The *Los Angeles Times* observed,

> A key factor in the plan is the expected continuance of a healthy economic climate that would enable the state to reap sizeable surplus funds over the next five years to provide the new school money.
>
> If an economic recession occurs, however, some critics say, there may be no alternative to requiring new taxes somewhere along the line to comply with a court mandate to reform school financing (6 January 1977).

Short of a recession, it was also possible that the taxpayers of California might regard the growing state budget surplus as a sign the government was overfunded. The surplus was Brown's keystone; it allowed him to support an ambitious reform plan without a tax increase.

As discussions ensued, the basic features of Brown's proposal became clearer. The proposal contained strong *Serrano* equalization features. It indexed the state's contribution to inflation and held the state's share steady at about 45 percent against erosion from increasing local property values. It eliminated the $125/ADA basic aid allotment that went to districts regardless of wealth. It proposed a Guaranteed Yield Program for low-wealth districts, designed to assure that for 80 percent of the ADA in the state, tax rates would yield equal revenue for expenditures above the foundation level. It provided for maintenance of the provision in SB 1641 that power-equalized voted overrides for districts above 150 percent of the foundation and provided that the percentage be decreased annually to 130 percent. It also proposed that tax rates in high-wealth districts be frozen (inflated property values coupled with revenue limits in these districts meant that tax rates were steadily declining) and the surplus revenue generated be allocated entirely to equalization. This provision was called "full recapture." Finally, the proposal gave tax relief to low-income families living in high-wealth districts.

Brown's plan also contained ambitious provisions for restructuring the schools. To be eligible for an increment of about $80/ADA to the foundation program, school systems would have to establish school-site councils, staff development plans, annual assessments of effectiveness, and individual instructional objectives for students. The state superintendent was authorized to deny school systems their inflation adjustment in the foundation program for any year in which they failed to meet the objectives of their plans. The new restructuring program was to be financed by eliminating the Early Childhood Education (ECE) program and two other small categorical programs for reading and gifted children.

The Educationally Disadvantaged Youth (EDY) program and the Bilingual Education program were to be collapsed into a single Economic Impact Aid program to provide supplemental assistance to districts with high concentrations of students requiring special attention. The State Department of Education would be required to develop evaluation requirements that could deny funds to districts that were not providing adequate services to disadvantaged children. Additional funds were added to the Economic Impact Aid program to soften the effects of equalization on large urban districts with high property wealth (Department of Finance 1978).

Insiders were surprised at both the audacity and the political naivete of the proposal. An assembly staff member commented:

> It was clear that when the Department of Finance put the proposal together they started with the basic items they wanted and then asked, "Who do we need to buy off in order to get it passed?" They thought they'd get Riles with the restructuring program, the big cities with the urban factor, and the low-wealth districts with the *Serrano* provisions. It was a Christmas Tree bill, but a pretty good one. You only get reform when you bribe people.

The Department of Finance group did make some questionable political judgments in constructing the proposal. By eliminating ECE and making the restructuring program an appendange of the foundation program, they reduced the visibility of Riles's school reform strategy and undercut his local political constituency in the ECE site councils. By giving Riles the authority to deny inflation adjustments to school systems, the finance group played into the hands of senate critics of ECE, who already objected to the State Department's heavy-handed intervention in local school systems. By collapsing the EDY and bilingual programs into a single program, they backed into a delicate political situation in which blacks and Chicanos, who increasingly saw themselves as competitors for state funds, were tossed into the same program. The equalization provisions of the proposal put Brown and the finance department in the camp of *Serrano* hawks as far as the legislature was concerned. Although the Guaranteed Yield Program and recapture provisions did not produce a level of equalization that would satisfy the *Serrano* lawyers, they were substantially more than the legislature had accomplished to that point.

Negotiations between Greene's Assembly Education Committee staff and Brown's Department of Finance staff were critical in shaping what eventually became AB 65. Brown needed Greene's sponsorship, especially since it was clear that Rodda would not sponsor the governor's proposal. The assembly staff, represented by James Murdoch and Paul Holmes, saw their major goal as increasing the total size of the pot available because they saw that substantial school finance reform could be purchased only with substantial increases in overall funding. The finance staff, however, tried to hold the line against substantial increases by consolidating existing programs as a mechanism to acquire funds. Both staffs were in agreement that the bill should be comprehensive—that is, it should contain *Serrano* equalization, restructuring, and assistance to urban districts to offset the effects of *Serrano* compliance.

Greene introduced the result of the negotiations on March 31 as AB 65. The differences between Greene's bill and the governor's initial proposal were mainly technical. Greene's bill maintained the Guaranteed Yield Program but tightened it slightly and strengthened power equalization of tax overrides substantially, extending it by 1981 to 1982 to all districts with revenue limits above the foundation, rather than just to those whose revenue limits were greater than 130 percent of the foundation. To deal with the issue of tax equity, the bill mandated minimum tax rates for wealth districts and provided that revenues generated by those tax rates in excess of the districts' revenue limits would be fully recaptured by the state. These provisions increased the *Serrano* compliance aspects of the governor's proposal. The bill also held the state's share of the foundation program constant, instead of increasing it as the governor had recommended, to free funds for categorical programs. It reduced the full recapture of revenues accruing from property tax freezes to 90 percent in an attempt to mollify wealthy districts.

Greene's AB 65 also significantly changed the restructuring provisions of the governor's proposal. It dropped the provision authorizing the State Department to withhold funds from districts not meeting their objectives, and it made the development of proficiency standards an entirely local matter. A provision was added for one-year planning grants in addition to implementation grants. The governor's proposal to allocate restructuring funds through the foundation program was maintained as was the consolidation of ECE into the program. The negotiated bill also backed away from the governor's proposal to consolidate the EDY and bilingual programs and concentrated instead on modifying the existing provisions to give more money to large urban districts.

To describe the *Serrano* effects of their proposal, Brown and Greene coined the term "substantial compliance." Greene argued that no legislative proposal would strictly meet the state supreme court's standard but that AB 65 was the best, politically feasible approximation to that standard. Brown argued that the courts would recognize "a principle, a rule of reason, a latitude of substantial compliance. In my legal judgment, I am very confident that this program will obtain a favorable decision by the . . . Court. In fact, I'm extraordinarily confident" (*Los Angeles Times*, 1 February and 26 February 1977). *Serrano* attorney John McDermott retorted, "Substantial compliance is gobbledygook. . . . The governor says this is how much money we have; this is how far we can go; let's call it 'substantial compliance.'" All the arguments that Governor Brown and Assemblyman Greene raised against stricter compliance, McDermott said, had already been considered by the state supreme court before it made its decision. "The Supreme Court said phooey," he concluded (*Los Angeles Times*, 26 February 1977).

The term "substantial compliance" became the shorthand way of summarizing the differences between the legislature and the *Serrano* lawyers over the adequacy of the legislative response to *Serrano*. It captured many levels of meaning. In the first instance, it described the legislature's genuine uncertainty over what the court actually meant by fiscal neutrality. Was it an absolute standard, or was it subject to degrees of approximation? Second, by claiming there was no such thing as substantial compliance, McDermott seemed to be saying that the slippery complexities of coalition building were illegitimate. It had to be clear who the winners and losers were; the only acceptable result was one that clearly penalized wealthy districts and rewarded poor districts. This struck Sacramento's political actors as an absurdly naive and presumptuous attitude to take toward legislative politics. Third, the substantial compliance issue touched a raw nerve on the question of the separation of powers. In the words of one Sacramento lobbyist, "The typical state legislator regards himself as the equal of any state Supreme Court Justice when it comes to making important decisions. 'What's the Court?' they say, 'I'm going to be President some day—just re-elect me.' " Legislative staff and their bosses bridled at the notion that McDermott could so disdainfully dismiss their skillful technical and political work. They also took exception to the *Serrano* lawyers' arguments that the legislature had a large number of options open to it in complying with *Serrano*. "They were great at trotting out these hypotheticals in front of the Court to convince the judges that it was all very easy and straightforward, but they didn't have the slightest idea what it required to get legislation passed," said one staff member.

With the emergence of substantial compliance, then, the lines were drawn between the legislature and the *Serrano* lawyers. Legislative actors continued to think in terms of subtle gradations, increments on past law, adjustments to broaden the coalition, and approximations to some goal. McDermott became the spokesman for an uncompromising, either–or view of compliance—the legislature was either in compliance or it was not, and there could be nothing substantial about it.

On 10 March 1977 Senator Rodda, now chairman of the Senate Finance Committee, introduced his own bill. Following the traditional cleavage between the assembly and the senate, Rodda's bill contained no provisions for categorical programs whatsoever and focused exclusively on modifications in the foundation program. Rodda said the "first priority is to meet the Court's directive while achieving substantial tax relief without exhausting the State General Fund or destroying the many fine programs in the high-wealth districts" (Department of Finance 1978:124). Rodda was also blunt on the issue of substantial compliance:

> To comply totally with the mandate of the Court would result in, (a) either a massive infusion of new dollars, or (b) the virtual destruction of programs currently being offered by high wealth districts. Neither course is reasonable. What is being proposed is the adoption of a standard with an important difference from that of the Court, but still consistent with the Court's major concern (Department of Finance 1978:125).

It is the legislature's job, Rodda seemed to be saying, to decide how the financial resources of the state should be used. If complying with the court's mandate meant acting in a publicly irresponsible way, either by raising taxes to an unacceptable level or by undermining educational programs in certain districts, then the legislature was compelled to modify the court's standard. The difficulty with this position, of course, was that neither Rodda nor any other legislator would convince the court or the *Serrano* lawyers that the mandate was unreasonable. After all, the lawyers and the court argued, fiscal neutrality did not require any specific solution or any particular combination of tax increases or program cuts in wealthy districts. The lawyers were talking doctrine; the legislators were talking politics. The lawyers were satisfied that it was possible to comply with the court's decision in any number of hypothetical ways. The legislators saw compliance as the balancing of competing interests and were therefore not interested in hypothetical solutions, only real ones. These two competing views never seemed to converge.

Rodda's bill, SB 525, was different in two main respects from AB 65. It emphasized expenditure equalization more than equalization of tax yield, and it took considerably less away from wealthy districts. The bill produced its main equalization effect by boosting revenue limits in low-spending districts to the level of the seventy-fifth percentile over three years. This outsized leveling up was possible because the bill did not provide any additional funding for categorical programs or any new categorical authority.

Although SB 525 and AB 65 were about the same cost, the senate bill used its resources mainly for leveling up, and the assembly bill used a substantial share for categorical programs and produced more of its equalization effect by recapture or leveling down. Both bills incorporated the Guaranteed Yield Program by which low-wealth districts would levy a statutory tax rate and the state would pay the difference between the district's revenue limit and the amount raised by the tax. SB 525's guaranteed yield covered 78 percent of the state's ADA; AB 65 covered 81 percent. Both bills also had recapture provisions. AB 65 recaptured 90 percent of the difference between a statutory minimum tax rate and the wealthy district's revenue limit, and SB 525 recaptured 20 percent of the difference between the state foundation and the district's revenue limit. SB 525 recaptured about 40 percent of the amount AB 65 would recapture from wealthy districts. Both bills contained provisions for power-equalizing voted overrides.

The response to SB 525 was positive from the major interest groups and from Legislative Analyst Alan Post because of the bill's emphasis on the foundation program and its lack of categorical programs. Post said he had qualms about the Early Childhood Education program, based on his staff's analysis of its effects, and thought SB 525's approach was a more efficient use of state resources (Department of Finance 1978). James Donnally, CTA lobbyist, publicly criticized AB 65's emphasis on categorical programs, saying he favored increased funding for such programs as EDY and bilingual programs that targeted money on special district needs but opposed expansion of, for example, ECE (*Los Angeles Times*, 18 March 1977).

James Murdoch, Assembly Education Committee staff member, observed of the difference between AB 65 and SB 525, "They were close together in total cost and in equalization language; that meant that the Senate was ready to compromise."[14] The pattern of negotiations between senate and assembly established in previous school finance measures would hold for this one. The assembly would wade in with heavy emphasis on categorical programs, the senate would counter with heavy emphasis on the foundation program, and the result would be somewhere between.

In late March and early April 1977 after the introduction of AB 65 and SB 525, education lobby activities began to heat up. The Tuesday Night Group formed a Technical Committee, composed of George Downing (ACSA), Beth Louargand (LA Unified), James Donnally (CTA), and Mike Dillon (Low-Wealth Districts). According to Donnally, "Our approach to AB 65 was completely different than with earlier bills. Instead of each organization introducing its own bill and developing its own list of 'must' provisions, we decided to concentrate on developing a prototype that the group could agree on and lobby for in unison."[15] This task devolved to the Technical Committee. Communication among the Technical Committee and staff from the legislature, the State Department of Education, and the Department of Finance was frequent. Gerry Hayward, Rodda's chief school finance staff member; James Murdoch, Greene's leading staff member; Jack Kennedy from the Department of Finance; and Jack Ross from the State Department were all regulars at Technical Committee sessions even though they were careful to dissociate themselves from Tuesday Night Group decisions. The Tuesday Night Group came to be the major conduit through which legislative ideas were tested and lobby proposals were communicated to the legislature. Everyone but Governor Brown seemed to understand the structure for consultation and communication. One veteran education lobbyist said, "We tried to communicate directly with the governor

14. James Murdoch 21 September 1978: personal communication.
15. James Donnally 22 January 1980: personal communication.

and we got a reply that we should deal with him through Wilson Riles. He tried to treat us as if we didn't exist."

As AB 65 and SB 525 began to move through the assembly and senate, two major trouble spots emerged: the problem of high wealth districts and the debate over coupling school restructuring to finance reform. According to Murdoch, the assembly staff member:

> We spent most of our time in the school finance portion of the bill on what to do about high-wealth districts. It was clear that it wasn't just an issue of equity, but also one of the impact of reform tax rates. Politically, we had to devise a system that had a neutral impact on tax rates statewide and that slowed or stopped the decrease of property tax rates in high-wealth districts occurring because of the sharp rise in property values. The whole issue of equity was a matter of concern to only a few of us.[16]

In other words, the equity requirements of *Serrano* set off an enormously complicated barrage of political problems. It was not politically just as simple as taking money away from rich districts and giving it to poor districts. Legislators would look at the net fiscal effect on their constituencies and on what proposals did to taxes. Ironically, the improved data analysis and computer modeling capability that resulted from collaboration among units of state government added to the political complexity of the legislation. "Before, we could say, 'Trust me, you'll do all right,' when they asked us what effect a proposal would have on their district," said one staff member. "Now, with all this computer capability everybody *knows* pretty well how they will make out. You can't hide much."[17]

The issue of linking school restructuring to finance reform raised problems with the education lobby and with the senate. Brown and Greene were adamant that no additional money should be channeled into the educational system without some provision for school reform. In response to Rodda's proposal, Greene said, "I will not support a bill that merely puts money in the pot, because I want to know where the money is going" (Department of Finance 1978: 136). Greene knew, however, that after the senate's hearings on ECE school reform proposals were in for rough sledding. His solution to this problem was to put heavy demands on his staff to justify the proposals he made and to be prepared to make concessions that

---

16. James Murdoch 21 September 1978: personal communication.
17. John Mockler 6 February 1979: personal communication.

would make restructuring more attractive to its opponents. Linda Bond, Assembly Education Committee staff member, said:

> Leroy was basically committed to the idea, but his approach with his staff was to play devil's advocate. He sometimes used us like a punching bag. He'd say, "I don't like this," and we'd come back with support from the research, and he'd change his ground and come at us another way, and we'd come back with more research. If we could get him to agree with us, he would defend it like it was part of his own soul.[18]

The notion of school restructuring soon came to include emphasis on staff development. Assemblyman Gary Hart (D–Santa Barbara), himself a former teacher, constituted a Staff Development Advisory Committee composed of representatives of the major education interests to advise him on the development of a bill. According to one staff member who worked on the staff development proposal, "The interest groups were basically opposed to school site councils and the Riles approach. They tried to use the Advisory Committee to drive a wedge between Hart and the State Department, but they didn't succeed." The result of Hart's consultations was AB 551, a staff development program linked to local site councils. Another staff member observed, "gradually the interest groups moved from opposition to neutrality on this restructuring issue; they knew there had to be a bribe in the bill for Wilson Riles, and they swallowed their medicine." The senate staff, fresh off their ECE oversight hearings, also started strongly opposed to restructuring and gradually modified their position. A senate staff member said, "No one over here was all that hot on the idea. Most of us felt it might have been a good idea at some point, but the State Department made a mess of it with its heavy-handed control. We accepted it as a political necessity."[19]

As AB 65 was readied for the assembly floor, debate was delayed when Greene found that he was some twelve votes short of the required two-thirds majority. The major opposition came from the four-member Chicano Caucus, which objected to the bilingual/EDY consolidation because they thought it favored blacks, and a group of legislators from high-wealth districts, who argued that with its surplus revenue the state should accomplish more of the required reform by leveling up and less by recapture. Greene put Chicano

18. Linda Bond 21 September 1978: personal communication.
19. Catherine Minicucci 21 September 1978: personal communication.

Caucus Chairman Richard Allatorre (D–Los Angeles) together with Assemblyman Willie Brown to negotiate a compromise on the bilingual/EDY consolidation and agreed to insert a variable cost provision to stem some of the objections of high-wealth districts. The variable cost proposal was the brainchild of John Mockler, Riles's chief legislative advisor and newly appointed head of the State Department's School Finance Equalization Project. A State Department staff member recalled the origins of the variable cost proposal:

> John was amazing. He carried a lot of numbers around in his head. We were puzzling over what to do about the variable cost problem—we called it "differential cost" at first—and John came up with this figure that 530 of the smallest districts, out of 1042, had something like 3 percent of the population and were getting something like 4 percent of the total revenue limit. It seemed to us that these were exactly the districts you wanted to protect from across-the-board expenditure equalization. The problem was that any formula you constructed to account for variable cost had Los Angeles in it. When they come in, the cost goes out of sight. L.A. gets five times more than the second district, which was San Diego, and San Diego was 50 percent bigger than the third. Then you started getting into the little guys. We went ahead with it, knowing it was a good idea in principle, but not a very good formula.[20]

These changes were apparently enough to still the opposition of the Chicanos and the high-wealth districts because on April 25 AB 65 passed the assembly with the required two-thirds majority (*Los Angeles Times*, 19 April and 26 April 1977). Three days later the Senate Education Committee reported out Rodda's SB 525 (*Los Angeles Times*, 28 April 1977). Rodda's bill passed the senate in late May with no major amendments, setting the stage for the assembly–senate conference to work out the differences between the two versions.

One of the sternest critics of AB 65 was Alan Post. Post argued before the Assembly Education Committee that the bill would not constitute *Serrano* compliance, that it would allow wealthy districts to continue "getting away with murder," and that it would require a tax increase to finance it in three years (*Los Angeles Times*, 13 April 1977). One of the staff who did analyses of AB 65 for Post was Steve Rhoads, who said of the legislature's consideration of AB 65, "It had something for everyone. You couldn't oppose it or you were in left

20. William Whiteneck 23 January 1980: personal communication.

field. We made the strongest case we could, but at that point no one was listening." [21]

When the senate–assembly conference committee was appointed on June 21—composed of Leroy Greene, Dixon Arnett, and Gary Hart from the assembly and Albert Rodda, Ralph Dills, and William Campbell from the senate—the battle lines were drawn. The major issues were the extent of recapture from wealthy districts (AB 65 would recapture about $760 million, SB 525 about $200), the trade-off between increasing the foundation and funding categoricals (AB 65 put a larger proportion into categoricals, SB 525 had no categoricals at all), and the question of whether restructuring, now called the School Improvement Program, would be linked to school finance reform. AB 65, with its heavy categorical funding, carried a price tag for five years in excess of $4.5 billion; SB 525 carried a five-year price tag of about $3.8 billion.

In late July and early August, as the conference committee was reaching final agreement on a compromise bill, the fiscal assumptions underlying the legislation came unstuck. When the school finance conference committee was appointed, another conference committee was appointed on the tax relief measure moving through the legislature. Together, these two pieces of legislation threatened to wipe out the state's revenue surplus. The governor and the legislative leadership asked their financial advisors, the Department of Finance, and the legislative analyst for estimates of the surplus. On August 1 Roy Bell, head of finance, and Alan Post, legislative analyst, presented their estimates to a joint meeting of the two conference committees. The estimates differed by substantial amounts, and the two were sent back to arrive at a common figure (Department of Finance 1978). Two days later Bell and Post returned with an agreed upon estimate that showed that, at current projections, the school finance and tax relief proposals would incur a $900 million deficit by 1980—a politically unacceptable result for both the legislature and the governor (*Los Angeles Times*, 3 August 1977).

The school finance conferees returned to their negotiations and trimmed their compromise proposal to about $4 billion over five years. Speaking for the Department of Finance, Charles Gocke said he was very pessimistic about the conferees' decision, declining to say whether he would recommend that the governor veto it (*Los*

21. Stephen Rhoads 21 January 1980: personal communication.

Angeles Times, 12 August 1977). From middle to late August, conference committee negotiations bogged down in a welter of competing cost and revenue estimates. Rodda said his committee was trying to "kick the stuffing" out of their proposal (*Los Angeles Times*, 17 August 1977). Finally, on August 24 Governor Brown, Assembly Speaker Leo McCarthy (D–San Francisco), and Senator Rodda compromised, trimming $442 million from the school finance bill and $350 million from the tax relief bill to put it within agreed upon revenue projections. The education bill suffered a 3 percent across-the-board cut in proposed foundation and categorical support, a delay of the guaranteed yield and recapture provisions, and a reduction in economic impact aid (*Los Angeles Times*, 25 August 1977).

During this period, the education lobby and the Tuesday Night Group played a fairly circumspect game. One legislative staff member said, "They stayed in touch on the inside and played a fairly constructive role on the outside."[22] In early June the lobby mobilized some 600 teachers, administrators, and board members to march on Sacramento in support of a well-funded bill (*Los Angeles Times*, 2 June 1977). They managed to achieve their major objective, a substantial increase in overall funding for schools, and to blunt the effect of the restructuring proposals by obtaining concession favorable to teachers and administrators in the design of the School Improvement Program.

On September 2 the compromise version of AB 65 passed both houses of the legislature. On the same day, the accompanying property tax reform measure failed to acquire the required two-thirds vote in the senate (*Los Angeles Times*, 3 September 1977). The major objections to the tax reform measure were that it did not give enough attention to middle- and high-income families. In these two actions, the legislature further confirmed what tax revolt planners had alleged: The legislature could agree on ways to spend the surplus revenue generated by the tax system, but it could not agree on ways of returning that surplus to the taxpayers.

The final compromise version of AB 65 had all the earmarks of coalition politics. Foundation increases were pared back from both the assembly and senate versions to meet the requirements imposed by the revised revenue estimates. The senate recapture provision was included, but its implementation was delayed one year. The mini-

---

22. James Murdoch 21 September 1978: personal communication.

mum tax rate for high-wealth districts from both the senate and assembly versions was included, but its implementation was also delayed one year. The Guaranteed Yield Program from the assembly version was incorporated and delayed a year. The provisions of both bills preventing slippage of the state's contribution in the face of increasing local property values were incorporated. The School Improvement Program was included, but its funding was reduced from the assembly version, and its structure was changed to give more authority to local school administrators. EDY and bilingual education were consolidated, and the new Economic Impact Aid program received a substantial increase in funding, an important concession to big city school systems. The variable cost provision developed by Mockler was included to provide compensation to districts with high property wealth and high expenses. Governor Brown signed the bill on September 17, vetoing only the variable cost provision.

REFORM IS IN THE EYE OF THE BEHOLDER

Serrano lawyer John McDermott's reaction to AB 65 was quick and devastating. "The legislature blew it," McDermott said, characterizing the bill as "a gigantic fraud on California taxpayers" (*Los Angeles Times*, 7 September 1977). John Serrano said he was very happy to see the legislature take the first step toward compliance but likened the claims that AB 65 constituted substantial compliance to saying a person is a little bit pregnant. "Either you're complying with the decision or you're not," he said (*Sacramento Bee*, 15 September 1977).

McDermott returned to the California Supreme Court in December 1977, asking the court to invalidate AB 65 on the grounds that it failed to meet the requirements of *Serrano II* by leaving the basic aid system in place, by permitting high-wealth districts to enact permissive overrides, and by allowing high-wealth districts to reach the foundation level with less tax effort than low-wealth districts. Appended to McDermott's brief before the court was Alan Post's analysis of AB 65, showing that compared with the SB 90 system in place at the time of its enactment, AB 65 would result in a modest convergence of tax rates and expenditures between high- and low-wealth districts.[23] Using the *Serrano* lawyers' favorite example,

---

23. Petition in the Supreme Court for the state of California, Sidney Wolinsky and John McDermott, no date.

AB 65 would result in a 1981–82 per pupil expenditure difference between Beverly Hills and Baldwin Park of $1178 (Beverly Hills = $2870; Baldwin Park = $1692) and a tax rate difference of $.60 ÷ $1000 assessed valuation (Beverly Hills = $2.79; Baldwin Park = $3.39). Under the old system the per pupil expenditure difference would have been $1265 (Beverly Hills = $2809; Baldwin Park = $1544) and the tax rate difference $2.34 (Beverly Hills = $2.42; Baldwin Park = $4.76). In aggregate terms, AB 65 would bring 95 percent of the state's enrollment to within a $200 per pupil expenditure range. Next to the court's $100 per pupil, eight-year standard, these figures clearly showed AB 65's shortcomings. McDermott took this as evidence that the legislature had deliberately failed to craft a remedy consistent with the court's ruling. The supreme court refused to rule on McDermott's petition and instead designated Los Angeles Superior Court Judge Max Deutz to hear the complaint and determine legislative compliance.

One notable effect of McDermott's assault on AB 65 was to further solidify the reform coalition that had formed around the bill. Wilson Riles, previously on the plaintiff's side in *Serrano*, publicly took the position that AB 65 was "the greatest hope to improve the quality of education in the state" and said the bill would "meet the constitutional test" (*Los Angeles Times*, 27 September 1977). Jerry Brown, preparing to campaign for reelection to the governorship, embraced AB 65 as his long-promised school reform measure. Legislators and legislative staff who had worked on the bill took the position that it was the best, most comprehensive education measure ever passed by the California legislature. The position of the high-wealth districts was summarized by one lobbyist who said, "The writing was on the wall. They knew they were going to have to take a cut. When it was over they felt they'd done the best they could." The position of the low-wealth districts was summarized by another lobbyist:

> Every legislator, except for four or five, has a high-wealth district in his constituency. In a lot of areas there is a fifty-fifty split of high- and low-wealth districts. Even though as many as 80 percent of the school districts in the state would be better off with greater equalization, there is a limit on how far you can go and still get broad political support.[24]

The Tuesday Night Group emerged from the AB 65 debate with a feeling of enhanced unity and influence; their position was summarized by a veteran Sacramento lobbyist who said, "I was surprised

24. Mike Dillon 6 May 1980: personal communication.

that AB 65 got through. I didn't think the legislature and governor would be willing to commit that much money to schools. It was remarkable how much broad-based constituency support it generated. Most lobbyists felt after it was all over that the pulling together had payed off."[25] In other words, the combination of forces that had been knit together to bring AB 65 about fell in line behind it and defended it as the most feasible solution to the *Serrano* problem.

Staff members in the Department of Finance and the Legislative Analyst's Office, who were *Serrano* hawks by and large, saw the coalition politics of AB 65 as the steady dilution of the bill's equalization provisions. One finance staff member said:

> Leveling up was the only politically feasible option. Low wealth districts saw equalization as a way to move up, not as a way to take money away from high wealth districts. We couldn't get support from low wealth districts for power equalization. The only thing they would support was across-the-board increases in state aid.
>
> As a consequence, there wasn't broad support for real redistribution. The recapture provisions were watered down from 50 to 20 percent, which is tokenism. But we thought that if we got it into law the Court could order it increased to 100 percent. Basic aid was left in. The categoricals were not equalized. And urban impact aid went to a lot of high wealth districts. We weren't happy with the final result, but our official position was that it constituted substantial compliance.

A staff member of the Legislative Analyst's Office said:

> Our role was consistently that of outside critic and conscience on *Serrano*. We didn't take a position on the legislation but we repeatedly reminded the legislature in the late summer and early fall of 1977 that you're not getting enough *Serrano* compliance for the amount of money you're spending. It obviously didn't have much effect.[26]

At a meeting of the Education Congress of California in October 1977, John McDermott appeared with leading legislative staff members to debate the adequacy of AB 65. McDermott described the bill as good for education but not a *Serrano* compliance measure. James Murdoch argued that the significance of AB 65 lay not so much in the absolute level of compliance as in the establishment of mechanisms for reallocating funds from wealthy to poor school districts

---

25. Gordon Winton 6 May 1980: personal communication.
26. Hal Geiogue 23 January 1980: personal communication.

despite strong political opposition. The legislature had gone as far as it could go in the short run, Murdoch argued, and any further equalization would require a major political decision to seek a tax increase.

Catherine Minicucci, senate staff member, said she found encouragement in the fact that McDermott did not attack the major elements of the AB 65 system but only argued that it did not go far enough. Reform should be introduced incrementally over a period of years, she argued, and AB 65 provides a firm basis for that approach. Gerald Hayward argued that the debate over AB 65 had revealed the weakness of the court's preoccupation with property wealth and its failure to clarify its position on the tax-equity/expenditure-equity issue. The court should rethink its decision, he argued (Education Congress of California 1977).

The basic outlines of this debate are deeply rooted in the differing perceptions of reform lawyers and legislative actors, and they continue to the present. AB 65 was an incremental reform. Rather than taking any of the substantially different options sketched out by the court and the *Serrano* lawyers, the legislature felt its way along using the revenue limit mechanism established in SB 90, modifying the voted override recapture established in SB 1641, and adding guaranteed yield and the minimum tax rate recapture mechanism in AB 65. Money that could have been used to increase the leveling up effect was used to draw together a broad coalition by channeling economic impact aid to urban districts and expanding Wilson Riles's school reform program. To people within the legislature, these were political necessities. To the reform lawyers, they were distractions for the court's mandate. Whether AB 65 is adequate or not, whether indeed it is even a reform measure, depends on whether one accepts the political view that reforms are made by coalitions or the legal view that reforms are made in compliance with legal doctrine.

5 TAX REVOLT AND FISCAL RETRENCHMENT

PROPOSITION 13—NEW REALITIES, NEW PROBLEMS

On 6 June 1978, in a record-breaking 67 percent turnout, Californians approved the Jarvis–Gann tax limitation initiative, Proposition 13, by a two-to-one vote.[1] Although only 500,000 signatures were required to qualify the Jarvis–Gann initiative for the June 1978 ballot, the initiative's organizational sponsors, the United Organization of Taxpayers and People's Advocate, Incorporated, collected approximately 1.25 million signatures with no extraordinary expenditures.

1. Article II of the California constitution establishes the right of citizens to enact laws and constitutional amendments independent of the governor or the legislature. An initiative petition to amend the state constitution must be signed by 8 percent of the number of voters participating in the previous gubernatorial election. To place a proposed statute on the ballot, 5 percent of the voters must sign the petition. Initiative measures may not relate to more than one subject and cannot be vetoed or changed except by public vote unless the measure itself makes other provisions.

There are twenty-one states with some type of initiative process to place measures on the ballot; sixteen of these, including California, permit voters to change their state constitutions without legislative approval, according to the Council of State Governments. The tax reform movement has taken hold rapidly in these states.

For a full discussion of the passage and implementation of Proposition 13, see Lipson (1980). An analysis of direct legislation in California is found in Lee (1978).

With a mere 400 words, Proposition 13 eliminated approximately 60 percent of local revenues. By imposing a de facto statewide property tax, it also wiped out the result of months of analysis, delicate negotiation, and coalition building—Assembly Bill (AB) 65. With the passage of Proposition 13, AB 65's complex distributional formulas and tax levy scheme became obsolete.[2]

The roots of Proposition 13 lie in the state's economic history and in the legislature's inability to provide property tax relief. California's economy boomed during the 1970s, and the state's efficient appraisal system duly noted the burgeoning of real estate values. As a result, property tax inflation rose many times faster than did personal incomes.[3] Although the legislature was aware that the state's property taxes had become onerous, it was unable to reach agreement on a tax reform measure (Lipson 1980). Consequently, with an unusual show of solidarity—and despite predictions of doom and charges of mean spiritedness or degrading hedonism—California voters imposed their own solution (see Lipset and Raab 1978).

This voter initiative left state political leaders less than one month to devise a solution before the July 1 budget deadline. Legislative response to the demands of Proposition 13 was impressive. In three frantic weeks, policymakers developed a plan to allocate the $4.4 billion in remaining property taxes, to replace approximately 60 percent of expected local revenue loss with $4.1 billion from the state's surplus, and to reduce the $16 billion state budget. These decisions, embodied in Senate Bill (SB) 154, collectively are known as the "bailout." They averted fiscal chaos in local budgets and significant disruption in local services. They also fundamentally altered the

2. The major provisions of Proposition 13's amendment to California's constitution are:

• Taxes on residential, commercial, and business property are limited to 1 percent of 1975–76 assessed market value.

• Property tax assessment increases are limited to no more than 2 percent a year.

• Property is permitted to be reappraised at current market value when it is sold, ownership is transferred, or newly constructed.

• State or local governments are prohibited from passing new property taxes.

• A two-thirds vote is required for imposition of special taxes.

• A two-thirds legislative vote is required for changes in state taxes.

3. For example, in the five years preceding Proposition 13, housing market inflation doubled assessed property values (from $67 billion in 1973 to 1974 to $120 billion estimated in 1978 to 1979), with single-family residences bearing a disproportionate burden (see Lipset and Raab 1978).

structure of intergovernmental finance and decisionmaking in California, most particularly in the area of public education.

Proposition 13 created a radically new climate for school governance and finance. It shifted public school financing from local to state sources and placed a new burden on state-level resources. With the bailout, the state assumed 70 percent of the cost of California's public school system. The fiscal and taxing restrictions of Proposition 13 further modified the structure of school control. With the imposition of a statewide property tax, stringent limitations on the levying of new taxes, and consequent dependence on the state to provide most of their operating funds, local residents and school boards could no longer decide how much to spend on education. They feared that they would also be unable to decide how the bulk of the money should be spent. Proposition 13, as many locals noted, made the state legislature the great school board in the sky.

More important, the Jarvis–Gann initiative heralded a new era of fiscal stringency. No longer could state planners count on the growth of assessed valuation to fund vital local services. Consequently, even though the disasters predicted by opponents did not immediately materialize, Proposition 13 substantially changed the political context of education decisionmaking. Traditionally, decisions about the level of state support for public education were made apart from other allocation choices. With Jarvis–Gann the question debated by the legislature changed from, How much *should* we spend on education? to How much *can* we spend on education given other responsibilities? Even the deliberations surrounding SB 90, also a general revenue measure, focused on the fiscal requirements of public schools, independent of other state-funded activities. Further, funds for SB 90's education support component were raised through a new sales tax, not from the state's general fund. As James Murdoch explained:

> Before Proposition 13 and SB 154, school finance was separated from general revenue measures. But tying school finance to the general budgetary surplus, which was the precedent set by SB 154, took school finance out of the hands of the education committees and opened the field to tradeoffs among different pieces of the state budget.[4]

Proposition 13 forced the schools to compete for the first time with police, fire, libraries, garbage collection, parks, street repair, courts,

4. James Murdoch 7 May 1980: personal communication.

welfare, and every other local government service for a share of the state's general fund resources.

Proposition 13 ended the isolation of education decisionmaking and changed the tenor and logic of school finance reform. A finite state surplus and new restrictions on revenue raising constrained legislative discretion in determining the level of state support for education or the extent of district equalization. Legislators feared that meeting *Serrano* through substantially reducing the budget of high-spending districts would destroy basic education programs. Allocating sufficient general surplus dollars to low-spending districts to raise their expenditures to a level comparable to those of high-spending districts was politically unrealistic because it consumed too large a slice of the state's pie. James Murdoch expressed the view of most bailout architects: "With Proposition 13, the problem changed from equalization to survival. We could not afford *Serrano* anymore."[5]

The Jarvis–Gann initiative presented state policymakers with a blank slate—a rare and unforeseen opportunity to reformulate priorities, rethink procedures, and identify new efficiencies. "Proposition 13 created a climate that permits serious consideration of major change and substantive reform" (*California Journal* Tax Revolt Digest Supplement, November 1978: 4). However, major change or full *Serrano* compliance did not result from Jarvis–Gann. But Proposition 13's effects on general reform, education decisionmaking, and the affordability of *Serrano* were not inevitable. They must be explained in terms of the state's overall response to post–Proposition 13 realities and the legislative politics of retrenchment.

Senate Bill 154: The Bailout

Before the June 6 vote, Governor Jerry Brown and Democratic legislative leaders campaigned vigorously against Proposition 13, predicting that it would cripple vital state and local services. Brown and legislators told the voters that the state could not afford to rescue local services and that passage of the Jarvis–Gann initiative would result in severe cutbacks, especially in crucial areas such as local fire,

---

5. Similarly, Linda Bond, then a member of Assemblyman Leroy Greene's staff, observed, "After *Serrano II*, there was a lot of room for moralizing and commitment to equity. Because of Proposition 13, there is a lot less room" (Linda Bond 24 September 1978: personal communication).

police, and education services. Most lawmakers were confident that the Jarvis–Gann tax limitation measure would be defeated. However, after the votes were tallied, both the governor and the legislature acted promptly to carry out what they called the will of the people.

Politically, the Proposition 13 mandate presented Brown with two choices: continue his opposition to the measure and face probable defeat in November by Evelle Younger, his Republican gubernatorial opponent and Proposition 13 supporter, or convert to the spirit of 13.[6] Governor Brown's immediate and complete conversion to Proposition 13 earned him the epithet "Jerry Jarvis." In a message to a joint legislative session on June 8, Brown seized the initiative and underscored his commitment to make Proposition 13 work:

> Over 4 million of our fellow citizens have sent a message to City Hall, Sacramento, and to all of us. The message is that government spending, wherever it is, must be held in check. We must look forward to lean and frugal budgets. It is a great challenge and we will meet it. We must do everything possible to minimize the human hardship and maximize the total number of state jobs created in our economy (Brown, Jr. 1978).

Thus to the plaudits of Howard Jarvis and Paul Gann, Brown picked up the banner and "brought himself back to full political health with one of his patented Brownstone the Magnificent magic acts" (Salzman 1978:264).

Brown immediately went to work. First, he vigorously cut his own state budget proposals. Then he froze state hiring, banned state pay increases (thus preventing local agencies from granting them), and "let loose of his security blanket," the as yet unspecified but huge state surplus (Salzman 1978:265).[7] After pledging the surplus and proposing that $4 billion be made available to aid local governments and $1 billion set up as a loan fund, Brown left the structuring of the bailout program in the hands of the legislature. The state's response to Proposition 13 would be purely a legislative solution.

---

6. At the time of the June 6 primary election, public opinion polls showed Younger and Brown in a dead heat. On the day of the election, a Los Angeles television station asked voters whether they would vote for Brown or Younger; Younger came away with a 4 percent lead.

7. State Treasurer Jesse Unruh called Brown "the father of Proposition 13" because Brown apparently chose to hoard the enormous state surplus to use to his political advantage in seeking reelection. Unruh considered this surplus a standing public invitation to Proposition 13 (Lipset and Raab 1978:42).

Immediately after the governor's message to the joint legislative session, Assembly Speaker Leo McCarthy announced the formation of a legislative innovation to deal with Proposition 13, a coalition of legislative leadership. McCarthy appointed a six-man joint conference committee of Democratic and Republican leaders from both houses.[8] With three weeks until the July 1 budget deadline, the joint committee held nine days of intensive hearings. They heard from fiscal experts presenting alternative financial plans, from affected interest groups pleading protection for their special interests, and from legislators proposing their own funding priorities.

Among the most impressive presentations, according to participants, was that of Superintendent Wilson Riles. "Riles was the only one who had done his homework. He was the only agency head who had a proposal and a plan."[9] This was in sharp contrast to the presentations of other interests, especially the special districts who, observers report, spent most of their time complaining.

Riles's presentation was both statesmanlike and consistent with the broad three-part strategy he formulated before AB 65: equalization, categorical support, and school reform. He observed, "Recent polls revealed that if cuts were to be made in public services 82 percent of those polled would prefer that they be made in areas other than education" (1978:1).[10] "Nevertheless," he continued, "we all know there must be reductions and education must assume its share" (1978:1). Education's fair share, Riles maintained, should be determined against the funding history of public education relative to other local government activities:

> It is important to recognize that schools have made reductions and foregone improvements to ease the statewide burden of property taxes longer than

8. The committee chairman was Senator Albert Rodda (D-Sacramento), who was also chairman of the Senate Finance Committee. Members included: Assembly Speaker Leo McCarthy (D-San Francisco); Senate President pro tem James Mills (D-San Diego); Senator William Campbell (R-Hacienda Heights); Assemblyman Dan Boatwright (D-Concord), chairman of the Assembly Ways and Means Committee; Assembly Republican leader Paul Priolo (R-Malibu).

9. Gerald Hayward 22 September 1978: personal communication.

10. Riles refers to a post-Proposition 13 poll by the Field Institute. Field's poll found that 82 percent of California citizens did not want to see money for schools cut back. Pollsters also concluded that concern for public schools was one of the few restraining influences that kept the yes votes from being higher. Conversely, those who favored Proposition 13 indicated a lower regard for the schools. However, 57 percent of Field's respondents added that they did not think that more money would necessarily improve the schools (the Field Institute 1978).

other elements of local government. In 1972 tax rate limits were replaced by stringent revenue limits and expenditure controls [SB 90]. As a result, the growth in school revenues was less than the rate of inflation (Riles 1978:2).

Indeed, as Riles maintained, with declining school enrollments and an inflation factor limited by SB 90 to less than an average 6 percent increase a year, education spending diminished relative to total public expenditures, which grew according to increases in assessed value and inflation.

Riles's first priority in a bailout plan was the preservation of AB 65's support for categorical funding, school reform, and foundation support. He argued that the categorical programs should not be thrown into a general funding pot, as urged by many senators and representatives from the Association of California School Administrators, California School Boards Association, and the California Teachers Association. Instead, Riles proposed that "categorical programs, with restricted funding, should each assume an equal reduction over levels previously established in AB 65" (1978:2). He also recommended a state funding strategy that would address *Serrano* equalization concerns and "reduce disparities in expenditures among districts" (1978:3). He proposed that districts spending at or below the foundation program level established in AB 65 assume a 6 percent reduction and that districts exceeding the foundation level be funded on the basis of a sliding scale with a maximum reduction of 15 percent applied to districts spending one and one-half times the foundation level or more.

Finally, Riles argued that reductions in education funding should be based on 1978–79 district information and take into account AB 65's new apportionment provisions. He concluded, "These recommendations can be accomplished by the allocation of $2.2 billion of the state's surplus and would probably mean a total statewide cut of 10 percent for schools. I believe this to be a fair and equitable portion of the surplus for education and as much of a cut as we ought to ask our schools to assume (1978:3).

After hearing fiscal experts and spokesmen for affected local agencies, the conference committee closeted itself with legislative staff to develop a bailout plan. The committee communicated with senate and assembly caucuses on major policy and partisan matters, but other Sacramento actors were not involved. Although lobbyists anxiously crowded capitol corridors during the hectic weeks following June 6, they had little role in designing the bailout. As principal consultant to the Assembly Education Committee James Murdoch explained: "Events were simply moving too fast for interest groups to have much input."[11] The concerns of education interests were indirectly represented. Even though education lobbyists could not actively participate in the bailout process, their point of view was well known to legislative staff who had worked closely with them in the development of AB 65. Gerald Hayward of the Senate Finance Committee commented:

> It was not difficult for us to understand what the education interest groups wanted; we were sensitive to their concerns as the bailout was put together. In this sense, education was much better off than other special interests. Our long-standing relationship with education interest groups was in contrast to the cities and counties, who had always held the legislature at arm's length.[12]

However, this indirect representation did not translate into special treatment for education interests. Committee ground rules established for bailout planning required that all local government entities be treated equally; no special interest hobby horses were allowed. "A decision was made early on," remembered one participant, "not to pick on anyone in particular. Because it was an election year, a high priority was given to getting by and not hurting anyone too much."[13]

Because Proposition 13 made the state banker for all local services, it changed the nature of the coalition support necessary to pass an education measure. All special interests demanded their fair share of the finite state surplus. As a result, the support necessary to approve an education measure now included not only education advocates but also other special interest advocates. A dollar allocated for education was a dollar lost to other interests.

Committee members represented an array of central legislative concerns. For example, Senator Campbell had particular interest in welfare, Assemblyman Priolo in fire and police protection. Senator Rodda and Assembly Leader McCarthy had a soft spot for education

11. James Murdoch 7 May 1980: personal communication.

12. Gerald Hayward 22 September 1978: personal communication. Hal Geiogue of the Legislative Analyst's Office also emphasized the indirect role of the Tuesday Night Group in the bailout deliberations. However, Geiogue believes that the relationship between legislative staff and education lobbyists had grown too close: "The legislative staff that dealt with the education bailout is very intertwined with the education establishment and does not work as an independent unit" (Hal Geiogue 23 January 1980: personal communication).

13. Catherine Minicucci 5 May 1980: personal communication.

and Senate President pro tem Mills was "a fanatic on transportation; he was concerned that the redevelopment districts not go into deficit."[14] Although legislative staff, as well as the committee members, were especially familiar with education concerns and knowledgeable about school finance, this close relationship could not result in disproportionate extra dollars for schools. It could only mean education bailout components that were sound technically and particularly sensitive to the complexity of local school finance.

Special interest lobbyists and even the administration were excluded from bailout planning. The policies contained in the Proposition 13 fiscal relief plan were solely the handiwork of committee members and their staff. One long-time staffer commented that this was the first time legislative staff "played such an out-front role on a piece of major legislation."[15] Indeed, the expertise, trust, and analytical sophistication of California's key legislative staff were put to the harshest test—developing a fiscally comprehensive, sound, and equitable financial plan for the state between June 7 and July 1.

Legislative leaders and their staff succeeded in devising a bill two weeks after the committee convened. On June 22, one week before the budget deadline, the joint conference committee passed the first major piece of bailout legislation—SB 154. That evening in a televised address Governor Brown described to Californians what had been done to make Proposition 13 work—asserting that the adopted measure conformed to the plan he had submitted earlier to the legislature. In a move that even his detractors called a master stroke, Brown underscored his commitment to the spirit of 13 by calling for a constitutional amendment to limit the growth of state and local spending to changes in personal income and announced the formation of a blue ribbon Commission for Government Reform to be headed by the recently retired A. Alan Post.[16] The Post commission was charged with the thorough review of state and local governance and finance and the development of proposals for substantial gov-

14. Catherine Minicucci 5 May 1980: personal communication.

15. James Murdoch 7 May 1980: personal communication.

16. Commissioners on the Post panel included Mayor Tom Bradley of Los Angeles; publisher Helen Copley of San Diego; Darlene Daniel, member of the board of directors, California League of Women Voters; labor leader John Henning of San Francisco; President Fred Heringer of the Farm Bureau; conservative UCLA economist Neil Jacoby; appellate Justice Cruz Reynoso of Sacramento; Superintendent of Public Instruction Wilson Riles; William Matson Roth, a businessman and a 1974 Brown gubernatorial opponent; Nathan Shapell,

ernmental reforms by early 1979. The following day, the governor
signed the bailout bill, and it took effect immediately.[17]

The Bailout and the Schools

The state's school system was particularly imperiled by Jarvis–Gann.
California's 1,045 school districts, which received approximately
60 percent of their revenue from local property taxes, were expected
to lose almost 30 percent of their total revenues as a result of Proposition 13 (Lipson 1980). Because schools relied more heavily on
property tax revenues than did other local services, this loss was
greater than other local agencies had to bear. Unlike cities, counties,
or special districts, which could levy special user fees or institute
other money-raising mechanisms before July 1, school districts had
no alternative revenue sources. Furthermore, Proposition 13 prevented districts from setting their own tax rates (to make up revenue loss) and from floating school construction bond issues. Indeed,
Jarvis–Gann left California with no capacity to build new schools.
Nor could permissive taxes be increased without public vote.

California's public schools also had the largest number of public
employees who would be hurt by Proposition 13 layoffs; on the
average, personnel costs amount to 85 percent of school district expenditures (Legislative Analyst 1978). To further complicate budget-

---

businessman and chairman of the Commission on Government Organization and Economy
(known as the Little Hoover Commission); Rocco Siciliano, head of the Ticor financial firm;
Caspar Weinberger, former secretary of the U.S. Department of Health, Education and Welfare and former director of the California Department of Finance; and former Governor
Ronald Reagan.

17. The $4.1 billion bailout gave schools, counties, and cities an amount that was
expected to limit their revenue loss to about 10 percent. The major provisions of the one-
year bill included:

- Specification of a formula for allocating the estimated $4.4 billion in remaining property
  taxes to schools, counties, cities, and special districts
- Clarification of the way remaining property taxes would be established and collected by
  defining assessment procedures and other questions left ambiguous by Proposition 13
- Allocation of $4.1 billion in additional state aid from the state's surplus to local govern-
  ments, thereby substantially damping the effect of the expected first-year $7 billion loss
- Specification of restrictions on the use of bailout funds to assure they would be spent in
  accord with state-determined priorities
- Establishment of an emergency loan fund to aid local agencies unable to borrow from
  private lenders to meet their cash flow requirements

balancing matters, state Education Code requirements specifically constrain the process by which school districts can lay off permanent employees because of revenue reductions.[18] Certificated employees can be laid off only after they receive preliminary notices of intent on two separate occasions and after holding hearings. Only the Los Angeles and San Diego school districts had issued necessary notices of intent by late May. As a result, most districts in the state were faced with a complex legal dilemma if state replacement funds did not materialize. Their problem was further exacerbated by the fact that schools are required by state law to remain open 175 days per year, meet class size standards, and offer certain minimum courses of study. In short, local districts depended solely on the state surplus, and there were few legal options to make the enormous cuts required by a post-Proposition 13 budget.

The committee needed to make two major decisions to develop the education portion of the bailout: What fiscal base should be used to determine district allocations? What *Serrano* mechanisms should be included?

Determining the Allocation Base

The committee wanted to make education's fair share as large as possible. Given the labor intensive character of public education, they feared Proposition 13 cuts would force staff dismissals. "We were worried about layoffs. We were worried about the district employees," explained Catherine Minicucci.[19] "The legislature is not going to let school districts lay off certificated employees," said James Murdoch, "that's just not good public policy."[20] Thus, although 1977 to 1978 was used as the base budget year for all other local government entities, the committee elected to use 1978 to 1979 as the base year for education. Because district 1978–79 budget estimates were based on AB 65's estimated overall 10 percent funding increase, this decision increased the total allocation to schools. Calculating the 10 percent aggregate Proposition 13 forced cuts on the 1978–79 school budget year meant that Proposition 13 reductions

18. Cal. Educ. Code section 44892 (West 1978).
19. Catherine Minicucci 5 May 1980: personal communication.
20. James Murdoch 7 May 1980: personal communication.

would have no effect on many districts, which would receive almost their entire expected budget.

Staff soon found that even this inflated base was not large enough to reduce the threat of teacher layoffs in urban areas. Like other states, California is experiencing an annual decline in school enrollment, most rapidly in suburban areas. Because the state support formula is based on district average daily attendance (ADA), year-old enrollment figures would channel funds away from the state's urban areas by giving more to suburban areas than their actual ADA merited. Computer simulations also showed staffers that even using current data, urban districts would suffer politically unacceptable funding losses unless other factors could be created to direct allocations among districts.

Paradoxically, their comprehensive data base and strong analytical capacity created more difficult problems for legislative staff than they faced seven years before when SB 90 was put together and district information was primitive. More knowledge about school district budgets and expenditure patterns simply made the problems more complex and solutions more difficult. Staff were able to foresee district budget problems with considerable accuracy.

Ironically, as a result of this better knowledge, bailout architects needed to invent information to make up for what they knew. Thus, committee staff quickly developed another factor to add to the formula, the phantom ADA. Districts around the state had canceled summer school and adult education programs in response to Proposition 13 uncertainty. Projected enrollments attributed to these canceled activities could be used to inflate enrollment figures without inflating costs, hence the term "phantom ADA." Phantom ADA was found primarily in urban districts, allowing legislators to direct more funds to these areas. These data base manipulations reflected committee concern that the bailout money go to the neediest districts. This concern also was politically motivated. As Gerald Hayward put it:

> The state had to use the 1978–79 budget figures for education because they had to get the money where the votes were. If the 1977–78 figures had been used, the money would not have flowed correctly. For example, if 1977–78 figures had been used, along with no adult and summer school ADA, most of the money would have flowed to elementary school districts in rural areas. With adult and summer school ADA put into the formula, unified and urban districts picked up. By calculating the school district formula on the basis

of 1977–78 summer and adult ADA and 1978–79 expenditures, the state was able to get more dollars to the right districts and give the districts more flexibility.[21]

The Bailout and *Serrano*

Proposition 13 transformed the *Serrano* issues. In a *Los Angeles Times* opinion-editorial, John McDermott wrote that Proposition 13 "could produce total compliance with the Supreme Court order almost overnight—if the legislators do not tamper with the process" (McDermott 1978).

Proposition 13 gutted the AB 65 equalization mechanism. The tax rate limits prevented districts from raising the revenues needed to reach their AB 65 spending levels. The foundation program concept then became meaningless because Proposition 13 put an absolute limit on local revenue-raising capacity, leaving the state's contribution the same. Furthermore, the AB 65 equalization provisions designed to stabilize tax rates in high-wealth districts and recapture tax revenues were struck down in the majority of school districts by the initiative's mandatory tax reduction and by imposition of a uniform statewide tax rate. With Jarvis–Gann, the issue of taxpayer equity became moot. "Equalization" now could be defined solely in terms of student expenditures.

Proposition 13 also made high-wealth districts low-wealth districts (see Table 5–1). High-wealth districts derive a greater proportion of their revenues from property taxes; thus, their percentage reduction in revenues was greater. Without state assistance to make up for lost property tax revenue, Baldwin Park would spend $155 more per ADA than Beverly Hills. Furthermore, high-wealth districts tend to spend more per ADA than low-wealth districts. As a result, their absolute dollar loss per ADA was greater, even if the percentage loss was about the same. For example, the reduction in property tax revenues in Baldwin Park was 62.1 percent; Beverly Hills suffered a 65.7 percent reduction in property tax revenues as a result of Proposition 13. However, Baldwin Park derives $383 per ADA from local tax levels compared with $2679 per ADA in Beverly Hills. Under the Jarvis–Gann initiative Baldwin Park lost $237 per ADA, and Beverly Hills lost $1759.

21. Gerald Hayward 22 September 1978: personal communication.

Table 5-1. 1978–79 Fiscal Effect of Proposition 13 on a Selected Number of Unified Districts.

Unified District	ADA	MAV[b] per ADA	Total[c] Revenue Limit per ADA	Total Property Revenue per Average Daily Attendance (ADA)[a]	
				Current Law	Proposition 13
San Bernardino	30,088	$ 13,825	$1,526	$ 636	$ 257
Baldwin Park	11,811	7,742	1,498	383	145
Stockton	25,104	20,455	1,544	893	341
Fresno	55,259	19,913	1,528	909	343
ABC	26,427	15,883	1,500	709	238
Sacramento	42,485	22,316	1,611	965	335
San Juan	50,276	20,209	1,549	913	289
San Diego	121,849	30,223	1,630	1,359	595
Los Angeles	578,511	27,235	1,700	1,269	419
Long Beach	55,871	34,674	1,658	1,488	483
Orange	32,427	24,607	1,669	1,202	576
Oakland	52,528	29,301	1,788	1,422	474
San Francisco	61,270	71,298	2,133	2,006	722
Piedmont	2,619	35,172	2,013	1,789	610
Berkeley	10,399	46,794	2,459	2,149	752
Beverly Hills	6,062	89,758	2,866	2,679	919
Emery	643	161,754	3,417	3,280	1,129
TOTAL	1,163,629[d]				

a. Does not include debt service.

b. Modified Assessed Value under current law.

c. Includes base revenue limit, voted overrides as of July 1976, State Teachers' Retirement System adjustment, necessary small high school adjustment, declining ADA adjustment, and permissive tax revenues. Does not include debt service.

Table 5-1. continued

Total Property Revenue per Average Daily Attendance (ADA)[a]				
Loss			Percentage of Reduction in Property Tax Revenue	Reduction as Percentage of Total Revenue Limit
General Purpose Revenue	Permissive and Adult Revenue	Total Revenue Loss		
$ 320	$ 59	$ 379	59.5	24.8
194	42	237	62.1	15.9
487	64	552	61.8	35.3
469	95	565	62.2	37.0
421	49	470	66.4	31.4
532	97	630	65.3	39.1
520	103	623	68.3	40.3
644	118	762	56.1	46.8
731	118	849	66.9	50.0
938	66	1,005	67.5	60.6
533	92	625	52.0	37.5
808	139	947	66.6	53.0
1,120	163	1,283	64.0	60.2
1,042	137	1,179	65.9	58.6
1,150	246	1,396	65.0	56.8
1,648	111	1,760	65.7	61.4
1,974	176	2,151	65.6	63.0

d. Represents 26.8 percent of the total ADA in 1978 to 1979.

Source: Office of the Legislative Analyst.

The state was under no legal obligation to replace lost district revenues, so Proposition 13 became an unexpected opportunity for California to achieve full *Serrano* compliance.[22] With traditional relationships between wealth and expenditures overturned, the legislature had a chance to make California's school finance system completely wealth neutral. Education bailout dollars could be allocated to equalize district expenditures either by full state assumption or by replacing revenues to high-wealth districts sufficient only to bring their spending to the level of low-wealth districts.

The joint conference committee chose neither of these full compliance strategies. Instead, the committee adopted a sliding scale. Depending on their relative expenditure levels, districts would take a cut of 9 to 15 percent in their projected budgets.[23] The critical considerations of maintaining jobs and protecting high-spending districts' basic education program determined the committee's *Serrano* response. As James Murdoch put it, "With Proposition 13, San Francisco's 'wolf' became real."[24] Staff did multiple computer simulations showing the effect of various *Serrano* strategies. They found that 15 percent was as high as the scale could go without precipitating layoffs or substantial budget deficits in high-wealth districts.

There was also a conscious effort to reduce if not eliminate cuts in the Los Angeles Unified School District (LAUSD) budget. In light of Los Angeles's size and voting strength, such cuts were seen as politically unacceptable. Michael Kirst, president of the State School Board, remembers: "The only political action taken in terms of allocating the surplus was in the case of Los Angeles. Those involved made sure that Los Angeles was at the 'kink' on the sliding scale." Similarly, Hal Geiogue, education program analyst in the Legislative Analyst's Office, commented, "One of the important lobbyists in the design of the bailout was Beth Louargand, deputy budget direc-

22. Cal. Const. art. 16, section 8, states: "From all state revenues there shall first be set apart monies to be applied by the state for support of the public school system and public institutions of higher education." However, this provision refers to the priority for distributing state funds, not the amount distributed. School money must be set apart first (in whatever amount) before funds are allocated for other purposes. Consequently, although the state might choose to replace a portion of the lost revenues, there is no legal requirement to do so.

23. It was found that a scale with a lower end of 6 percent, as Riles proposed, gave some districts more money than they had in 1977 to 1978. Accordingly, the committee decided that all districts must take at least a 9 percent cut.

24. James Murdoch 7 May 1980: personal communication.

tor from Los Angeles Unified. LAUSD wanted to make sure that they took a minimal cut on the sliding scale and they wanted adult and summer ADA [the phantom ADA] included in the base because both were big programs in Los Angeles."[25] According to the legislative staffers, "We played with the numbers until Los Angeles came out in the middle."[26] The 9 to 15 percent sliding scale met the committee's guideline to hold LAUSD harmless in any equalization scheme.

The 9 to 15 percent sliding scale adopted by the committee insured that no California district suffered major fiscal or programmatic disruption. It also achieved more equalization than would have come about under AB 65 because it leveled down at a sharper rate than previous school finance bills. James Murdoch commented:

> The "Serrano thing" has taken a back seat to everything else in the wake of Proposition 13. But Proposition 13 has resulted in a greater leveling down than AB 65 would have accomplished. We knew we could equalize more in five years with SB 154 than with AB 65.[27]

Until Proposition 13, it had been politically impossible to level down more than a small portion of high-spending districts. With Jarvis–Gann, high-spending districts became dependent upon the state, and state policymakers had new leverage.

> Because of Proposition 13, the schools are going to come a lot closer together in their expenditure patterns. In this sense, Proposition 13 helped meet the Serrano mandate. In the past, the legislature has had to fight to take money away from high-wealth districts. Now high-wealth districts have to come to the legislature to obtain money. The state has more leverage over high-wealth districts than it ever did in the past. A district like Beverly Hills was basically in the position of being a pauper and a beggar (Gerald Hayward 22 September 1978: personal communication).

The bailout formula adopted by the committee put the state in a tenuous position with regard to the Serrano mandate. To insure that no district received more than a 15 percent budget reduction, thereby ameliorating program and staff cuts, the state gave substantially more bailout funds to high-wealth districts than to low-wealth districts. In fact, the state bailout to Beverly Hills approximated

25. Hal Geiogue 23 January 1980: personal communication.
26. Paul Holmes 22 January 1980: personal communication.
27. James Murdoch 7 May 1980: personal communication.

Baldwin Park's total budget. Although the gap between Beverly Hills and Baldwin Park was reduced more by SB 154 than by AB 65, it still remained substantial. Under SB 154 Beverly Hills spent approximately $1000 more per ADA than Baldwin Park (see Table 5-2).

Because the bailout allocations were calculated upon the wealth-based disparities of the past, *Serrano* hawks questioned the constitutionality of a standard that perpetuated the inequalities the court had declared illegal.[28] The bailout scheme clearly did not satisfy the principle of wealth neutrality. As John Serrano observed in a post-bailout interview: "The result [of SB 154] is that we have the same inequalities, only now by an act of the legislature" (as quoted in Stanfield 1979:1928). However, despite his belief that the SB 154 allocation scheme was unconstitutional, *Serrano* attorney John McDermott (who reportedly was relieved that the committee chose a sliding scale instead of an even less equalizing across-the-board 10 percent cut) decided not to mount a court challenge because the bailout was a one-year emergency measure (see McDermott 1978). Reformers decided to wait and see. "In regard to the effect of SB 154 on *Serrano*," said John McDermott, "to paraphrase Mark Twain, Serrano's death has been greatly exaggerated" (as quoted in *California School Board Association Journal* 1979:8).

Tax Limitation: A New Era

The allocation plan that resulted from committee deliberations was, in the view of members, fair to all and would see the schools through their first post-Proposition 13 year with minimal disruption. SB 154's education bailout provided:

- A district revenue base that included 1978–79 AB 65 revenue limit for expected K–12 pupils, revenue limit for adult and summer school pupils credited in 1977 to 1978, plus the permissive override taxes actually collected in 1977 to 1978.

- A statewide aggregate revenue base of 90 percent of pre-Proposition 13 budget. A sliding scale would be used to fund those dis-

28. McCurdy and Speich report widespread relief in the education community as a result of SB 154 ("Outlook Brighter for Schools and College," *Los Angeles Times*, 14 June 1978).

Table 5-2. Senate Bill 154 Guarantee for a Selected Number of Unified Districts.

Unified Districts	1978-79 ADA	Senate Bill 154 Guarantee		Per 1978-79 Average Daily Attendance (ADA)	
		Local Property Tax Revenue	Apportion-ment Aid	Senate Bill 154 Surplus Aid	Total Aid
San Bernardino	29,566	$ 297	$ 894	$ 214	$1,405
Baldwin Park	11,567	133	1,182	145	1,405
Stockton	24,333	436	593	409	1,438
Fresno	51,240	361	618	402	1,381
ABC	25,138	289	900	340	1,528
Sacramento	40,950	451	623	532	1,607
San Juan	49,060	350	581	477	1,408
San Diego	117,260	591	341	462	1,393
Los Angeles	525,497	585	322	737	1,644
Orange	30,815	545	485	402	1,432
Oakland	51,006	522	379	738	1,639
Long Beach	55,949	575	136	761	1,472
San Francisco	59,769	822	133	945	1,901
Piedmont	2,357	647	156	1,111	1,914
Berkeley	10,234	752	145	1,246	2,143
Beverly Hills	5,732	1,116	136	1,288	2,541
Emery	599	1,571	126	1,270	2,968

Source: Office of the Legislative Analyst.

tricts under 1.1 times the foundation level at 91 percent of their base and those over 1.5 times the foundation level at 85 percent. Districts in between were prorated.

- A guaranteed foundation level determined by subtracting the local property tax received and providing the remainder in a state block grant.

- Funding of all categorical programs at 90 percent, except special education and teacher retirement, which would be funded at 100 percent.

- A requirement that all districts with unrestricted revenues (contingency funds) over 5 percent of their previous year's budget allocate one-third of the amount over 5 percent to offset the state block grant.

Education, which would have received about 52 percent of pre-Proposition 13 local property tax revenues, received approximately 53 percent of the available state surplus. Thus the education bailout figure of $2.267 billion was consistent with the committee goal to allocate the surplus in such a way that all local government entities got their fair share.

MAINTAINING THE STATUS QUO

With local school district expenditures unhitched from local property taxes—the traditional stumbling block to reform—Proposition 13 left the state free to equalize school district expenditures by either leveling up low-spending districts or leveling down high ones. Jarvis-Gann presented an opportunity for the legislature to achieve the wealth neutrality mandated in *Serrano II*.

However, the legislature did not use the opportunity inherent in Proposition 13 to introduce reform either in school finance or in general government services. Instead, the bailout legislation functioned to preserve the status quo. The legislative ground rule—that no local governmental entity take a disproportionate cut—guided decisions about bailout allocations. There could be no winners or losers. A leveling up strategy—the only policy that would not cripple many school districts and cause certificated employees to be laid off—was rejected for two reasons. It was inconsistent with the general principle that everyone take their fair cut. It also was politically impossible given the limited funds available for the bailout. Leveling up would require that education receive more than its proportionate share of the state surplus, thereby disrupting local government services. In one sense, the unwillingness of the legislature to take what Catherine Minicucci called "the obvious Serrano steps" reflects the California legislature's unwillingness to engage in a more general rethinking of governmental objectives and the distribution of public goods.[29]

There are several reasons why the legislature did not use the opportunity of Proposition 13 to consider more general reform. The most obvious was lack of time. The bailout package was put together under intense pressure in two weeks. There was little time to consider reform. Furthermore, Proposition 13 signaled fiscal retrenchment, thereby raising critically different public policy questions from those considered during preceding years of expansion. The state government had no experience in funding many of the local services rescued by the bailout. Appreciating the errors that could occur in the design of a policy to manage retrenchment—even one that sustained the status quo—legislators wisely saw SB 154 as a temporary, one-year measure.

Nor was fundamental rethinking forced by fiscal constraints. The state surplus was sufficiently large to accommodate the status quo and to preclude hard choices about priorities. Fewer state resources might have pried the legislature loose from perpetuation of existing structures and commitments. Less money might have required legislators to reconsider the ways in which various local services were delivered and the relationships among them.

Because 1978 was an election year, reform would have important political costs. According to Gerald Hayward, "The election year had a major effect on the bailout. It put a lot of pressure on the legislature to get a solution as fast as possible and to keep it simple."[30] Resolving the conflicts among competing interests, as typically required by substantive reformulation of governmental objectives and routines, is nothing less than a reallocation of society's values. Sacramento actors saw Proposition 13 as a pocketbook war; legislators did not perceive a constituency for significant governmental overhaul. In the absence of fiscal necessity or constituent pressure, change in the

29. Catherine Minicucci 5 May 1980: personal communication.
30. Gerald Hayward 22 September 1978: personal communication.

distribution of social values was viewed as an unnecessary political risk.[31]

For all of these reasons, the legislature bypassed major reform opportunities as the bailout was put together. It was easier and more politically expedient for the legislature to treat the new economic problems of Proposition 13 as a disbursement problem than as an opportunity for a major change in the distribution of resources.

This legislative posture had critical consequences for school finance reform. Legislative ground rules put the reform of *Serrano* on a collision course with the reform of Jarvis–Gann. The fiscal retrenchment precipitated by Proposition 13 significantly curtailed the legislature's flexibility to frame school finance reform solutions, given legislative commitment to treat all of the various local government entities equally. The responses of the past, in which some districts gained but none were hurt, were no longer possible. Past solutions to *Serrano* had always meant more money. In a world constrained by Jarvis–Gann, school finance reform assumed significant new political and public policy costs. Leveling down, possible now that high-wealth districts had lost over 60 percent of their funds, threatened to destroy district programs and force employee layoffs. Legislators took this possibility seriously. Leveling up could be achieved only at the expense of other governmental services. Proposition 13, in short, created a decisionmaking environment in which equalization and tax limitation could become mutually exclusive and competitive.[32]

Exactly how the legislature would resolve the conflicts between these two reform movements in the long run cannot be accurately predicted by the hectic coping that followed the June 6 vote. The legislature was faced with new problems and a short time in which to solve them. The result was a purely legislative solution, molded by little of the administrative jockeying, special interest lobbying, or partisan negotiations that characterize other exercises in coalition politics.

---

31. Asked about the secret of political longevity in an 11 June 1980 television interview, retiring Republican leader Paul Priolo suggested that such revisions are risky in any event. He neatly summed up this political logic by advising: "Do nothing and you'll get elected forever."

32. Michael W. Kirst (1980) traces the development and conflict of the school finance reform movement and the tax limitation movement. He points out that the only area of partial agreement between school finance reform and adherents of tax reform and spending limits is in dislike of the local property tax as the major means for financing education.

ASSEMBLY BILL 8: THE POLITICS
OF RETRENCHMENT

The economics of retrenchment were top priority as Sacramento actors reconvened for the 1978–79 legislative session. Most policy-makers agreed with Senator John Dunlap (D–Napa) that the bailout legislation "did a pretty good job" of portioning out the available money (*Los Angeles Times*, 2 August 1978). They also believed that a long-term legislative response to Proposition 13 should emerge from an open process of consultation and bargaining. The closed-door sessions that spawned SB 154 could be defended as an emergency strategy but were contrary to the basic ground rules of coalition politics.

Both the legislature and the state board of education moved quickly to solicit the views of practitioners and citizens. But the concerns centered on providing adequate funding for the public schools, not upon a remedy for *Serrano*. Senator Dunlap called upon the Educational Congress of California to conduct statewide hearings to plan public school financing in the aftermath of Proposition 13 (*Los Angeles Times*, 2 August 1978). The state board of education convened a thirty-three-member citizens' advisory panel to study school finance methods. Senator Ralph Dills (D–Gardena), "one of the education establishment's biggest supporters in the legislature," turned to the Tuesday Night Group to develop a school finance proposal (*Los Angeles Times*, 23 January 1979). Dills called upon CTA's James Donnally. Donnally remembers:

> Around December of 1978, Dills called and said, "Write me a school finance bill." I promised Dills a good coalition bill. We had already begun working on a bill right after the passage of SB 154. I was chair of the technical committee that put together the prototype for Dills' bill.[32]

In response to Dills's request, Donnally closeted himself with LAUSD's Beth Louargand to develop a wish list and a comprehensive proposal.

The administration, which had strategically excluded itself from development of the bailout, was anxious to assert its position on the management of retrenchment. Governor Brown directed the Department of Finance to develop a bill to fund schools and local gov-

33. James Donnally 22 January 1980: personal communication.

ernments. Meanwhile, staff for both the Senate and the Assembly Education Committees were put to work on proposals.

Four Finance Alternatives

Senator Dills was first off the mark. On 22 January 1979, Dills introduced the long-term school finance bill, developed by the Tuesday Night Group Technical Committee, SB 234. The bill was backed by the education lobby: Superintendent Wilson Riles and the State Department of Education (SDE), the State Board of Education, California Teachers Association (CTA), California Federation of Teachers (CFT), LAUSD, and United Teachers of Los Angeles. It called for $796 million in state support for the schools, $400 million more than proposed by the governor's budget. The bill also assumed that the state would provide another $2.2 billion in bailout funds for education (*Los Angeles Times*, 23 January 1979). Dills's proposal would grant an average 11 percent funding increase to school districts. To ensure Riles's support, the bill included funding for the School Improvement Program and the categorical structure pushed by the SDE even though fiscal hard times had effectively eliminated the lukewarm support for categoricals that existed within the Tuesday Night Group (see Kirst and Somers 1980).

SB 234 acknowledged *Serrano* through a weak squeeze factor. As a product of the Tuesday Night Group Technical Committee, SB 234's minimization of *Serrano* issues is not surprising. As the AB 65 debates showed, *Serrano* equalization was something the Tuesday Night Group was willing to abide as long as the high-spending districts and politically powerful LAUSD were not seriously hurt. With the exception of the Association of Low-Wealth School Districts, few members of the Tuesday Night Group even pretended *Serrano* concerns. For example, Charles Mitchell, Oakland's legislative advocate, remarked: "The Tuesday Night Group really didn't think about *Serrano*. That was the Legislature's headache, not ours."[34] Another district lobbyist asked, "*Serrano* who?"[35] Or Steve Rhoads, a legislative staffer and *Serrano* advocate grown somewhat bitter about the educators' priorities said: "The lobbyists don't give a damn about *Serrano*. All they want is more money."[36]

34. Charles Mitchell 20 August 1979: personal communication.
35. Mike Dillon 6 May 1980: personal communication.
36. Steve Rhoads 21 January 1980: personal communication.

Governor Brown laid out the Department of Finance developed proposal with much fanfare at a March 6 news conference (*Los Angeles Times*, 24 March 1979). "The days of hard choices are upon us," counseled the governor in explaining his plan. Brown's proposal called for another one-year bailout. Schools, again, would get slightly more than one-half of the funds, with an average increase of 7.1 percent for the state's school systems. Unlike the education lobby's initiative, Brown's proposal also called for a vigorous *Serrano* squeeze. Brown wanted to solve *Serrano* once and for all within the fiscal constraints of Jarvis–Gann. The governor, like the legislature, wanted to eliminate as much uncertainty as possible from the post-Proposition 13 environment. A strong *Serrano* measure could defuse a possible *Serrano III*. The stringent administration plan, based on extremely conservative Department of Finance estimates of the state's surplus, was seen as penurious and had trouble finding sponsorship (Kirst and Somers 1980). It was finally carried by Senator John Holmdahl (D–Castro Valley) as SB 550.

About the same time, Assembly Education Committee Chairman Leroy Greene introduced long-term finance bill AB 8 in response to Proposition 13's ban on local school construction bonds. Greene's bill, primarily a capital outlay measure, proposed a $650 million funding level for public education, more than the governor's proposal but less than the generous Dills measure.

Unhappy with the administration proposal and with Dills's SB 234 and fearful that a long-term bill, such as Greene's could not gain approval, Senator Albert Rodda introduced a fourth finance bill, SB 186, in March. Rodda said his bill, which would provide $47 billion in second-year bailout funds to local government and the schools—$354 million more than proposed by Brown—was simply a back-up measure that might be needed only if no acceptable long-range measure emerged (*Los Angeles Times*, 28 April 1979).

Legislative response to these four substantively different finance proposals began to define California's response to the politics of Jarvis–Gann, the reality of fiscal retrenchment, and the future of school finance reform. The governor's proposal, SB 550, which some participants called "laugh tracks," was never seriously considered by the legislature (see Kirst and Somers 1980). Republicans and Democrats, as well as the education lobbyists, strenuously objected to the administration's proposal on a number of grounds. They felt that the proposed funding level was unnecessarily low. Brown's proposal, in the view of many legislators, underestimated the available state sur-

plus and imposed unnecessarily tight budgetary guidelines. Legislators and their staff agreed with Wilson Riles who called Department
of Finance estimates "flaky" (*Los Angeles Times*, 23 January 1979).

In addition, legislators, even former *Serrano* supporters, objected
to the bill's equalization scheme which would equalize expenditures
for approximately 93 percent of the state's public school students by
1983 to 1984 (*Los Angeles Times*, 20 April 1979). SB 550 allowed
little or no growth in the revenue limits for high-spending districts.
Some districts would actually take a cut. For example, although the
governor's proposal gave an average 7.1 percent increase in education
spending, San Francisco, home of Assembly Speaker Leo McCarthy,
would assume a 0.7 percent reduction. Opposition to the scheme was
immediate and vigorous. State board of education member Louis
Honig, Jr. protested: "You're going to kill the public schools in
those areas" (*Los Angeles Times*, 24 March 1979). Even school
finance reform advocate Assemblyman Leroy Greene expressed adamant opposition in an exchange with Department of Finance Chief
Richard Silberman: "We were choking those high-spending districts
pretty hard. . . . What you're asking us is to squeeze the life right out
of them" (*Los Angeles Times*, 20 April 1979). Greene and others
saw the bill's equalization measures as a meat axe that would unnecessarily destroy the basic educational programs in high-expenditure
districts.

Finally, legislators objected to a one-year measure. Although legislative leaders recognized that a longer term measure would be hard to
pass, they felt it was important to try. A short-term measure would
leave local governments and school districts uncertain about long-
range plans; more important, leaders believed that it would not be
possible to pass as good a bill in 1980, an election year (California
School Boards Association 1979).

For all of these reasons, the legislators felt no enthusiasm for the
governor's proposal. "The drubbing given to SB 550 in the legislature," said Assemblyman Leroy Greene, "shows that there is relative
unanimity in what we *won't* do" (Educational Congress of California
1979a: 5, emphasis in the original). The legislature would not enact
an unnecessarily stringent budget; it would not, in Leroy Greene's
words, "squeeze the hell out of high-wealth districts."[37] It would

---

37. Mary Bergan, legislative director, CFT, to Senator John Holmdahl, 10 May 1979.

not accept a one-year plan without some serious effort to reach agreement on a long-range measure.

Although the governor's bill, SB 550, quickly died, Senator Dills's SB 234 received a great deal of attention. Visible and vocal support from the education establishment, orchestrated by Tuesday Night Group teacher union lobbyists, insured the measure broad attention from the press. California teachers initiated an intensive five-month lobbying effort as soon as the bill was introduced. At a Sacramento kickoff rally by the 157,000-member CTA, teachers stressed that "kids were not the target" of Proposition 13 (*Sacramento Bee*, 2 February 1979). To the music of a banjo and guitar, the teachers sang, there will be "no more Proposition 13 over me" (*Sacramento Bee*, 2 February 1979). Wilson Riles emphasized the importance of a long-term school finance measure: "Now is the time to establish a funding system which is free of the disruption and uncertainty of year-to-year funding" (*Los Angeles Times*, 23 January 1979).

Educator lobbying efforts apparently paid off. On 7 March 1979, SB 234 zipped through the Senate Education Committee on an eight to zero vote. However, Senator Rodda, member of the Senate Education Committee and chairman of the influential Senate Finance Committee, abstained from voting, calling the measure "fiscally irresponsible" (*Los Angeles Times*, 8 March 1979).

SB 234 cleared Senate Finance on April 16, on an eight to two vote. At this point, members of the education lobby redoubled their efforts to win support for the bill. For example, the California Federation of Teachers sent flyers to their members, telling them that "before April 26 [the Senate floor vote] every senator should be contacted and asked to vote for SB 234. Contacts should be made by students, parents, teachers, trustees, and school administrators. A vote for SB 234 on the Senate floor is a vote for California's students."[38]

Again, educators were successful in winning support on the senate floor. However, as SB 234 headed off for the Assembly Education Committee, influential and possibly fatal objections to the bill were surfacing in Sacramento. Department of Finance Chief Silberman warned that the governor would never sign such a costly bill. Senator Rodda continued to attack the bill as fiscally irresponsible because it

---

38. California Federation of Teachers, "Long-Range School Money Bill Reaches Senate Floor," undated memo.

allocated too much money to the schools. Assembly Speaker Leo McCarthy took up Rodda's argument. He declared SB 234 incompatible with the fiscal logic of Proposition 13 in which lawmakers must consider the state pie as a whole:

> I don't think we can vote out a $1.3 billion school finance bill in a vacuum unless we are prepared to say where that $1.3 billion comes from. . . . In the Assembly, we're trying, on a bi-partisan basis, to put it all in one place and get everybody to say, "OK, if you want this number of school dollars, you've got to be prepared to vote against dollars in these other areas" (*Los Angeles Times*, 3 April 1979).

Senator Dills, the CTA, CFT, LAUSD, and the State Department of Education kept pushing hard for a separately funded school finance bill that would give school districts a level of funding they could have expected if Proposition 13 had failed. The coalition supporting SB 234 had a narrow focus: more money for the schools. Dills defended this single interest orientation: "I would hope [that these activities would] not be tied together because school finance and local government finance really don't belong together" (*Los Angeles Times*, 3 April 1979).

To paraphrase James Murdoch, with Proposition 13 the educators' wolf became real. Although educators chronically report fiscal crisis, with Proposition 13 growth in funding for California's public school dropped for the first time since the Depression year of 1934. Jack McCurdy of the *Los Angeles Times* reported:

> The state's schools in 1978-79—the first year of the Proposition 13 era—will receive $200 million, or 2.3 percent less than the $9.4 billion they received from local property taxes, federal aid and state aid in 1977-78, according to state calculations.
>
> The 2.3 percent drop is a sharp reversal of 44 years of steady spending growth. For the past five years alone, funds for schools have increased at an average 9 percent annual rate.
>
> Even with the $200 million overall loss, however, a majority of school districts in California will have more money to spend this year than last—though in nearly all cases it will be less than they would have received if Proposition 13 had failed (1 October 1978).

However, the plight of the schools was not substantially different from that of the cities and counties (*Los Angeles Times*, 1 October 1978). To legislative influentials, Dills's position and that of his supporters harked back to another era—the salad days of growth-financed public policy. The SB 234 stance created tension within the legislature and within the Tuesday Night Group. Catherine Minicucci, Senate Office of Research, said that the aggressiveness of SB 234 supporters angered key legislators and made it harder for legislative staff education advocates to make a strong case for education:

> Rodda and the others were really angry with the educators. They thought that they asked for too much. The education lobby alienated a lot of the staff. The [SB] 234 people didn't know when to stop; they became a walking joke. From our perspective, they were kind of bogus all along. Their prototype was bogus; it represented LAUSD. It didn't represent statewide interests. Also, the schools thought they could get a bill alone, without the municipalities. That ended up being quite divisive. It weakened support for the education provisions Senate and Assembly staff were trying to put together.*

Dissension in the Education Coalition

The issues Minicucci outlined were among those that began to rupture the Tuesday Night Group by mid-spring. For the first time since its inception, Tuesday Night Group members were unable to reach agreement on an acceptable school finance strategy. The teachers' unions and the big districts, notably LAUSD, lobbied energetically for SB 234. Their support was straightforward. SB 234 meant a large funding increase for schools. However, other important members of the Tuesday Night Group did not agree with this funding strategy. Disagreement centered on the share of state revenues suggested for education, the bill's cursory *Serrano* component, and inclusion of categorical support for the School Improvement Program. For example, the Association of California School Administrators (ACSA) opposed SB 234 primarily because, like Rodda and McCarthy, they thought it fiscally irresponsible. Gordon Winton, director of ACSA's Legislative Office, explained: "ACSA thought that Dills's bill was impossible. We thought it better to work for the possible. But we went along to keep the coalition together."[39] Neither did the Association of Low-Wealth Schools support Dills's bill. Mike Dillon, legislative advocate for the Association of Low-Wealth Schools, commented: "The low-wealth districts didn't support SB 234. We

*Catherine Minicucci 5 May 1980: personal communication.
39. Gordon Winton 6 May 1980: personal communication.

couldn't support it because it really didn't have any *Serrano* mechanisms. But we kept our disagreement within the group."[40]

Two Tuesday Night Group participants went public with their opposition, causing bitterness. Cal–Tax, California taxpayers' public-expenditure control organization, announced early resistance to the bill on the grounds that it was too expensive and failed to address two central issues: *Serrano* equalization and the $9 billion unfunded liability of the State Teachers' Retirement System (see Parks 1979). Bonnie Parks, then senior research analyst, reports that she was subsequently encouraged not to attend Tuesday Night Group sessions "so I wouldn't learn their strategies."[41]

Although Tuesday Night Group members were annoyed at Cal–Tax's disavowal of their bill, public lack of support from a major education group, the California School Boards Association (CSBA), caused the most dissension. The CSBA had established a finance task force after the passage of Proposition 13 to "study the immediate needs of schools and develop long-range proposals to meet the funding needs of all districts. . . . [The task force proposal] was adopted by CSBA's governing body and later used to compare the four main school finance proposals . . . before the Legislature" (California School Boards Association 1979:6). Because of their task force report, CSBA Sacramento representatives were unable to support SB 234. Dills's measure was inconsistent with a number of CSBA principles for school finance legislation. Most important, CSBA believed the SB 234 funding level was unrealistic and would jeopardize working relationships with other local governmental entities. They were also concerned that SB 234 did not address the unique funding needs of small school districts (California School Boards Association 1979:7).

In addition, the CSBA was troubled by the lack of SB 234 attention to *Serrano* equalization. CSBA's feelings on this point came not from strong *Serrano* advocacy but from a belief that the group should support a bill that was legislatively feasible. Herbert Salinger, CSBA executive director, put it: "[SB] 234 didn't grapple with *Serrano*. We knew there was no way that the legislature would pass a bill that didn't deal with *Serrano*." Salinger says that the CSBA tried to minimize their position in order to maintain the cohesion of the

40. Mike Dillon 6 May 1980: personal communication.
41. Bonnie Parks 5 May 1980: personal communication.

Tuesday Night Group: "We tried hard to make it clear to the group that we didn't *oppose* [SB 234], that we were just taking a 'watch' position, but our position led to a major breaking of the ranks. We were also angry when people, especially Marion Joseph's troops, started making end-runs, contacting local board members and so on."[42]

Wilson Riles and the State Department of Education were also prominent defectors from the SB 234 bandwagon. Riles had come under fire from Senate Education Committee Chairman Paul Carpenter, his long-time political foe, for using the Friends of Public Education group to organize support for Riles's categorical initiatives. Friends of Public Education was supported by SDE funds and staff, so Riles was charged with improper lobbying and illegal use of state funds. The Tuesday Night Group used Riles's political embarrassment to yield to legislative demands to abandon SIP. As the Tuesday Night Group dropped their support of SIP, Riles withdrew the department's support for the coalition measure (see Kirst and Somers 1980).

With these internal disputes and legislative rumblings apparent, SB 234 proponents should not have been completely surprised when the Assembly Education Committee killed the bill. In a hearing room packed with an estimated 500 persons—including school-aged children, parents, and teachers—the bill died on a three to one vote. Most members abstained. Dills immediately charged that the bill had been killed on orders from Speaker McCarthy. "Thank you very much for the charade," snapped Dills. "We're playing political games here that we should not be playing with our educational systems" (*Los Angeles Times*, 31 May 1979). Greene told Dills that McCarthy had not asked him to scuttle the plan and that "there's no chance in the world in my opinion that anything that approaches this amount of money can be in a long-range bill" (*Los Angeles Times*, 31 May 1979). Or as Greene later said to a meeting of the Educational Congress: "Dills's bill has all the good things in it . . . that we can't afford" (Educational Congress of California 1979a).

---

42. Herbert Salinger 5 May 1980: personal communication. Marion Joseph is Wilson Riles's influential assistant. She is primarily responsible for organizing the Friends of Public Education, a grass-roots organization also called Marion's Army. This group can mount extraordinarily effective—and from a legislator's perspective, irritating—lobbying efforts on short notice.

An Omnibus Bill Emerges

With the demise of SB 234, hopes for a long-term finance bill centered on Leroy Greene's AB 8. Early in April Speaker McCarthy had initiated meetings with assembly minority leader Paul Priolo (R–Malibu). The leaders hoped to fashion a bipartisan, long-term solution to Proposition 13. Greene's AB 8, originally a school finance, capital outlay bill, was amended to provide a long-term source of funding for all local government entities.

The assembly version of AB 8 contained a number of features aimed at winning support from assemblymen. In particular, LAUSD, other urban district lobbyists, and assembly Democrats were pushing hard for continuation of the Urban Impact Aid program, originally devised to win Assembly Ways and Means Chairman Willie Brown, Jr.'s support for SB 90. Urban Impact Aid, which goes to high-spending urban districts and is *not* included in the revenue limit calculations for *Serrano* equalization, was to have been phased out. Instead, to appease Willie Brown and other urban Democrats, it was continued in AB 8 and increased by $18 million.

AB 8 then went off to the Senate Education Committee. Chairman Paul Carpenter (D–Santa Ana) greeted the measure disdainfully:

> Somebody left a dead cat at the Senate doorstep this week and the Assembly leadership insists that it is alive. Backroom deals have wiped out a bold attempt to get classroom construction legislation and replaced that provision with costly, permanent funding of categorical programs whose merits are, at best, questionable. . . . Far too much is being given away to help employees become funded categorically, rather than to help children become funded wisely. . . . The political tradeoff involving the doubling, and making permanent, expenditures for "urban impact aid" is very troublesome. . . . These public policies should be debated on their merits, not as horsetrades made overnight and free of public scrutiny and testimony.[42]

Carpenter, like most of his senate colleagues, especially objected to the continuation of categorical funding for the School Improvement Program and for services targeted to disadvantaged and bilingual children. He did not like the side payment to urban districts — urban impact aid. Senators had battled with assembly leaders, strong supporters of categorical programs, during the AB 65 debates. The

---

43. Senator Paul B. Carpenter, 8 June 1979: press release.

senate acquiesced at that time because they felt there was enough money to fund the foundation program as well as categorical programs. In a time of fiscal stringency, however, they believed that continuation of categorical programs would erode the funds available for general support of the schools. Both Wilson Riles and assembly Democrats insisted that categorical programs should continue. William Whiteneck of the State Department of Education summed up the rationale of categorical program supporters:

> What was important to the State Department of Education [as AB 8 was debated] was the structure of school finance. It was important during AB 65 and it is even more important now. We are adamant that the structure we set in place move forward. It would take a bombshell to move Wilson Riles off that position. In California, given its diversity, we must have a base program plus dollars not open to bargaining. We will fight to keep the special programs out of the base. From AB 65 to AB 8, what the department has continued to say is that these pieces are interrelated and cannot be separated.[44]

Anticipating this problem, assembly leaders inserted a compromise they hoped would be acceptable: The categorical programs would be sunsetted in AB 8; their authorization would expire on a fixed schedule, and they would be reconsidered at that time.

The *Serrano* issue proved more difficult. Ironically, Proposition 13 created a new constituency for *Serrano*. An enlarged Republican caucus made it clear that they wanted *Serrano* addressed more vigorously than it had been before. Republican legislators primarily represent suburban bedroom communities that, because of their generally low-spending status, stood to gain from a forceful *Serrano* measure now that property was taxed at a uniform rate statewide. Chairman Carpenter and the Republican caucus advocated inclusion of the so-called Republican Plan developed by Steve Rhoads of the assembly Republican caucus. Rhoads's plan would have brought 97 percent of the state's students within the court-ordered $100 range by 1983 to 1984. However, the Republican proposal was politically and economically expensive. To pay for this equalization, the plan would have eliminated increases for many of the categorical programs, cut the size of the Urban Impact Aid increase, eliminated financial support for the School Improvement Program, and recomputed financial aid for districts with declining enrollment, thereby deflating the

---

44. William Whiteneck 5 February 1980: personal communication.

declining enrollment factor. Urban districts, consequently, would lose the most through the Republican plan.

On Wednesday, June 13 Carpenter invited *Serrano* attorney John McDermott to testify before the committee. McDermott called the Republican proposal, which the Senate Committee on Education had just amended into AB 8, "a historic . . . resolution of the *Serrano* case." McDermott agreed that the Republican plan Carpenter supported made it possible "for the first time for the legislature and the plaintiffs to consider the potential of a final resolution of the *Serrano* case" (*Sacramento Bee*, 14 June 1979). In a flurry of emotion and self-congratulation, Carpenter's proposal was passed and the committee adjourned for lunch.

This resolution of *Serrano* was shortlived. Opponents to the measure got busy as soon as the committee adjourned, pressuring members to change their votes. In what has been dubbed the "Wednesday Night Massacre," the committee voted eight to two when it reconvened to rescind its morning decision. According to Jim Browne, consultant to the Senate Committee on Education, "When Carpenter saw all of his amendments fall, he knew it had been orchestrated. Rodda absented himself from the vote, then he and Catherine Minicucci got on the telephone and got everyone except Jerry Smith (D–Saratoga) to change their votes."[45] The *Sacramento Bee* reports: "The Los Angeles Unified School District, the California Teachers Association, United Teachers of Los Angeles, and minority education lobbyists worked seven hours to get the Committee to change their position" (14 June 1979).

After rejecting the Republican proposal, the committee inserted the school finance provision of Rodda's SB 186, which was very much like the AB 65 inflation squeeze, and added portions of the Dills bill that the education lobby thought most critical, in particular the inflation factor and declining enrollment components. "Now we're back to the old education game — diving for dollars," protested Senator Jerry Smith (*Sacramento Bee*, 14 June 1979). However, the committee's action is precisely what some members of the education lobby hoped would happen. Ron Prescott, then lobbyist for LAUSD, said:

> SB 234 was a pressure strategy. It would have given us a trillion dollars. I don't think anyone thought it would pass. The CTA needed a bill. Mean-

45. Jim Browne 5 February 1980: personal communication.

while, AB 8 was happening. The press focuses on Dills's bill because of all the noise we are making. The educators are all jumping around and saying, "That's what we want." Therefore, the writers of AB 8 were willing to amend to include some of the things we thought were important.[46]

James Murdoch of the Assembly Education Committee agrees with Prescott's analysis: "Dills's bill served a useful purpose. It was the squeaky wheel. It kept pressure on for more money for schools. It had important psychological effects."[47]

In an effort to kill the categoricals, Carpenter reduced the assembly appropriations for SIP from $140 million to a token $2,[48] reduced Urban Impact Aid by $15 million, inserted language to warn planners that the Special Education Program may not be expanded, and cut driver-training programs. According to Paul McGuckin, then of the Senate Education Committee staff, a primary objective was to get the bill to the Legislative Conference Committee as quickly as possible by presenting the senate with the very bill it had approved earlier and then sending it promptly to the assembly for nonconcurrence (Education Congress of California 1979b).

These strategic purposes were realized and the bill was sent to a joint senate–assembly conference committee, chaired by Leroy Greene. Here the education lobby's pressure strategy guaranteed a place for Senator Ralph Dills to guard those portions of SB 234 amended into AB 8. As CFT's Mary Bergan put it: "The major contribution of SB 234 was to assure Dills's presence on the Conference Committee." Here a protracted debate centered on a *Serrano* mechanism. Tension mounted as the July 1 constitutional deadline for enactment of the state budget passed, and no resolution was in sight.

Republicans in both houses threatened to vote against the bill unless the *Serrano* component was strengthened. Urban Democrats, who represented districts that were home to a significant number of "John Serranos," protested that Rhoads's proposal would cost them

46. Ron Prescott 5 May 1980: personal communication.

47. James Murdoch 7 May 1980: personal communication.

48. Two dollars were appropriated for strategic reasons. If the committee completely eliminated SIP from the budget, appropriation for the program would have reverted to the level specified in AB 65—which was 10 percent more than the $140 million appropriated by SB 154. Shortly after this committee action, an education consultant to the Senate Finance Committee saw William Whiteneck from the State Department of Education and strong SIP supporter in a capitol corridor. He reached in his wallet and handed Whiteneck $2, saying, "Senator Carpenter didn't want you to have to wait for your appropriation" (Paul McGuckin 27 August 1980: personal communication).

crucial dollars. Both senate and assembly staff members continued to work with Steve Rhoads's Republican proposal trying to identify a compromise. That proposal departed from the previous school finance squeeze scheme by allocating funds on a sliding *dollar* scale rather than on a *percent* sliding scale. This strategy moved toward compliance at a much faster rate because a percent-based scale by definition perpetuated the old wealth-related revenue limits. For example, a district that received only 9 percent (the low end of the SB 154 scale) of its $2,500 revenue limit would receive $225 per ADA from the state. A district receiving the maximum SB 154 increase of 15 percent of its $1,300 revenue would receive only $156 per ADA. Rhoads's scheme gave high-spending districts absolutely fewer dollars rather than a smaller percentage of their revenue limit.

Rhoads's scheme as proposed had numerous difficulties. It was too expensive and cut categoricals as well as important political side payments, such as the urban impact factor and the declining enrollment component, in order to support the sharp proposed leveling up. It would certainly encounter stiff opposition in the assembly. The proposal also had technical problems with critical political implications: Staff could not fit Rhoads's model to the *Serrano* line or the equalization slope that the conference committee had established. The committee had already agreed how much of a squeeze would be placed on high-spending districts. Steve Rhoads said: "The 'political' problem with the Republican proposal was that somebody had to be a loser. And the loser was Los Angeles. L.A. went crazy so the proposal was withdrawn."[49] At least two members of the conference committee, Senator Milton Marks, a San Francisco Republican, and Assemblyman Howard Berman, a Los Angeles Democrat (whose district included Beverly Hills), would kill any bill that cut too sharply into high-spending districts either through reduction of urban-oriented categoricals or absolute dollar decreases. Catherine Minicucci said: "We had to devise some kind of system that [didn't fly in the face of *Serrano* but] didn't hurt Beverly Hills. Influential people like Howard Berman, they have to go home."[50]

The committee had reached agreement on an equalization slope that they believed suburban Republicans as well as urban Democrats would accept. At this point, according to Assembly Education Com-

49. Steve Rhoads 21 January 1980: personal communication.
50. Catherine Minicucci 5 May 1980: personal communication.

mittee consultant James Murdoch, "Bob Wells in the Department of Finance saved school finance for that year."[51] Wells took the Rhoads model and the total dollar amount for education that Murdoch told him he had to work with—education's fair share—and after forty-eight hours of computer runs emerged with dollar figures that could fit the conference committee line. Paul Holmes, Assembly Education Committee, said, "We had to get some version of the Rhoads' mechanism into AB 8. We couldn't get a two-thirds vote without the Republicans. Plus, the Department of Finance was squeaking about *Serrano*."[52] Although Republicans wanted to send more education dollars to their suburban districts, the Department of Finance was concerned that legislative disregard of Proposition 13's full compliance opportunity would lead to *Serrano III* and a finding for the plaintiffs that would cost the state more money.

With this distant cousin of the Republican proposal in place, the conference committee approved AB 8 on 18 July 1979. Now that the July 1 budget deadline had passed, the education lobby, worried that they might end up with no bill, quickly circulated a memorandum of support to legislators:

> The undersigned members of the educational community urge your support of AB 8. . . . Although the bill falls short of education's total needs, we recognize the political and economic realities and feel that the efforts of the Conference Committee resulted in a bill which gives equitable treatment to all involved entities.
>
> Now it is most essential that the bill be sent to the governor immediately so that school districts can prepare their budgets for the fiscal year which began on July 1.[53]

The $4.85 billion post-Proposition 13 omnibus funding package was sent to both houses, where it passed quickly with little debate. And somewhat to the surprise of education supporters, Governor Brown signed the bill on 24 July 1979.[54]

---

51. James Murdoch 7 May 1980: personal communication.

52. Paul Holmes 22 January 1980: personal communication.

53. Memo "To All Senators and Assemblymen," 18 July 1979.

54. In his message, the governor noted that the bill contains a deflator clause that provides for the reduction of funds to cities, counties, special districts, and schools if state revenues decline. Many Sacramento observers said it was this clause that caused him to sheath his blue pencil since AB 8 was $145 million more that he wanted (California Teachers Association 1979).

AB 8 allocated $2.8 billion to K–12 schools and community colleges, more than most education advocates dared to hope for. Significant provisions of AB 8 for K–12 districts are the following (drawn from Legislative Analyst 1979):

- A statutory cost-of-living adjustment for K–12 school district revenue per ADA of 8.6 percent in 1979 to 1980. Further increases are by minimum and maximum revenue limit increases with a 1980–81 minimum dollar increase of $85 per ADA and a maximum dollar increase of $175 per ADA.

- Funding sufficient to bring 76 percent of ADA in elementary school districts, 66 percent of ADA in high school districts, and 86 percent of ADA in unified school districts into compliance with *Serrano* requirements by 1983 to 1984.

- Calculation of 1979–80 school district revenue on the basis of authorized 1978–79 revenue rather than actual revenue.

- Continuation of funding for phantom summer school and adult education program attendance.

- Provision of a small district revenue limit increase for districts with high transportation costs.

- Provision of an additional $18 million for Urban Impact Aid and continuation of the program.

- Provisions to sunset categorical aid programs beginning in 1981 to 1982 unless programs are continued by legislative action.

- State assumption of the additional cost of a more fully funded State Teachers' Retirement System.

THE POLITICS OF RETRENCHMENT

The increasing governmental burden that taxpayers rejected with Proposition 13 was largely a result of the coalition character of representative government—of the side payments necessary to maintain the coalition and the consequent growth in governmental budgets. How does this form of government work when it is no longer possible to make side payments that require new funds? How does reform fare in a period of fiscal retrenchment?

After all the debate and horsetrading leading to AB 8, the legislature passed a bill that looked remarkably like the emergency bailout measure SB 154. AB 8 gave school districts just a little more than half the available state resources, as did SB 154. AB 8 continued, as did SB 154, the school finance structure that had been built by the bargains and compromises struck in SB 90 and AB 65 — categorical funding, the urban factor, and a differential squeeze factor. "AB 8 was essentially SB 154, bag and baggage," said Paul McGuckin, then with the Senate Committee on Education. "There was no attempt in AB 8 to rethink K-12 finance."[55]

AB 8 shows that the immediate — and almost politically reflexive — reaction of policymakers to Proposition 13 accurately foreshadowed California government's long-term response to fiscal retrenchment. It is not entirely surprising that the debates of an entire legislative session yielded the same result as the hectic two week joint conference committee session. This outcome reflects in large measure the character of California legislative decisionmaking. As the *Serrano* story illustrates, the California legislature has unusually impressive expertise. That plus the concomitant high quality of information available to decisionmakers produced a technically sound bailout measure. There were few serious technical difficulties to be fixed in the 1978–79 legislative session. Nor did SB 154 contain political problems that demanded resolution. A major feature of California school finance legislation was its incremental nature and strong coalition base. These carefully crafted measures resulted in uncommonly sturdy compromises. The technical quality and political durability of past decisions enabled the legislature to focus on the root problem precipitated by the fiscal crisis of Jarvis–Gann: How to introduce stability and predictability into a new policy environment.

The management of retrenchment defined as the introduction of stability generates new guidelines for policymaking. Because fiscal retrenchment removes all risk capital from the system, policy mistakes become unacceptably expensive. Legislative logic thus dictates that, where possible, policies continue the known and predictable. The technical and political robustness of past legislative actions allowed California legislators a high level of certainty in adapting past solutions to a new reality. In the California case, stability could be defined as maintenance of the status quo. Radically new solutions were not necessary to meet Jarvis–Gann or to bring order to the policy system.

55. Paul McGuckin 27 August 1980: personal communication.

Governmental stability also means that special interests can no longer play the role that was defined during expansion. Granting of special interest requests, according to Jarvis–Gann economics, no longer means a budget addition. The fiscal reality of Proposition 13 approximates a zero-sum game in which even a modest gain is made at the expense of other interests. Public interest lawyers Alan Rader and Dorothy Lang describe the new advocacy strategies dictated by Proposition 13:

> We will probably have to do more of what we always knew we should be doing anyway: working closely with active client groups on broad legislative and administrative advocacy strategies at both State and local levels. That lobbying will have to become more important. We and our clients will no longer be able to say simply that a program or an activity should be funded because it is critically needed. We will have to identify where — and from whom — the money is to come (1979: 393).

The new politics of retrenchment demands a different strategy on the part of the education lobby. Simply pleading need and asking for more, the tactic of the past, is no longer effective. Neither is it effective to act as if all parts of the education lobby can pursue their own objectives without damaging education's position relative to other sectors. All types of local government can plead the same case. According to legislative staffers, this stance neutralized the education lobby as AB 8 was put together. If an effective education coalition is to be maintained, urban representatives can no longer ignore the needs of small districts. Teacher groups cannot overlook administrator concerns. In the past, individual lobbyists were able to accommodate the interests of others through more money. For example, Los Angeles was willing to go along with a small school factor as long as it did not cost Los Angeles anything. In the debates surrounding AB 8, only the CSBA expressed a concern for California education as a whole. This CSBA view, believes legislative staffer Catherine Minicucci, "is on the ascendency. We have to look at the statewide picture. Los Angeles can't dominate education policy anymore."[56]

Coalition theorists would predict that Proposition 13's finite fiscal pie will severely diminish the effectiveness of the Tuesday Night Group (see Groennings, Kelley, and Leiserson 1970; Riker 1962), which was organized explicitly to coordinate education lobbyists' efforts to get more money for schools, the only issue lobbyists could

56. Catherine Minicucci 5 May 1980: personal communication.

agree upon. SB 234 was an effort to resurrect the pre-Proposition 13 era of school finance politics. The effort failed because the ground rules had changed. Bonnie Parks, former Cal–Tax analyst and Tuesday Night Group participant, said:

> The dynamics of the group changed dramatically after Proposition 13. With AB 8 and a limited pot, the group began to break down. It was no longer possible to make side payments to all of the competing interests. Some people had to lose with AB 8; it split the coalition. It doesn't seem likely that there will be enough money available in the future to glue it together again.[57]

The role of the education coalition as well as its ability to function as a group may be jeopardized as fiscal retrenchment makes passage of significant educators' bills unlikely. Furthermore, some legislators feel that the education lobby is not really concerned about the people—that the legislature must protect the public interest against a monolithic education establishment. To this point, the AB 8 experience suggests that an effective education lobby will need to adjust its strategies to the new politics of retrenchment. Education lobbyists must acquire statesmanship in representing the interests of education against other local government responsibilities and in reconciling competing concerns within the education sector. The AB 8 experience also shows that the education coalition because of its accumulated expertise, effective organization, and established relations with the legislature will be better able than most other special interest groups to make these adjustments to the politics and economics of fiscal limitation (Kirst and Somers 1980).

The politics of retrenchment also prescribed a new role for legislative leaders. Just as the role of special interests is diminished in a world constrained by Jarvis–Gann, single issue legislation is also limited. Omnibus legislation, such as AB 8, which shows clearly the fiscal interrelationships among local government entities, is the most effective legislative vehicle. Accordingly, the role of legislative leaders changes from advocating new initiatives or bargaining for special concerns, as seen in AB 65, to orchestrating the legislative coalition necessary for passage of a general state-funding package. SB 154 worked because the legislative leaders who constituted the joint conference committee were aware of critical member concerns and used these issues as glue to win support. AB 8 was fashioned in the same way. California government needed to pass a bill; legislative leaders needed

57. Bonnie Parks 5 May 1980: personal communication.

to ensure support for the long-term bailout package they devised. Jim Browne, Senate Committee on Education, explains:

> Omnibus legislation like AB 8 is a different thing. You can't debate it in the legislature; you can't take out one piece and look at it. So the bill becomes a question of leadership and coalition politics. This bill resulted from the leadership of Greene, Rodda, Carpenter, and McCarthy.[58]

Similarly, Assembly Education Committee's James Murdoch said: "AB 8 was very much like SB 154 in the way it was put together. More players were involved and it was more of an open process, but it was still a legislators' bill."[59]

To manage retrenchment, legislative leaders devised a winning bailout package built on past agreements: Assembly Democrats got their categorical programs, Willie Brown and urban legislators got their urban factor, Senator Dills and legislative friends of education got a larger inflation factor, and the relative funding among sectors remained stable so as not to anger legislators with other special concerns. Ironically, because Proposition 13 made the question of school finance reform independent of tax reform, it generated a new constituency for *Serrano*—Republican legislators. Thus, to fashion a successful coalition for AB 8, Republican lawmakers got a bit more *Serrano* for their suburban communities and special attention to small school districts.

To a very large extent, the features of a winning package to manage retrenchment were preordained. Senator Dills was not entirely wrong when he characterized the Assembly Education Committee hearing on his SB 234 a charade. Similarly, William Lambert of the United Teachers of Los Angeles understood the pivotal rule of legislative leaders: "I told them in February there should be a conference committee bill in February, to save six months of horseplay and hard work by staff people" (Education Congress of California 1979b: 9). The openness of the AB 8 process seems largely pro forma; it is difficult to imagine that the legislative conference committee would have reported a very different bill even without the preceding months of debate and posturing.

58. Jim Browne 5 February 1980: personal communication.
59. James Murdoch 7 May 1980: personal communication.

WHITHER SERRANO?

The California legislature, charges John McDermott, "has done little to bring the California school financing system into compliance with [*Serrano II*]."[60] However, most observers believe differently.[61] Contrary to McDermott's claims, there is substantial agreement that the state's legislature has through the series of school finance measures culminating in AB 8 made concrete progress in equalizing the distribution of California's educational dollars. According to James Kelly, Ford Foundation program officer whose education and public policy division has sponsored many of the studies that fostered reform, "We're a hell of a lot better off than we were. . . . What's happened in California was undreamed of just eight years ago" (as quoted in Stanfield 1979:1935). Even John McDermott, when not arguing before the court, grants California a modest compliment:

> In general, school finance reform has not reduced school district spending disparities in a terribly substantial way. California is one of the exceptions to the rule, but it still falls far short of the mark (Stanfield 1979:1936).

Figures from the California School Finance Model (the common data base used by all school finance technicians to simulate school finance formulas) show that the majority of California's school children receive substantially equal funding under AB 8.[62] These figures also show that one's conclusions about *Serrano* equalization depend on the funding range chosen to assess compliance ($100, $200, $300, or $400) and on the factors included in the expenditure model. *Serrano* doves use Table 5–3 which includes base revenue limits and excludes all categorical funding. *Serrano* hawks use Table 5–4, total revenue limits, which includes certain categorical factors. Both tables show that the gross inequities underlying *Serrano I* have been eliminated. The tables also illustrate the difficulties inherent in determining the state's compliance with *Serrano II*. There is no agreed upon

60. Petition for Enforcement of Prior Judgment in this Action and Statement of Facts Regard Noncompliance with the Prior Judgment, *Serrano v. Priest*, No. C938 254 (Cal., filed 23 June 1980).

61. To this point, Stanfield (1979:1935) writes: "California, where Serrano's lawsuit started the school financing reform movement, probably has made the greatest progress toward equity in education support. So most reformers agree."

62. We are grateful to Paul McGuckin, Assembly Office of Research, for supplying these figures.

Table 5-3. Dove Table: Assembly Bill 8—Percentage of Average Daily Attendance (ADA) Equalized 1983–1984 (*Using Base Revenue Limit per ADA*).

| District Type | Percentage of ADA Equalized by Expenditure Differentials | | | |
	$100	$200	$300	$400
Elementary	93.22	97.28	98.50	98.84
High School	79.48	96.57	98.51	99.43
Unified	94.49	99.05	99.27	99.33

Source: California School Finance Model.

Table 5-4. Hawk Table: Assembly Bill 8—Percentage of Average Daily Attendance (ADA) Equalized 1983–1984 (*Using Total Revenue Limit per ADA*).[a]

| District Type | Percentage of ADA Equalized by Expenditure Differentials | | | |
	$100	$200	$300	$400
Elementary	86.07	95.04	98.31	98.77
High School	42.49	66.69	88.81	94.78
Unified	79.84	93.14	97.05	98.70

a. Major categorical factors included: adult education, declining enrollment adjustment, meals for needy pupils. Excludes court-mandated programs and state fully assumed programs such as the State Teachers' Retirement System.

Source: California School Finance Model.

rule for determining what is in and what is out of the base used to compute *Serrano* compliance. Nor is there agreement on what compliance means. Many argue that the $100 range assumed by *Serrano II* is unrealistic (because of inflation in variable costs) in the 1980s. As a result of these fundamental issues, many Sacramento school finance actors conclude that *Serrano* is in the eye of the beholder.

Most Sacramento actors were pleased with AB 8's *Serrano* provisions. They also believed that in AB 8 the legislature went as far as it could to comply with the *Serrano* mandate. The reform of Jarvis–Gann complicated the reform of *Serrano* in ways legislators, plaintiffs, and the court could not have expected. The dialectic of reform and retrenchment that characterized SB 154 prevailed in AB 8. With local property taxes eliminated as a source of interdistrict disparity, the state controlled the allocation of school district revenues. To level down substantially the revenues of high-spending districts would produce employee layoffs and service disruption. Leveling up low-spending districts required either a disproportionate allocation of the state's resources to education or a new tax to raise additional revenues. The former strategy would disrupt the stability of local governments as a whole; the latter action, in the climate of Proposition 13, would lead California taxpayers to hurl epithets at legislators more rude than "Sacramento popcorn balls."[63]

As a result of Proposition 13, there were few if any major Sacramento actors willing to carry the *Serrano* banner except Republicans who stood to gain funds for their suburban communities. In the view of most lawmakers and their staff, Proposition 13 created irreducible political obstacles to further *Serrano* equalization. According to James Murdoch, who played a central role in developing the fiscal relief package:

> Everyone was reasonably satisfied with AB 8. We couldn't have done much better under the political circumstances than we did. The legislature thinks it has gone as far as it can, given the resources. Even Greene has mellowed on *Serrano*. He acknowledges the reality of the situation. I think the court will find us in compliance. Judges are part of the political process—they know what's been going on.[64]

Mike Dillon, legislative advocate for the Association of Low-Wealth School Districts, commented:

> The legislature has gone as far as it can. They say they're worried about "the people" and about tax increases. The legislature is not going to vote tax increases to meet *Serrano*. Let the courts mandate them. The legislature has always played chicken with the courts.[65]

---

63. Howard Jarvis favored this characterization of California's lawmakers during his Proposition 13 campaign.

64. James Murdoch 7 May 1980: personal communication.

65. Mike Dillon 6 May 1980: personal communication.

Paul Holmes, Assembly Education Committee staff said:

> I've changed from a *Serrano* hawk to a *Serrano* dove. It can't be done any-more in the legislative arena. It's hopeless to ask the legislature to solve this. Everybody's got a *Serrano* district. Plus you will never get this legislature to take money away from Beverly Hills. It will have to be done by the courts.[66]

Hal Geiogue of the Legislative Analyst's Office, the long-time *Serrano* advocate, said:

> The legislature has done all they could politically. They've done all right within the reality of the real world. With AB 8, the members have done what they can. They'll abdicate to the courts.[67]

Flaws in the *Serrano* decision compromised the reform's political viability from the outset. In a Proposition 13 environment it became impossible for it to win support from its logical allies—representatives from urban areas with low-income families. There was not enough free money in the policy system. The economics of Proposition 13 cost *Serrano* much of its ideological support. Now that the state was banker for the whole of local government, further equalization became a luxury public policy good, inconsistent with the requirements of fiscal retrenchment.

The court will hear the question in 1981. Shortly after the governor signed AB 8, *Serrano* attorney John McDermott charged that the new law failed to comply with the Jefferson mandate to reduce differences in per pupil spending to $100 or less by 1980 (*Los Angeles Times*, 14 August 1979). McDermott was joined in his objections by Cal–Tax's Bonnie Parks who alleged that AB 8 "does little to equalize" (Parks 1979: 3). Parks pointed out that although the revenue limit formula would bring 94 percent of the unified districts within a $150-per-ADA range by 1983 to 1984, the bill did not meet the 1980 court deadline.

In December 1979 McDermott reopened the case in Los Angeles Superior Court, arguing that even though dependence on local property tax rates ended with Proposition 13, state school finance aid continues to be calculated on wealth differences. These wealth differences, of course, spring from pre-Proposition 13 tax rate disparities.

---

66. Paul Holmes 22 January 1980: personal communication.
67. Hal Geiogue 23 January 1980: personal communication.

Consequently, John McDermott filed his petition on 23 June 1980, asserting:

> It is now 1980 and there are and will continue to be substantial disparities in spending among California school districts, in direct and blatant violation of the prior judgment in this action.[68]

Serrano hawks and doves alike credit the court for leveraging the change achieved thus far. Until the court-ordered change in *Serrano I* and *II*, there was little traction for the cause of school finance reform in California. Some hope that the court can provide impetus for additional change in *Serrano III*. John Serrano said:

> We have gone a step in the right direction. We identified a problem, won a victory, and now have a club to keep hitting the legislature over the head (as quoted in Stanfield 1979: 1935).

Unlike the situation that obtained in *Serrano II* when plaintiffs found allies in key members of the legislature, the superintendent of public instruction, the state controller, and even in the education lobby, the court and *Serrano* attorneys will be alone in *Serrano III*. *Serrano I* and *II*, music to the ears of reformers, legitimized reform. The coalition that had supported *Serrano* reform evaporated with Proposition 13. In fact, state response to Proposition 13 showed that there never had been a coalition for *reforming* California school finance. Alan Post of the Legislative Analyst's Office, Ronald Cox, school finance expert, and Assemblyman Leroy Greene were lonely advocates for equalization as a goal. Support for *Serrano* came principally as a way to increase funding for public education. Middle class taxpayers, the other early constituency for school finance reform, supported *Serrano* only as it involved tax reform. Jarvis–Gann eliminated both incentives for coalition support of *Serrano* and made it impossible for legislative advocates to compensate for *Serrano's* inherent political and technical problems with more money. With Proposition 13, the politics of school finance reform came full circle. Even long-time supporters gave up. School finance reform became, once again, bad politics. More important, even in the view of former advocates, full *Serrano* compliance became bad public policy.

---

68. Petition for Enforcement of Prior Judgment in this Action and Statement of Facts Regarding Noncompliance with the Prior Judgment, *Serrano* v. *Priest*, No. C938 254 (Cal., filed 23 June 1980).

6 COURTS, LEGISLATURES, AND REFORM
Connections Made and Lost

The course of school finance reform in California can be described as a series of interlocking puzzles—each solution reveals a new puzzle; each puzzle is more difficult than the last. The least difficult but most basic puzzle was that of explaining how a school-financing system that was originally designed to equalize expenditures could produce results that were so unequal. The answer lay in the substantial variations in property wealth among localities and in the basic aid provisions of the system that guaranteed an equal amount to all localities regardless of wealth. The features were only partly compensated for by the equalization features of the foundation system. Explaining these distributional effects opened up another more difficult set of questions. Were the expenditure and tax inequalities generated by the foundation system evidence of invidious discrimination or of a legitimate delegation of fiscal control from the state to the local level? Did the existence of extremes in expenditures and tax rates mean that any system based on property wealth was suspect, or only that the foundation system had failed to meet some reasonable standard of equity? What standard of equity ought to apply—equal expenditures and tax rates for all, equal expenditures for those with equal need, or equal expenditures for equal effort? If the foundation system was a creature of the legislature, how could it be induced to change the system?

Out of these questions grew the next puzzle: how to make the case for judicial intervention in school-financing policy. This was a more difficult problem, requiring not only an explanation of how the foundation system produced unequal results but also a constitutional argument that would support judicial action overturning that system. The puzzle was made more difficult by a growing reluctance on the part of the federal courts to intervene and by the chaotic and opportunistic nature of public law litigation. The theory and strategy developed by reform lawyers in *Serrano* was ideally suited to this turbulent legal environment. They focused litigation at the state level, and they proposed the simple negative standard of fiscal neutrality—educational expenditures should not be a function of property wealth, other than that of the state as a whole. Having made the case for judicial intervention, the reform lawyers opened up yet another set of questions. Was it only the wealth relatedness of educational expenditures that troubled reformers, or were they also concerned about the effects of unequal expenditures on individual students? Would the individual students who most needed special educational attention necessarily benefit from reform based on the fiscal neutrality standard? Did the relationship between property wealth and educational expenditures represent inequity in all cases, or in some cases did it represent legitimate differences in the cost of public services? Were tax inequities and expenditure inequities to be given equal or different weight in the construction of a new financing system?

Out of these questions grew the next puzzle—that of conceiving alternatives to the existing system and estimating their effects on local expenditures, tax rates, and revenue requirements. The solution to this puzzle required technical expertise and the ability to understand complex, multifactor relationships. These skills were a step beyond those of explaining the inequities of the foundation system and devising a strategy for proving them unconstitutional. As expertise developed, an abundance of alternatives to the foundation system surfaced. Some were completely consistent with the wealth neutrality principle, others less so. Some found political sponsorship; others did not. Reformers quickly discovered that conceiving alternatives to the existing system was one thing, but making them into policy was quite another. What constraints—fiscal, technical, and political—would operate on the development of a successful reform measure? What inducements could be offered to generate support for reform? Who were the actual winners and losers in a reform measure based on the principle of wealth neutrality? Could the principle be used to galvanize a political constituency in support of reform? From where would the major political support for reform come?

From these questions grew the next puzzle—that of building a reform coalition and finding a package of benefits that would bind that coalition together. This task required more than a mastery of legal theories, policy options, and distributional mechanisms although they were prerequisites. It required an understanding of the full range of inducements, within and beyond the basic financing system, that were available to construct a coalition and an ability to calculate the self-interest of potential participants in such a coalition. These are skills that come only with extended experience in legislative politics. Out of the interplay of genuine interest in reform, inducements, and self-interested bargaining grew the reform proposals that eventually became law. For better or for worse these were the results of judicial intervention in school finance policy. With these reforms came still more questions. Could the results of bargaining in the legislative arena be made to square with the wealth neutrality principle that emerged from public law litigation? Would the positive inducements that were used to construct a reform coalition continue to exist in the face of fiscal retrenchment? Would commitments to changes in the school-financing system hold in the face of drastic changes in the overall state structure of revenue and taxation?

These questions created the final, as yet unsolved, puzzle of maintaining reform in the face of retrenchment. The difficulty of this problem stems largely from its uncertainty. The skills required to construct a reform coalition with surplus resources are different from those required to maintain one in the face of resource decline. Support for greater equity in school finance, however that might be defined, seems to have declined appreciably with the increase in concern for maintenance of the basic educational program in all school systems, wealthy or poor. Some of the strongest advocates of reform when resources were abundant have become ambivalent about or critical of reform as resources shrink.

Laying out the course of school finance reform in this way—as a series of interlocking puzzles of steadily increasing difficulty—clarifies some general conclusions. First, individual commitment, expertise, and political skill make a great deal of difference in the success or failure of reform. Puzzles remain puzzles in the absence of people willing to engage and solve them. Too often analysts approach the explanation of political events by focusing on broad structural forces at the expense of individuals. This book's analysis shows how important individuals are. Scholars like Arthur Wise, John Coons, and Harold Horowitz combined a commitment to equity with a knowledge of and curiosity about the law to make connections between existing constitutional law and inequities of school finance. Litigators like Sidney Wolinsky and John McDermott demonstrated great tactical skill in forging the arguments and counterarguments necessary to keep *Serrano* alive in an increasingly hostile legal environment. Individual staff members in the legislature, the Department of Finance, and the Legislative Analyst's Office crafted alternatives and analyzed their effects. Key political actors like Leroy Greene, Albert Rodda, Wilson Riles, and the organizers of the Tuesday Night Group took public positions and made the bargains necessary to construct and maintain a coalition. In practical terms, one cannot expect either sustained attention to a complex issue like school finance reform or successful solutions to the puzzles it raises in the absence of strong incentives for individuals to engage in the issue. The incentives may consist of professional recognition, as in the case of the lawyers; the ability to influence important policy decisions, as in the case of staff members; or constituent credit, as in the case of elected officials and interest group representatives. The incentives must be strong enough to attract and bind individuals to the issue long enough for them to develop the expertise and skill required for problem solving and long enough for that expertise and skill to be applied to policy decisions. Broad political trends are fickle and unpredictable in this regard. In all but a few periods, as one legislative staff member put it, good school finance policy is bad politics because of its redistributive nature. The reform measures embodied in Senate Bill (SB) 90 and Assembly Bill (AB) 65, apart from their technical defects, represented rare occasions in which the availability of surplus resources coincided with the commitment, expertise, and skill of individuals necessary to introduce a marked shift in policy. One consequence of the post-Proposition 13 fiscal retrenchment and erosion of support for political leaders may be a slackening of incentives for individuals to engage in complex issues like school finance reform.

Second, solving one puzzle does not assure the solution to succeeding puzzles. Not only are the puzzles that constitute school finance reform different in content; they also involve different institutions of government and require different kinds of expertise and skill. Constructing a legal theory that connects inequities in expenditures and tax rates with existing constitutional law is different from constructing a winning argument in court; both these activities are considerably different from constructing policy options that remedy defects in the existing system and constructing the coalition necessary to turn reform proposals into legislation. Connecting these puzzles is critical to the overall success of school finance reform, yet strong individual and institutional factors work against these connections. Differences in expertise and skill are frequently translated into normative judgments that work against connections. Lawyers regard politicians as too ready to compromise principle for political gain; politicians regard lawyers as too preoccupied with principle to understand political feasibility; technical experts regard both politicians and lawyers as insufficiently alert to detail; and so on. Ironically, all these actors may be motivated by the same goal, but their individual views of the problem and their institutional affiliations tend to drive them apart. There is no guarantee that the multitude of complex puzzles involved in school finance reform will fall together in a useful way unless individuals consciously acknowledge that their solution is someone else's puzzle. The California case abounds with lost connections, and it also contains some examples of serious attempts to make connections between one puzzle and the next. These attempts to make connections will be explored in more detail. Making connections among puzzles explicit in technical, individual, and institutional terms is one useful way of concluding a study of this kind because it makes the process of reform more intelligible, less enigmatic, and more tractable. These connections are the aspect of reform that the participants in the process are least likely to see because of the forces that drive them apart, and hence they are the aspect in which analysis is most likely to be useful.

Finally, the term "solution" considerably overstates the precision and finitude of movement from one puzzle to the next. The puzzles of school finance reform are frequently not solved in any definitive sense, only made more understandable, less problematical, less uncertain. Furthermore, as one moves from legal to technical to political puzzles, the solutions become less determinate, more diffuse, and more difficult to define as prescriptions. Legal theories can be anchored on case law and, through a process of argument among legal scholars and litigation, refined to a single summary statement of principle. To be sure, the wealth neutrality principle left certain large questions unanswered, but as a solution to a puzzle of public law litigation it was exemplary. Developing policy options is a somewhat less determinate puzzle; it requires paying attention to the multiple effects of various distributional schemes, estimating revenue requirements, and laying out alternative courses of action rather than a single comprehensive principle. Nonetheless, the solutions to the puzzle can be reduced to relatively specific technical changes in existing legislation. The same cannot be said for solutions to the coalition-building puzzle. These depend on the commitment, skill, and values of the participants; on the benefits or costs to be distributed; and on the scope of the issues to be bargained. Solutions cannot be defined as simply as legal principles or policy options. Rather they take the form of packages of benefits that bind multiple, divergent interests together. Some of these benefits have only a remote relationship to the policy under discussion, such as when committee chairmanships are bartered for legislative support or when categorical programs are used to buy support for changes in the basic financing system. The package of benefits that will capture and bind coalition members together cannot be specified in advance in the same way as a legal principle or a policy option, but it is no less important to the process of reform because of this characteristic. In fact, coalition-building solutions are probably the most critical ingredient in the entire process since legal principles and policy options do not have much utility if they can not be translated into legislation. The movement from legal to technical to political puzzles means a loss of precision, an increase in complexity, and an increase in importance to the overall process of reform. From a practical standpoint this means that would-be reformers are well advised to invest as much, or more, in understanding the process of constructing packages of benefits that will bind reform coalitions together as they do in creating legal principles and policy options.

In the opening chapter, three themes were identified that could be traced through the California case. Each of these themes defines a connection that is critical to the process of reform. *Technical problems, political solutions* is the theme that describes the connection between the increasing technical complexity of school-financing systems and the political stakes entailed in changing them. *Judicial remedy, legislative response* describes the connection between public law litigation and legislative process. *Political capacity and coalition building* describes the connection between staffing, organization, and information, on the one hand, and political decisions, on the other. This final chapter returns to the three themes stated at the beginning and draws from them some conclusions about the practical problems of reform and retrenchment. The main concern is with connections among the interlocking puzzles of school finance reform.

TECHNICAL PROBLEMS, POLITICAL SOLUTIONS

Revenue and tax questions are among the most technically demanding and politically charged decisions that elected officials face. They require a combination of technical mastery and political calculation that few other decisions demand. School finance questions are surely among the most difficult of revenue and tax questions because, as the California case has demonstrated, it is impossible to separate equity from the structure and performance of the educational system. Hence, school finance questions present an occasion for decisions not only about the collection and distribution of revenue but also about how the educational system will be governed and organized and how effectively it is performing its function.

A major practical problem for political decisionmakers in dealing with these questions is the technical complexity of school-financing systems. School finance policy cannot be made simply by announcing a general set of objectives and charging some administrative body to work out the operational details, as is the case with most policy decisions. Changes in school finance policy must eventually be stated as changes in the complex technical mechanisms for raising and distributing revenue. The process of changing school finance policy can be characterized, somewhat schematically, as follows: Some defect in the system—in this case, inequities in tax and expenditure—becomes evident and is pushed onto the political agenda—in this case, by judicial action. That defect is traced to its source in mechanisms for raising and distributing revenue. This is the technical problem that requires a change in policy. In this case, the problem consisted of the basic grant to all school systems regardless of wealth and the wide variations in local property wealth that allowed rich districts to raise more revenue with lower tax rates than poor districts. At some point in the process of specifying the technical problem, general principles begin to emerge that describe what an adequate solution might be; in this case, the search took place in the courts and eventually resulted in the wealth neutrality doctrine. Proposals surface embodying various solutions to the technical problem and various degrees of approximation to whatever general principles guide discussion. Eventually, political interests begin to coalesce around certain solutions, and if sufficient inducements exist to form a winning coalition, a political solution emerges. There is no way for political decisionmakers to avoid confronting the technical complexity of the financing system if they are to change policy; the technical mechanisms for raising and distributing revenue *are* the policy. There is no necessary straight-line connection between technical problems, general principles, and political solutions. The technical problem grows out of the internal workings of the system, the general principles emerge from argument and debate over what an adequate solution might be, and the political solutions emerge from coalition politics.

Simply put, the tension between technical problems and political solutions arises from the illusion that if it is possible to specify a defect in school-financing systems that requires a remedy, then it must also be possible to frame a solution to that defect and make it into public policy. In fact, no such connection necessarily exists. Specifying defects requires only technical mastery of the system; framing solutions and making them into policy requires, in addition, political skill and inducements sufficient to form a winning coalition.

The solutions produced by the California legislature to the problem of school-financing inequities had several attributes in common. First, changes in the revenue-raising and -distributing mechanisms were incremental, both in terms of their effect on existing policy and their effect on tax and expenditure inequities. The SB 90 differential inflation adjustment, the AB 65 guaranteed yield formula, the SB 154 differential expenditure reduction, and the AB 8 sliding scale all treated local property wealth as the basis for local expenditures and attempted to make distributional changes by forcing the extremes closer together. By definition such mechanisms will always appear to be inferior solutions to the technical problem of the relationship between local property wealth, expenditures, and tax rates. That is, they will always appear to be inferior to solutions that simply eliminate any local claim on local property wealth. Second, the solutions all embodied the principle of increased sharing of property wealth between rich and poor districts. The SB 90 solution envisioned a long-term closure between rich and poor districts; the AB

65 formula instituted a modest recapture of revenues from rich districts; and the post-Proposition 13 solutions used the allocation of state revenues to compensate for locally generated inequalities. Hence, even though the solutions will always appear to be technically inferior to those that eliminate any local claim on property taxes, they have produced significant closure between rich and poor districts. Finally, the solutions all involved substantial side-payments that had no necessary connection to the narrow technical problem of inequities in tax rates and expenditures. The Educationally Disadvantaged Youth and Early Childhood Education provisions of SB 90; the School Improvement Program, bilingual, and compensatory education provisions of AB 65; and the large allocations to categorical titles in the post-Proposition 13 bills all involved the use of state revenues for side-payments. These funds might otherwise have been used to alter the wealth relatedness of the basic financing system. Hence, as long as the basic financing system is left in place, the solutions will always appear to place greater emphasis on pay-offs to educational constituent groups than on reforming the basic financing system.

Thus, if legislative actions are evaluated on the basis of how well they solve the technical problem or how closely they approximate the fiscal neutrality standard, one gets a different answer than if they are evaluated on the basis of how well they work as political solutions. As solutions to the technical problem, they are flawed and inferior: as political solutions, they look quite good. They have not eliminated the wealth relatedness of educational expenditures, but they have managed to mobilize a collection of interests around a package of benefits that substantially reduces the wealth relatedness of expenditures.

Which evaluation is the correct one? In one sense, evaluating legislative actions by how well they solve technical problems or how closely they approximate general standards is useful. It anchors one's understanding of solutions to school finance problems on something besides the shifting sands of politics. It offers, in other words, a relatively objective assessment of how well solutions are working. In another sense, it is a narrow and wrong-headed way of evaluating legislative actions. In the world of policymaking, there are no such things as technical solutions or solutions in principle to school-financing problems. All solutions are, of necessity, political because they require decisions on the distribution of benefits or costs among competing constituents. One can always demonstrate that such solutions are inadequate in technical or normative terms, but the more important and more difficult question is how well they work in political terms. If one grants that the guiding principle was reducing the wealth relatedness of the California system and that doing so required certain specific changes in mechanisms for raising and distributing revenue, the question still remains how these changes can be made into policy. That question can only be answered by finding some combination of changes in financing mechanisms and side-payments that will bind together a winning coalition. This is exactly what political actors did in California.

It is possible to argue that the shortcomings of legislative solutions stem not from the necessities of coalition politics but from a lack of commitment or knowledge on the part of political decisionmakers. This may be a plausible explanation in some states, but it does not hold water in California. While it is true that commitment to school finance reform varied widely among political actors and seemed generally to fade with the onset of fiscal retrenchment, it is not true that the legislature failed to produce a technically adequate solution because of a lack of a committed band of reformers. Legislators like Leroy Greene and Albert Rodda; finance experts like Alan Post and the technical staff of the Legislative Analyst's Office and the Department of Finance; legislative staff like John Mockler, Gerald Hayward, Paul Holmes, and James Murdoch; and political influentials like Wilson Riles were each committed strongly to school finance reform—some before *Serrano*—and were influential in shaping its outcomes. Their commitment, as is the case with all successful political reformers, was tempered by a distrust of simplistic solutions and an appreciation of the exceedingly narrow margin for political bargaining on redistribution. They faced certain irreducible political realities: First, most legislators had at least one high-wealth school district among their constituency, and, second, the amount of surplus money available at any given time was not great enough to comply with the wealth neutrality standard by leveling-up alone. Taken together these facts meant that, judged solely in terms of the basic financing system, there would be a substantial number of clear losers in any reform proposal. They solved this problem, as intelligent political actors would, by coupling incremental reforms in the basic financing system with generous side-payments to reduce the number of clear losers. This hardly qualifies as a lack of commitment.

Nor does it seem plausible to argue that technical inadequacies of the legislative solutions stemmed from a lack of knowledge. If anything, the political actors who specialized in school finance reform manifested a better technical grasp of school-financing alternatives than the reform lawyers. No fewer than two full-scale reviews of school-financing options were conducted by the State Board of Education, both of which concluded with solid endorsements of reform. The joint executive-legislative task force that preceded AB 65 discussed the full range of possible responses to *Serrano*. The Education Systems Unit in the Department of Finance prepared an exhaustive review of these options for Governor Brown prior to the introduction of his reform plan. The Legislative Analyst's Office provided a steady stream of technical criticism of all options put before the legislature. The range of options discussed within the executive and legislative branches was far broader than one would have predicted and more exhaustive than discussions anywhere else, including the courts.

To argue that the legislative actions in California are defensible as political solutions is not, however, they same thing as saying that they were the best possible political solutions. There are instances where, with a bit more will and skill, significantly greater reductions in inequalities of tax effort and expenditures might have been possible. Two such instances come readily to mind. Staff members in the Department of Finance who worked on Governor Brown's AB 65 reform proposal felt that the Governor conceded too much too early in negotiations with Wilson Riles and key legislators over the content of the bill. They watched with growing frustration as the relatively stringent recapture and guaranteed yield provisions of their proposal were watered down by successive compromises. Another example is the opportunity presented by the Rhoads proposal in AB 8, which would have significantly increased the rate of closure between high- and low-wealth districts. The reluctance of proreform Democrats to make an expedient alliance with Republican sponsors of the proposal resulted in its demise. In both instances, one could argue, political solutions could have been devised that came closer to solving the technical problem. The underlying political tradeoffs in both instances are relatively clear. Decisionmakers were working with a fixed pot of money. Both the Department of Finance proposal and Rhoads proposal accomplished a substantial amount of closure between high- and low-wealth districts by leveling-up. In order to finance this leveling-up, they effectively took funds that had been allocated to categorical programs and folded them into the basic financing system in order to increase the state-funded share of low-wealth district expenditures. This reallocation not only took money from urban areas, like Los Angeles and San Francisco; it also substantially reduced the pool of discretionary funds available to make side-payments. Hence, greater equity was purchased at the price of diminished support from urban areas and reduced bargaining power. Not surprisingly, when political actors began to bargain over the content of reform proposals, the effect was to divert funds away from leveling-up and toward categorical programs. Many of the major recipients of these categorical funds were not low-wealth districts although they might be judged to be in need of special support for other reasons. Los Angeles, a big beneficiary of funds for disadvantaged, bilingual, and school improvement lies at about the median of property wealth; San Francisco, a consistent supplicant for special state support, lies toward the high end of the property wealth distribution. The net effect of this tradeoff between categorical support and leveling-up was to dilute the redistribution effect of reform proposals.

An obvious alternative, given this reality, would have been to rely more heavily on leveling-down to achieve closure between high- and low-wealth districts. Each of the major reform laws—SB 90, AB 65, and AB 8—did contain some type of leveling-down mechanism, but their effect was concentrated at the extreme high end of the property wealth distribution, and they accomplished less redistribution than leveling-up. The political logic behind this reluctance to use leveling-down is very simple: No one, not even low-wealth districts, was in favor of leveling-down. The objective that bound the education coalition together was not school finance reform but more money for education. If low-wealth districts could be given a greater-than-equal share of this increase through leveling-up, then everyone reaped some benefit from reform. Low-wealth districts did not wish to be seen as taking their gains out of other districts' pockets except as a last resort. Even more significantly, zero-sum politics within the education coalition would only serve to diminish the influence of education relative to other competitors for state funding. Leveling-down, then, had very limited appeal as a political solution.

What this analysis suggests is that while one can identify instances in which greater equity might have been achieved, the knowledge required to force that result was political not technical. The Department of Finance and Rhoads proposals were exemplary in their attention to the technical problems of redistribution; their key weakness was their inattention to the political problems of using categorical funds to finance leveling-up. In strictly political terms, both proposals unravelled a complex collection of prior agreements giving preferential treatment to certain interest groups, school districts, and state-level political figures. Their weakness lay not so much in this unravelling of prior agreements as in their failure to replace them with a new set of agreements sufficient to realign political forces within the education coalition in support of using categorical programs to level-up. This is the domain of political judgment and persuasion, not of technical expertise. Furthermore, it presents an extraordinarily complex problem of political calculation—balancing certain opposition against reductions in categorical programs against uncertain support for leveling-up. A less complex approach would be to pursue both categorical funding and leveling-up until available funds were exhausted, which is what the major reform laws did. Those who would argue that the legislature could have done more to close the expenditure and tax rate gap between low- and high-wealth districts are obliged to demonstrate an alternative alignment of political forces, not simply to demonstrate that the existing alignment produced a technically inferior solution. Such an alternative alignment is difficult to see.

JUDICIAL REMEDY, LEGISLATIVE RESPONSE

Whatever else may be said about the role of the courts, it was they who initiated school finance reform in California. *Serrano* legitimized reform as a policy objective, made binding the principle that educational expenditures should not be a function of local property wealth, and forced the legislature to act after a fashion and in its own way. It is doubtful that any of these things would have occurred without judicial intervention. In this sense, *Serrano* satisfies the standards that advocates of public law litigation set for themselves. Having made this point, one is still left with the questions raised in Chapter 1 about the connection between courts and legislatures in the process of reform: How well does public law litigation work as a device for initiating reform? How much do lawyers and judges know about the system for which they are making policy? How well does the litigation process work to expose the weaknesses of competing arguments? How useful are judicial decisions as guides to policy? How effective are the courts in monitoring compliance? Saying that judicial intervention worked in California, in other words, is not the same thing as saying that it worked well or that it ought in all respects to serve as an example to would-be reformers in other settings.

While *Serrano* was indispensable as an action-forcing device in the California case, it did not contribute much to the clarification of policy issues or to the shaping of reform policy. As the litigation progressed, the fundamental questions raised by legal scholars were progressively narrowed to questions of legal strategy and doctrine that had very little to do with the task of constructing a new school-financing system. The knowledge, skill, and analytic resources brought to bear on the school-finance question in the courts, while impressive in some instances, were unequally distributed among the lawyers and judges who worked on *Serrano* with the result that many of the questions that would later trouble policymakers were not adequately addressed in litigation. This steady narrowing of focus aggravated the inherent differences that separate those who see reform as the creation of legal principles and those who see it as the realignment of old coalitions or the construction of new ones. Consequently, there was a steadily widening gap between litigators and political actors who nominally shared the same reform objective, rather than convergence on a single solution.

The questions raised by legal scholars at the beginning of the school finance reform movement went to the heart of the legitimacy, organization, and financing of local government. Were inequities of expenditure and tax rates really instances of invidious racial and economic discrimination? Was judicial intervention required to change these inequities? Did judicial intervention have to be justified on the grounds that it would result in tangible benefits to children, or was the existence of expenditure inequities sufficient? Were local school districts wholly creatures of the state, or were there compelling reasons to treat them as autonomous units of government, capable of making their own revenue and expenditure decisions? These were questions of both legal principle and policy. They concerned both the issue of what organizing principles should govern the construction of financing systems and the issue of what the systems themselves should look like. One can find traces of these questions recurring throughout the whole course of litigation in *Serrano*, but the general trend as the case progressed was to subordinate these issues to narrower, more manageable questions of strategy and doctrine.

From the beginning the objective of the litigators, as distinguished from the legal scholars, in *Serrano* was to win in the California Supreme Court, not necessarily to initiate a broad-scale debate on school-financing options or to inform the content of future public policy on school finance. The plaintiffs' case in *Serrano* was skillfully constructed, fitted, and trimmed to the constraints of existing case law and accepted conventions of legal argument. The legal environment in the courts was unrelentingly hostile to judicial intervention, as evidenced by *McInnis* and *Rodriguez*, and forced the litigators to invest much of their effort in distinguishing their case from others that had failed. The plaintiffs, recruited deliberately to demonstrate the coincidence of race, ethnicity, and inequities of school finance, played little or no role in the litigation. When the crucial substantive questions of the relationship between income and expenditure inequities and the relationship between expenditures and school achievement were addressed in court, they were argued on the level of aggregate data at a safe distance from any tangible effect on individual plaintiffs. The legislature's action in SB 90 further complicated the litigators' job by forcing them to demonstrate and explain the law's long-term effects. As the case progressed through the court system, the *Serrano* lawyers' success at deflecting the defendants' arguments, their clear advantage in analytic support, and the withdrawal of key political figures from the defendants' side left defense lawyers with a weak and abstract argument. The state supreme court's decision in *Serrano II*, in contrast with its eloquent decision in *Serrano I*, dealt with a long list of doctrinal issues that might have excited constitutional lawyers and *Serrano* litigators but did little to answer the questions of political actors.

The wealth neutrality principle that emerged from litigation was a model of judicial elegance, parsimony, and negativity. It described with compelling simplicity what a school-financing system should *not* do. Purely from the standpoint of legal strategy, it was a stroke of genius. It got to the heart of the problem of expenditure and tax inequities, it deflected all the messy questions about the connection between finance and schooling, and it left the plaintiff's lawyers and the courts in the position of indefinitely withholding approval of any scheme the legislature produced that did not eliminate the claim of local districts to property tax revenues. After *Serrano I*, the principle seemed to be the saving grace of the reform movement. As successive court decisions emerged and the political climate surrounding school finance became more turbulent, executive and legislative advocates of reform began to feel the same way about wealth neutrality as the Greeks must have felt about the utterances of the oracle at Delphi. Everyone knew the court's word was authoritative, everyone suspected it was pregnant with meaning, but no one was quite sure how to get from it to a real piece of legislation. What began as muted dissatisfaction among reform proponents grew to impatience, exasperation, and finally rejection. In the debate over AB 65, Senator Albert Rodda, whose views were important in shaping legislative opinion on reform, stated that if wealth neutrality put the legislature in the position of having to choose between a level of expenditure it regarded as excessive or policies that undermined the educational program in high wealth districts, then the principle ought to be replaced by another, more manageable one. This statement, more than any other, captured the fundamental lack of connection between reform as litigation and reform as coalition building.

The very idea that anything as complicated and politically nettlesome as school finance reform could be adequately captured by a principle as cryptic as wealth neutrality struck legislative actors as increasingly absurd. From a strictly legal point of view it was anything but absurd. The forces that drove school finance litigation to progressively higher levels of abstraction were the same ones that drove the courts and the legislature further apart. In practical terms, the result was to weaken the case for reform and, potentially, the authority of courts to remedy inequities. The implications of Rodda's argument are that the courts undermine their own legitimacy when they offer the legislature nothing but a politically impossible choice.

The roots of this predicament lie in the dilemmas of judicial intervention that were sketched in Chapter 2. The more public law litigation deals with the actual complaints and damages to real plaintiffs, the less capable it is of enunciating the elegant general principles that lawyers and judges aspire to. The more technically complex the underlying policy issue, the more fertile the field for public law litigation, but the more the courts push against the limits of their competence to digest data and understand the consequences of their decisions. The more attractive the issue as a target for judicial intervention, the less likely the courts are to control the means of implementing their own decisions. The more persistent the courts are in pressing for remedies that are politically infeasible, the more likely they are, when faced with competent political adversaries, to produce a series of impasses rather than a change in policy.

What makes *Serrano* such a superb example of public law litigation and such a dubious example of the connection between litigation and legislation is precisely the fact that it pushed against the outer limits of each of these dilemmas. When arguments become instrumental to winning in court, they tend to lose their utility as guides to policy. If the litigation were not intended to influence policy, this lack of closure between legal argument and public policy would not be a matter for concern. Since the entire purpose of public law litigation is to use the courts to initiate broad-scale changes in policy, it is a serious matter indeed.

The questions of who the plaintiffs were and what their precise interest in school finance reform was were too pedestrian for either side to spend much time on. They were playing for higher stakes. The early association of the case with the interests of the poor, the disenfranchised, and minority groups became less and less easy to maintain as it became clearer and clearer that a large proportion of people meeting that description stood to gain little or nothing from the elimination of property wealth-related inequities. It was clear, however, that certain school districts stood to gain something, so the interests of individuals and districts were confounded to accommodate this inconvenience. When questions were raised by the defendants about the association between school expenditures and school performance, these too were treated at the level of aggregate effects on students and schools without ever establishing the precise connection between the complaints of individuals and the remedies that reform lawyers sought. Finally, when urban school districts expressed some concern about the way their special fiscal situation would be treated in a reformed financing system, they were reassured that nothing in the state supreme court's precluded attention to their needs. All these adjustments were well suited to winning in court. They made the reformers' arguments stronger because they made it appear inconceivable that anyone—except possibly Beverly Hills—could lose from school finance reform. They also diminished the litigation's utility as a guide for policy and drove a wedge between the courts and the legislature. Political actors knew that there would have to be losers—in relative, if not in absolute terms—and that some of those losers might in the short term be the very people *Serrano* seemed originally designed to help. The political actors also knew that they were being manuevered under the guise of deference to legislative prerogatives into answering a basic legal question that the reform lawyers and courts had successfully evaded: If the inequities of the existing system damaged certain individuals, who were they and to what remedy were they entitled?

As long as the courts were grappling with the defects of the existing system, they were on relatively solid ground. Indeed, the state supreme court's analysis of that system in *Serrano I* was clear and lucid. As the legal agenda expanded to include such issues as the long-term effects of SB 90 and the relationship between school expenditures and school performance, the tactical advantage shifted to those with the analytic resources necessary to address those issues, and the courts became more dependent on the reform lawyers rather than their own resources. By the time the case was argued in Los Angeles County Superior Court, the reform lawyers had the analytic resources of both the State Department of Education and the Berkeley Childhood and Government Project at their disposal as well as their own considerable technical expertise and skill in litigation. The critical determinations of fact and law in Judge Jefferson's decision looked a bit too much like the plaintiffs' argument to be persuasive as a careful judicial weighing of arguments and counterarguments. Judge Jefferson did what anyone faced with the same overload of data and the clear superiority of the plaintiffs' case probably would have done. He deferred. His findings of fact and conclusions of law then became the basis for the state supreme court's decision in *Serrano II.*

The greatest strength of the reform lawyers' strategy from a purely legal point of view was also its greatest weakness from the point of view of influencing policy. Wealth neutrality was designed to force legislative action without drawing the courts into the construction of a new financing system. As Sidney Wolinsky, one of the *Serrano* lawyers said, the legislature had "thousands of options" available to reach compliance. The list included the statewide property tax, district power equalization, and vouchers. These options, and many others, were dutifully reviewed and rejected one by one in the process of constructing legislative reform proposals. All this exercise demonstrated was that no matter how many thousands of options were available to comply fully with wealth neutrality, coalition politics, not legal argument, would determine the outcome. The courts, for all their authority in legal matters, were virtually powerless to affect the process by which political interests are formed and aggregated. While school finance was an attractive target for public law litigation, because of the size of the inequities and the fact that they could be measured in dollar terms, it was also an area in which the limits of the courts' competence and their ability to influence political outcomes were clear.

As the litigation dragged on and the search for a politically feasible solution proceeded in the legislative arena, the two sides seemed to become more rigid and divergent. With each successive legislative action, political actors had more experience by which to measure the distance between what they perceived as politically feasible and what the wealth neutrality principle seemed to require. As their understanding deepened, defections from *Serrano* hawk to dove increased. This process speeded up considerably after Proposition 13 and SB 154 introduced the education lobby to the fiscal realities of retrenchment. The key defection was Wilson Riles, who turned the resources of the State Department of Education against the reform lawyers, but this defection was preceded by a number of others in the legislative arena. This shift left the courts with an unpleasant and awkward choice—as yet unresolved. They could assume full responsibility for reforming the school-financing system, or they could accept an impasse. Either course leaves them with diminished authority and emphasizes the tenuousness of their influence on political processes.

There is a plausible alternative to this situation of impasse and unconnectedness, but it requires a rethinking of legal strategy and the nature of public law litigation that is so fundamental that it is not likely to occur. The alternative lies with Derrick Bell's suggestion, quoted at the end of Chapter 2, that litigation cannot be expected to affect policy unless it results in the mobilization of a political constituency that will actively press for legislative reform. The slipperiness and vagueness of the plaintiffs' stake in the outcome of reform coupled with the elegant abstraction of the wealth neutrality principle meant that no strong external political constituency developed to support reform. The reform coalition, as this book has described it, was composed of a handful of individuals who were committed to reform on principle and a large number of political interests who were more concerned about raising state support for education than they were about equity. There never emerged a strong, articulate external political constituency around the nucleus of the *Serrano* plaintiffs that would press for legislative action consistent with the reformers' objectives. The absence of such a constituency left the courts in the position of advocating a principle for which there was no clearly defined political support. In a democracy that is a perilous position.

POLITICAL CAPACITY AND COALITION BUILDING

If the connection between litigation and legislation is tenuous, the many political connections required to construct and maintain a reform coalition are even more so. If ironies and dilemmas abound in public law litigation, they are even more prolific in coalition politics.

School finance reform politics in California were until recently characterized by a steady growth on all measures of political capacity. Prior to SB 90 only a handful of individuals had any technical knowledge of school finance policy, no formal or informal organization existed for consultation and coordination among interests affected by changes in policy, and the ability of decisionmakers to estimate the effects of various reform measures was primitive or nonexistent. SB 90 itself introduced education policymakers and interest groups to the costs of this lack of capacity. Deep divisions within the education lobby diluted their influence. Political and technical naivete led legislators and interest groups to accept a school-financing system that left them at a substantial disadvantage in an inflationary economy. Major policy decisions were made with little or no information about their short- or long-term effects. Immediately after SB 90 signs of growth in political capacity began to appear. Divisions within the education lobby began to moderate, and interest groups began increasingly to see the benefits of concerted action. Organizations appeared that connected divergent interests—the mobilization committee for SB 1641, the Education Congress of California, and the rudiments of what eventually became the Tuesday Night Group. Legislative staff who had received their baptism of fire with SB 90 became hardened veterans in its aftermath; the number of legislative and executive staff assigned to work on school finance increased markedly. The joint executive–legislative task force appeared, demonstrating a command of the range of options available for responding to *Serrano*. The Education Systems Unit in the Department of Finance followed shortly. By the time of the debate on AB 65, staff members had created a data retrieval and analysis system that would permit an exhaustive analysis of any proposal and an organizational structure that guaranteed the system's accessibility to everyone working on finance policy. In the immediate aftermath of Proposition 13 the tight organization of the Tuesday Night Group, the speed and technical competence of education staff members' responses to legislative requests, and the experience of both lobbyists and staff all meant that education emerged in better shape than any other function of state government. With AB 8 the first signs of a pulling apart of the political organization spawned by AB 65 began to emerge. The very success of the Tuesday Night Group meant that it attracted more members than it could easily accommodate and still do business. The politics of retrenchment surfaced issues that proved difficult to resolve within the Tuesday Night Group and between the group and staff members in the legislative and executive branches. An increasing number of decisions were taken by staff and members without formal consultation. It is easy to overstate the significance of these signs of declining political capacity, however. The network of expertise, organization, and analytic capacity that exists around school finance policy in California remains extraordinarily well developed.

While the growth of political capacity can be plotted with relative certainty, it is more difficult to explain the relationship between political capacity and the construction of a reform coalition. A high level of political capacity is not a necessary condition for the formation of a reform coalition; divergent interests can agree to collaborate temporarily without any of the advantages of expertise, organization, or analytic resources that characterized the California reform coalition. A high level of political capacity, however, carries with it a number of advantages for coalition members. Interest group representatives, legislators and their staff, and education department personnel were able by giving up only a small amount of autonomy to gain access to inside information on positions taken by others, to discussions in which positions could be influenced, to information on the effects of alternative proposals, and to decisions affecting the distribution of money. Most participants recognized these benefits self-consciously. Only two important political actors consistently rejected the benefits of close collaboration—Governors Reagan and Brown. Both took the position that education was inefficient and self-serving, and both adopted a strategy of making their political calculations privately and announcing their proposals unilaterally. Reagan was only slightly more flexible in this regard than Brown. Both were influential despite their unwillingness to collaborate, but both also sustained defeats which could be traced directly to their unwillingness to play coalition politics. From the participants' point of view, the main internal benefits of increased political capacity were access and influence.

Running through this analysis is another set of benefits, external to the coalition itself, which has to do with the influence of education relative to other interests. One of many lessons that education people learned from SB 90 was that they suffered considerably from having school finance reform treated as part of a general revenue and tax package. One of the benefits they gained from a higher degree of political capacity was the ability to force school finance onto the political agenda as a separate item. AB 65 showed the benefits of this strategy. After Proposition 13, with SB 154, school finance was once again lumped together with other revenue and tax questions, but this time education had a substantial edge on other interests in staff expertise, organization, and analytic capacity. By the time of AB 8, however, the zero-sum politics of retrenchment had begun to take their toll. Certain interest groups began to seriously calculate the benefits of acting independently and to question the motives and actions of other groups more openly. Legislators began to voice concern that the education lobby had become too powerful and self-serving for its own good. In other words, as the external benefits of participation declined, signs of stress increased and political capacity began to diminish.

Given this preliminary evidence, one finds it difficult to avoid drawing the conclusion that the single strongest determinant of the growth of political capacity was the prospect of controlling the distribution of a large state revenue surplus. Within a year after SB 90, legislators and interest group representatives knew that education had been burned badly by revenue limits and the inflation factor. School administrators and board members were smart enough to compare their own projected revenue shortfalls against the projected revenue surpluses at the state level. They also knew that with the state supreme court's impending decision in *Serrano II* the legislature would be forced to act again and that the most politically feasible way for the legislature to comply was to level-up. In simple terms, leveling-up meant more money for most school districts. For political actors like Wilson Riles the existence of a state surplus meant the prospect of achieving both *Serrano* compliance and structural reform of elementary and secondary schools. For teachers the surplus meant more money on the bargaining table. For key legislators the surplus meant the prospect of *Serrano* compliance without the difficult tradeoffs involved in leveling-down. The only voice left out of this rising wave of expectations was that of property taxpayers, who would be heard from later. Determining the precise size of the surplus and deciding whether it would be committed to education were in the hands of Governor Brown—not exactly an enthusiast of increased educational expenditure. However, Brown's no-reform–no-money position acted as an additional stimulus for education interests to pull together. The direct benefits of coalition formation—measured both as expected expenditure increases and as influence in the distribution of those increases—far outweighed the costs—measured in lost autonomy. After Proposition 13 this benefit–cost ratio tended to decline as school finance politics shifted from distributing shares of a surplus to deciding on the redistribution of a fixed or declining pot. Capacity, in other words, grew out of the mutual benefit to be gained from collaboration, and that benefit declines with the decline in surplus resources.

Nor is it clear that increased capacity resulted necessarily in dramatic changes in access to political decisionmaking or in policy changes more consistent with the equity objectives of school finance reformers. Advocates of reforms designed to reduce wealth-created disparities in expenditures became more influential in political decisions after *Serrano*, but they did not become much more numerous. To the degree that key legislators like Leroy Greene and Albert Rodda were able to capitalize on increased political capacity to serve the objectives of *Serrano*, one could argue that increased political capacity contributed to the achievement of reform. But large amounts of that political capacity were also put in the service of other political objectives: more revenue for fiscally pressed school districts (regardless of wealth), higher teachers' salaries, structural reform, aid to special target populations, and so forth. In some instances these objectives were consistent with the courts' instructions in *Serrano*; in many instances they either had nothing to do with them or ran counter to them. The level of political capacity was to a large degree independent of the propensity of coalition politics to produce results consistent with the equity objectives of reformers. In fact, one could argue that there were a number of instances in which increased capacity undercut equity objectives. The watering down of the AB 65 guaranteed yield and recapture provisions that so bothered their authors was abetted in large part by an information system that allowed legislators to calculate the effect of the bill on school systems in their districts.

One could imagine a situation in which this imperfect relationship between capacity and reform might be different. That situation would be characterized by the mobilization of a large external political constituency that would press for the reform objectives stated in *Serrano*. If such a constituency had gained access to the information, organization, and expertise of the reform coalition, much as the *Serrano* lawyers capitalized on these assets to strengthen their litigation strategy, the complexion of school finance politics in California might have been much different. Probably the most significant feature of the California case is the fact that this did not happen. No political constituency of John Serranos emerged in Sacramento. Those who did come to Sacramento lobbied mainly for more money, not for greater wealth neutrality in the distribution of that money. The lobbyist for low-wealth school districts, Mike Dillon, was one of many participants in the Tuesday Night Group, and the districts themselves took the position that they did not want to realize revenue increases at the expense of other school systems. The strongest political advocates of *Serrano* reforms were essentially the same handful of people who had championed reform before *Serrano*, supplemented by a growing contingent of staff. Ironically, it was these reformers, not their opponents, who absorbed the brunt of the litigators' criticism for failing to produce a legislative solution more consistent with *Serrano*.

The overall effect of this brand of coalition politics was what might be called the half-full or half-empty problem. Legislative leaders and Governor Brown looked at the difficult tradeoffs required to achieve modest progress toward *Serrano* objectives and at the enormous cost of that progress and announced that they had created a system in substantial compliance with the decision. Litigators looked only at the distributional effects of that system and announced that substantial compliance was a ruse. After Proposition 13 one could produce data showing either that significant progress had been made or that significant amounts remained to be done; the conclusion depended on one's judgment about what constituted equity. The courts and legislature achieved only a stand-off with litigators and judges playing the role of shadow participants in the reform coalition—reserving their veto power over successive reform measures but never directly negotiating outcomes. The missing link in this stand-off was a strong political constituency for reform measures consistent with the courts' mandate. The absence of this constituency and its failure to develop in the wake of *Serrano* can be traced to the roots of school finance reform in public law litigation. The final irony of the California case is that school finance reform lawyers got precisely what they bargained for, or, to put it more accurately, what they failed to bargain for: a series of reform measures in which equity was a subsidiary objective to increases in educational expenditures.

REFERENCES

Allison, Graham. 1971. *Essence of Decision: Explaining the Cuban Missile Crisis.* Boston: Little, Brown.

Assembly Education Committee. 1978. "Impact of Proposition 13 on Public Education." Sacramento, May 10.

Aufderheide, JAlan. 1974. *State Policy Making for the Public Schools of California.* Columbus: The Educational Governance Project, Ohio State University.

Bardach, Eugene. 1972. *The Skill Factor in Politics.* Berkeley: The University of California Press.

_____. 1977. *The Implementation Game.* Cambridge, Mass.: MIT Press.

Benson, Charles S.; Paul M. Goldfinger; E. Gareth Hoachlander; and Jessica S. Pers. 1974. *Planning for Educational Reform.* New York: Dodd, Mead & Co.

Benson, Charles S., et al. 1965. *State and Local Fiscal Relationship in Public Education in California.* A Report of the Senate Fact Finding Committee on Revenue and Taxation, Senate of the State of California, March. Mimeo.

Berke, Joel. 1974. *Answers to Inequity: An Analysis of the New School Finance.* Berkeley: McCutchan.

Berne, Robert, and Leanna Stiefel. 1978. "A Methodological Assessment of Educational Equality and Wealth Neutrality Measures." In *Papers in Education Finance*, no. 17. Denver: Education Commission of the States, July.

Brown, Edmund G. 1970. *Reagan and Reality: The Two Californias.* New York: Praeger.

Brown, Edmund G., Jr. 1978. "Address Before Joint Session of the Legislature," June 8.

243

California Journal. 1970. April: 112-113.

_____ . 1970. May: 134.

_____ . 1970. August: 215-236.

_____ . 1970. December: 330-341, 350.

_____ . 1971. January: 8-9, 15-19.

_____ . 1971. September: 237-239, 252.

_____ . 1971. October: 269, 276.

_____ . 1973. February: 44-49, 65-71.

_____ . 1973. August: 261-265.

_____ . 1974. November: 360-366.

_____ . 1975. August: 277-279, 280-282.

_____ . 1978. Tax Revolt Digest Supplement, November.

California School Boards Association. 1979. *Legislative Report* 79, no. 4 (April 23): 16.

California School Board Association Journal. 1979. March.

California Teachers Association. 1979. *Politics and Legislation* 2, no. 28 (July 31).

Chambers, Jay G. 1978. "Educational Cost Differentials and the Allocation of State Aid for Elementary/Secondary Education." *Journal of Human Resources* 13, no. 4: 459-481.

Chayes, Abram. 1976. "The Role of the Judge in Public Law Litigation." *Harvard Law Review* 89, no. 7 (May): 1281-1316.

Cohen, David. 1969. "Defining Racial Equality in Education." *UCLA Law Review* 16: 255-280.

_____ . 1974. "School Finance and Social Policy: *Serrano* and its Progeny." In *School Finance in Transition*, edited by John Pincus, pp. 286-314. Cambridge, Mass.: Ballinger Publishing Company.

Coleman, James. 1968. "The Concept of Equality of Educational Opportunity." *Harvard Educational Review* 38: 7-21.

Coons, John. 1962. *Civil Rights U.S.A.: Chicago.* Washington, D.C.: United States Commission on Civil Rights.

Coons, John; William Clune; and Stephen Sugarman. 1969. "Educational Opportunity: A Workable Test of State Financial Structures." *California Law Review* 57: 305-421.

Coons, John; William Clune; and Stephen Sugarman. 1970. *Private Wealth and Public Education.* Cambridge, Mass.: Harvard University Press.

Cubberley, Ellwood P. 1905. *School Funds and Their Apportionment.* New York: Columbia University.

Department of Finance, Educational Systems Unit. 1978. *California and the Serrano Issue,* July.

Education Congress of California. 1977. *Newsletter,* November 1.

_____ . 1979a. *Newsletter* 7, no. 7 (May).

_____ . 1979b. *Newsletter* 7, no. 8 (June).

Fenno, Richard F., Jr. 1973. *Congressmen in Committees.* Boston: Little, Brown.

The Field Institute. 1978. *Californians Look at Public Schools Following the Passage of Proposition 13.* San Francisco, December.

Fuhrman, Susan, with contributions by Joel Berke; Michael Kirst; and Michael Usdan. 1979. *State Education Politics: The Case of School Finance Reform.* Denver: Education Commission of the States, Report No. F 79-12, December.

Gamson, William. 1961. "A Theory of Coalition Formation," *American Sociological Review* 26:373–382.

Garms, Walter I.; James W. Guthrie; and Lawrence C. Pierce. 1978. *School Finance: The Economics and Politics of Public Education.* Englewood Cliffs, N.J.: Prentice–Hall, Inc.

Glazer, Nathan. 1975. "Towards an Imperial Judiciary." *Public Interest* 41: 104–124.

Groennings, Sven; E.W. Kelley; and Michael Leiserson. 1970. *The Study of Coalition Behavior.* New York: Holt, Rinehart and Winston.

Hall, Kenneth F. 1973. "Presentation to the Association of California School Boards," December.

Horowitz, Donald. 1977. *The Courts and Social Policy.* Washington, D.C.: Brookings Institution.

Horowitz, Harold. 1966. "Unseparate but Unequal—The Emerging Fourteenth Amendment Issue in Public School Education." *UCLA Law Review* 13: 1147–1172.

Horowitz, Harold, and Diana Nietring. 1968. "Equal Protection Aspects of Inequalities in Public Education and Public Assistance Programs from Place to Place Within a State." *UCLA Law Review* 15:787–816.

Kirp, David. 1968. "The Poor, the Schools and Equal Protection." *Harvard Educational Review* 38:635–668.

_____. 1973. "Judicial Policymaking: Inequitable School Finance and the *Serrano* Case." In *Policy and Politics in America*, edited by Allan Sindler, pp. 83–112. Boston: Little, Brown.

_____. 1977. "Law, Politics, and Equal Educational Opportunity: The Limits of Judicial Involvement." *Harvard Educational Review* 47:117–137.

Kirp, David L., and Mark G. Yudof. 1971. "Whose Priorities for Educational Reform?" *Harvard Civil Rights and Civil Liberties Law Review* 6:619–630.

Kirst, Michael W. 1970. *The Politics of Education at the Local, State and Federal Levels.* Berkeley: McCutchan.

_____. 1979. "The New Politics of State Education Finance." *Phi Delta Kappan* 60, no. 6 (February):427–432.

_____. 1980. "A Tale of Two Networks: School Finance Reform Versus the Spending and Tax Limitation Lobby." *Taxing and Spending* 3, no. 1:43–49.

Kirst, Michael W., and Stephen A. Somers. 1980. "Collective Action Among California Educational Interest Groups: A Logical Response to Proposition 13." Stanford University, School of Education, October (draft manuscript).

Kurland, Philip. 1968. "Equal Educational Opportunity: The Limits of Constitutional Jurisprudence Undefined." *University of Chicago Law Review* 35:
583–600.

Lee, Eugene C. 1978. "California." In *Referendums: A Comparative Study of
Practice and Theory*, edited by David Butler and Austin Ranney. Washington, D.C.: Enterprise Institute for Public Policy Research.

Legislative Analyst. 1969–70. *Analysis of the Budget Bill of the State of California*. FY Report of the Legislative Analyst to the Joint Legislative Budget
Committee.

_____ . 1970. *Public School Finance.*

_____ . 1970–71. *Analysis of the Budget Bill of the State of California*. FY
Report of the Legislative Analyst to the Joint Legislative Budget Committee.

_____ . 1971. *Public School Finance*, vol. 1–4.

_____ . 1979. "Analysis of Assembly Bill No. 8 (Greene), as amended in Senate
June 21, 1979 and as further amended by LCR No. 104589, 1979–80 Session." July 19.

Lehne, Richard. 1978. *The Quest for Justice.* New York: Longman.

Lindblom, Charles E. 1965. *The Intelligence of Democracy.* New York: The
Free Press.

Lipset, Seymor, and Earl Raab. 1978. "The Messages of Proposition 13." *Com-
mentary* 66, no. 3 (September): 42–46.

Lipson, Albert J., with Marvin Lavin. 1980. *Political and Legal Responses to
Proposition 13 in California.* Santa Monica, Calif.: The Rand Corporation,
R–2483–DOJ, January.

Los Angeles Times. 1971. January 21.

_____ . 1972. January 25.

_____ . 1972. January 26.

_____ . 1972. February 21.

_____ . 1972. March 10.

_____ . 1972. April 15.

_____ . 1972. May 10.

_____ . 1972. May 19.

_____ . 1972. July 19.

_____ . 1972. July 25.

_____ . 1974. November 18.

_____ . 1974. November 29.

_____ . 1975. January 7.

_____ . 1975. January 8.

_____ . 1975. February 25.

_____ . 1975. February 27.

_____ . 1975. March 7.

_____ . 1975. April 1.

_____ . 1975. June 26.

_____ . 1975. June 28.

_____ . 1975. June 29.

_____ . 1975. July 1.

_____ . 1975. July 3.

_____ . 1975. July 9.

_____ . 1975. August 1.

_____ . 1975. August 5.

_____ . 1975. August 15.

_____ . 1975. August 19.

_____ . 1975. August 22.

_____ . 1975. September 7.

_____ . 1976. June 26.

_____ . 1976. July 3.

_____ . 1976. August 26.

_____ . 1976. September 11.

_____ . 1976. October 6.

_____ . 1976. December 3.

_____ . 1976. December 31.

_____ . 1977. January 1.

_____ . 1977. January 5.

_____ . 1977. January 6.

_____ . 1977. January 7.

_____ . 1977. February 1.

_____ . 1977. February 26.

_____ . 1977. March 18.

_____ . 1977. April 13.

_____ . 1977. April 19.

_____ . 1977. April 26.

_____ . 1977. April 28.

_____ . 1977. June 2.

_____ . 1977. August 3.

_____ . 1977. August 12.

_____ . 1977. August 17.

_____ . 1977. August 25.

_____ . 1977. September 3.

_____ . 1977. September 7.

_____ . 1977. September 27.

_____ . 1978. August 2.

_____ . 1978. October 1.

_____ . 1979. January 23.

_____ . 1979. March 8.

_____ . 1979. March 24.

_____ . 1979. April 3.

Los Angeles Times.(continued)

_____ . 1979. April 20.

_____ . 1979. April 28.

_____ . 1979. May 31.

_____ . 1979. August 14.

Luther, Claudia. 1980. "Education Lobbyists Final Strength in Togetherness." *Los Angeles Times*, February 3.

Madigan, Vonnie. 1975. "Riles' 'Impossible' Task: Taming of the Bureaucracy." *California Journal*, January: 23–25.

Mayhew, David. 1974. *Congress: The Electoral Connection*. New Haven: Yale University Press.

McCurdy, Jack, and Don Speich. 1978. "Outlook Brighter for Schools and Colleges." *Los Angeles Times*, June 24.

McDermott, John. 1978. "Suddenly, California Must Again Reslice the School-Finance Pie." *Los Angeles Times*, June 18.

Meltsner, Arnold J.; Gregory W. Kast; John F. Kramer; and Robert T. Nakamura. 1973. *Political Feasibility of Reform in School Financing: The Case of California*. New York: Praeger.

Meltsner, Arnold J., and Robert T. Nakamura. 1974. "Political Implications of Serrano." In *School Finance in Transition*, edited by John Pincus, pp. 257–286. Cambridge, Mass.: Ballinger Publishing Company.

Michaelsen, Jacob B. 1980. "Financial Reform in California." *American Journal of Education* 88, no. 2 (February): 145–178.

Michelman, Frank. 1969. "The Supreme Court 1968 Term, Foreward: On Protecting the Poor Through the Fourteenth Amendment." *Harvard Law Review* 83: 7–59.

Mockler, John, and Gerald Hayward. 1978. "School Finance Reform in California: Pre-*Serrano* to Present." *Journal of Education Finance* 3 (spring): 386–401.

Nagel, Robert. 1978. "Separation of Powers and the Scope of Federal Equitable Remedies." *Stanford Law Review* 30: 661–690.

Owens, John; Edmund Constantini; and Louis Wechsler. 1970. *California Politics and Parties*. New York: Macmillan.

Parks, Bonnie. 1979. "School Finance Traffic Jam Heads for Assembly Bottlenecks." *CAL-TAX News*, June 1–14.

Pincus, John. 1976a. "Brown Falters on Education." *Los Angeles Times*, August 15.

_____ . 1976b. "Brown, Riles Jockey for Reforms in RISE Dispute." *Los Angeles Times*, September 19.

_____ , ed. 1974. *School Finance in Transition*. Cambridge, Mass.: Ballinger Publishing Company.

Post, A. Alan. 1972. "Statement to National Legislative Conference, Special Committee on School Finance," Los Angeles, May 19.

_____. 1974. "Serrano and Finance: Implications for the Future." Paper presented to the Fifth Annual Summer Seminar for School Superintendents, The University of Southern California, July 12.

Post, A. Alan, and Richard W. Brandsma. 1973. "The Legislative Response to *Serrano* v. *Priest,*" *Pacific Law Journal* 4:28–46.

Rader, Alan, and Dorothy Lang. 1979. "Proposition 13 and the Poor: The New Alchemy in the Golden State." *Clearinghouse Review* (February):681–693.

Rebell, Michael, and Arthur Block. Forthcoming. *Education Policy and the Courts: An Empirical Study of the Effectiveness and Legitimacy of Judicial Activism.* Chicago: University of Chicago Press.

Reinhold, Robert. 1972. "John Serrano et al., and School Tax Equality." *New York Times Educational Review*, January 10, E–26.

Report of the Governor's Commission on Educational Reform. 1971. Sacramento, California, January.

Riker, William. 1962. *The Theory of Political Coalitions.* New Haven: Yale University Press.

Riles, Wilson. 1978. "Statement to the Joint Legislative Conference Committee on SB154." June 14.

Sacramento Bee. 1977. September 15.

_____. 1979. February 2.

_____. 1979. June 14.

Salzman, Ed. 1975. "The Greening of Governor Brown." *California Journal* (May):149–152.

_____. 1976a. *Jerry Brown: High Priest and Low Politician.* Sacramento: California Journal Press.

_____. 1976b. "The $800 Million Everyone Wants." *California Journal* (July): 214.

_____. 1976c. "Property Taxes and *Serrano*—Danger Signals for the Democrats." *California Journal* (December): 403–404.

_____. 1978. "Life After Jarvis." *California Journal* (August):264–267.

School Services of Sacramento, Inc. 1979. "The High Price of Leveling Down: An Analysis of the Impact of Expenditure Reduction in High Revenue Districts." Sacramento, January.

Serrano/Priest Task Force: Summary of Findings. 1977. January.

Stanfield, Rochelle L. 1979. "The School Financing Revolutions—More Help for Taxpayers than Schools." *National Journal* 11, no. 46 (November 17): 1935–1939.

State of California, Department of Finance. 1971. *How to Get More Out of Your School Dollars.* Sacramento, August 1.

Stowe, Noel J. 1975. *California Government: The Challenge of Change.* Beverly Hills, Calif.: Glencoe Press.

Tron, Esther O. 1978. *Selected Papers in School Finance, 1978.* Washington, D.C.: U.S. Office of Education.

Turner, Henry A., and John A. Vieg. 1971. *The Government and Politics of California*. New York: McGraw-Hill.

Tyack, David B.; Michael W. Kirst; and Elisabeth Hansot. 1980. "Educational Reform: Retrospect and Prospect." *Teachers College Record* 81, no. 3 (spring): 253–269.

Uslaner, Eric M., and Ronald E. Weber. 1977. *Patterns of Decision Making in State Legislatures*. New York: Praeger.

Weiss, Janet A. 1979. "Access to Influence." *American Behavioral Scientist* 22, no. 3 (January/February): 437–458.

Wechsler, Herbert. 1959. "Toward Neutral Principles of Constitutional Law." *Harvard Law Review* 73:1–35.

Wise, Arthur. 1967. *Rich Schools, Poor Schools: The Promise of Equal Educational Opportunity*. Chicago: University of Chicago Press.

Wyner, Alan. 1973. "Legislative Reform and Politics in California: What Happened, Why and So What?" In *State Legislative Innovation*, edited by James Robinson, pp. 46–100. New York: Praeger.

Yudof, Mark. 1973. "Equal Educational Opportunity and the Courts." *Texas Law Review* 51: 411–504.

_____. 1978. "School Desegregation: Legal Realism, Reasoned Elaboration, and Social Science Research in the Supreme Court." *Law and Contemporary Problems* 42, no. 4, Part V (autumn): 57–110.

_____. 1981. "Implementation Theories and Desegregation Realities." *Alabama Law Review* 32: 441–464.

Yudof, Mark G., and Daniel Morgan. 1974. "*Rodriguez v. San Antonio*: The Politics of School Finance Reform." *Law and Contemporary Problems* 39: 383–414.

RAND EDUCATIONAL
POLICY STUDIES

PUBLISHED

Averch, Harvey A.; Stephen J. Carroll; Theodore S. Donaldson; Herbert J. Kiesling; and John Pincus. *How Effective is Schooling? A Critical Review of Research.* Englewood Cliffs, N.J.: Educational Technology Publications, 1974.

Carpenter-Huffman, P.; G.R. Hall; and G.C. Sumner. *Change in Education: Insights from Performance Contracting.* Cambridge, Mass.: Ballinger Publishing Company, 1974.

Crain, Robert L.; Rita E. Mahard; and Ruth E. Narot. *Making Desegregation Work: How Schools Create Social Climates.* Cambridge, Mass.: Ballinger Publishing Company, 1982.

Elmore, Richard F., and Milbrey Wallin McLaughlin. *Reform and Retrenchment: The Politics of California School Finance Reform.* Cambridge, Mass.: Ballinger Publishing Company, 1982.

Gurwitz, Aaron S. *The Economics of Public School Finance.* Cambridge, Mass.: Ballinger Publishing Company, 1982.

McLaughlin, Milbrey Wallin. *Evaluation and Reform: The Elementary and Secondary Education Act of 1965, Title I.* Cambridge, Mass.: Ballinger Publishing Company, 1975.

Pincus, John, ed. *School Finance in Transition: The Courts and Educational Reform.* Cambridge, Mass.: Ballinger Publishing Company, 1974.

Timpane, Michael, ed. *The Federal Interest in Financing Schooling.* Cambridge, Mass.: Ballinger Publishing Company, 1978.

OTHER RAND BOOKS IN EDUCATION

Bruno, James E., ed. *Emerging Issues in Education: Policy Implications for the Schools.* Lexington, Mass.: D.C. Heath and Company, 1972.

Coleman, James S., and Nancy L. Karweit. *Information Systems and Performance Measures in Schools.* Englewood Cliffs, N.J.: Educational Technology Publications, 1972.

Haggart, Sue A., ed. *Program Budgeting for School District Planning.* Englewood Cliffs, N.J.: Educational Technical Publications, 1972.

Levien, Roger E. *The Emerging Technology: Instructional Uses of The Computer in Higher Education.* New York: McGraw–Hill Book Company, 1972.

INDEX

ABOUT THE AUTHORS

Richard F. Elmore, a Rand consultant, is an associate professor of Public Affairs at the University of Washington and associate director of the University's Institute for Public Policy and Management. Dr. Elmore has done extensive research and writing on problems of public policy implementation, most particularly in the areas of education and youth employment. He received his Ed.D. in Education and Social Policy from the Harvard Graduate School of Education in 1976.

Milbrey Wallin McLaughlin is a senior social scientist with the Rand Corporation. Her research has focused on questions of policy implementation, planned change in education and the role of the states in federal education programs. Dr. McLaughlin received her Ed.D. in Education and Social Policy from the Harvard Graduate School of Education in 1973.